FROM MY SEAT

ON THE AISLE

Movies and Memories

FROM MY SEAT
ON THE AISLE
Movies and Memories

JACK GARNER

Save My Seat

Jack Garner

RIT PRESS
ROCHESTER, NEW YORK
2013

From My Seat on the Aisle: Movies and Memories
Jack Garner

Published and distributed by
RIT Press
90 Lomb Memorial Drive
Rochester, New York 14623-5604
http://ritpress.rit.edu

Printed in the U.S.
ISBN 978-1-933360-99-7 (print)
ISBN 978-1-939125-002 (e-book)

Library of Congress Cataloging-in-Publication Data

Garner, Jack, 1945-
From my seat on the aisle : movies and memories / Jack Garner.
    pages cm
Includes index.
ISBN 978-1-933360-99-7 (alk. paper) -- ISBN 978-1-939125-00-2 (e-book)
1. Motion pictures--Reviews. 2. Motion pictures. I. Title.
PN1995.G286 2013
791.43'75--dc23
                              2013025042

For Bonnie—for a thousand reasons

That's part of your problem…you haven't seen enough movies.
All of life's riddles are answered in the movies.

Movie producer (Steve Martin) in *Grand Canyon.*

Critics are like eunuchs in a harem; they know how it's done,
they've seen it done every day, but they're unable to do it themselves.

Brendan Behan

CONTENTS

ROBERT FORSTER

Nobody Says "No You're Not!"

YOU TELL PEOPLE YOU'RE A TROMBONE PLAYER, THEY SAY "TAKE OUT YOUR AX...
let's see what you got!" You say you're a magician, they say "Let's see a trick!" But if you tell
people you're an actor... nobody says "No you're not!" – except for this guy, Jack Garner. He
can say, "No you're not" with authority... and for a living! A guy to be scared of!

I had made a movie in 1986: *Hollywood Harry.* ("Not much, but not junk," I always
say). I had spent every penny I had or could borrow to make and finish it, and I brought it
to Rochester. When I started the project I fantasized that its success would bring with it a
house in Malibu. By now, though, like my career, my hopes were more realistic, and I was
peddling my little movie to any audience I could find. I'd come to Rochester to show it to
several investors and to my family.

Almost broke, I'd borrowed my ex-wife's car to get to the west side multiplex. She'd had
some little accident with the car... the passenger door was inoperable and the driver's side
door was wired shut. I was still agile in those years, and as I clambered out the driver's side
window, a big guy walked by. He was considerate enough not to stare, but my embarrass-
ment could not have been greater. Straightening and dusting my clothes, I walked toward
the brightly lit lobby whose marquee announced: Special Screening – *Hollywood Harry.*

In the lobby, I encountered a smattering of family, friends, curious others, and uh-oh –
the big guy! "Hi," he says, "I'm Jack Garner."

Now I had always thought that protocol required talent to keep their distance from the
assayers of it. (Hollywood, of course, does it in reverse — they butter up anyone with as little
as one column inch, the way those who want plenty of butter on their popcorn say "a little
extra in the middle, please.") I was old school though, and none too sure of myself, so I said,
"Hi, thanks for coming" — and retreated. In New York, they wait in Sardi's for the reviews.
I went to Nick Tahou's for a hot dog. Tick, tock...

Years later I learned much more about Jack and read plenty of his reviews and essays, which are the subject of this book. It's remarkable how many things we have in common.

We were both born in the 1940s. We both had fathers, it turns out, who valued the lessons so tightly revealed in Rudyard Kipling's masterpiece, *If* ("If you can keep your head when all about you are losing theirs," etc.). Like *If*, Jack's crisp offerings speak simply and plainly to me. For 30 years he enthused, he tempted, and he warned his readers in regards to his favorite subject: the movies.

To many an actor like me, he has been that breath of fresh air in the midst of movie critics whose job description surely include words like "cut," "stab," and "savage." Substitute the words "love," "delight," and "discover," and you start to know Jack. His is a passionate approach to his subject, and a knowing one. Take, for instance, his review of *Apocalypse Now Redux*.

Apocalypse Now and *Mulholland Drive* were mysteries to me when I first saw them, even though I appeared in the latter. From someone close to David Lynch I overheard an explanation of *Mulholland Drive* that made me want to watch it again. Seems that the disappointed actress, who is also a disappointed lover to another girl, decides to commit suicide. In the short moment between pulling the trigger and her head hitting the pillow, her life unfolds to her *the way it ought to have been*! Likewise, Jack's review of *Apocalypse Now Redux* operates like a key in a lock. It makes the classic film understandable, and one that I now look forward to seeing with new eyes.

We both had a passion for the movies as boys. My mother told me at least 50 times in my youth, "Bob, you're going to grow up to be an usher in a show!" (I tried hard, Ma.)

Jack, in a different way, succeeded. He spends lots and lots of quality time watching movies. He, like me, loves 3-D. I was heartbroken when my father explained to me that it was a fad and it would not last … like Smell-o-Vision, its life would be short. I'm sorry the old man did not get to see the resurgence of 3-D in recent years. It's better than ever

Jack saw many of his early movies at the Capitol Theater. So did I – in different towns, though. My Capitol (in Rochester) was a bus ride away, so mostly I went to a third-run house, fondly remembered as the stinkin' Lincoln. I saw the scariest movie of my life there: *The Thing*. I've got a theory about that: One movie, and one movie only, scares you the most. It comes along at about age 12 or 14 and nothing thereafter can scare you as much . . . by then, you know more about how they're made and how actors go from one movie to another, and, sad as it is, you will never crap your pants (or toss your Milk Duds) again in the movies.

Jack's scariest was *Psycho*. And, wouldn't you know it, I was in the remake. One of the scariest days of my career. I played the psychiatrist who sums up and explains the picture in medical jargon that even in 1960 made little sense. Less, now. The script was an exact duplicate of the original. I thought it was a mistake, and asked my agent to get the studio to send me the new one. It arrived. It *was* the same. They were reshooting the movie almost exactly, including the timing of scenes. I arrived on the set at Universal. I knew the scene. I'd worked very hard on it (I remind actors that you need to know the words so well they can come out of your mouth the way thoughts come out of your mouth). I'd watched the picture and seen the way it was edited. Simon Oakland's four-and-a-half-minute speech was broken up into several cuts, so I figured I'd be able to handle the scene in manageable chunks.

The first shot got us into the room. The next shot, I was told, was to be my uncut moving close-up … a Steadycam shot … they didn't have Steadycam in the old days. Gripping pressure! The first take was shaky, and too long. I needed to shave 14 seconds off. The second take might have been worse. Total tension … shake it off, Bob. All the work I had done on the scene finally kicked in. Two false starts and then a real good take. Cut, print.

So, *Psycho,* for both Jack and me, goes into the category: *scariest ever!*

Another Hitchcock movie Jack writes about is *Rear Window.* As with *Psycho,* I was in the remake (a Hallmark made-for-TV film), this time starring Christopher Reeve. (May I say as an aside that there has never been a tougher guy … this was after his paralyzing horse-riding accident, but he did his work as an actor, his work as producer, and the grindingly difficult tasks of just getting to the set each morning with charm and cheer. I have never been prouder of an actor.)

The Hitchcock films and all that followed *Jackie Brown* have to be credited to Quentin Tarantino, another in my pantheons of benefactors and tough guys. I told him at the very beginning that I might be damaged goods and that the distributors would probably not let him hire me. He didn't hesitate. "I hire anyone I want!" he said. I could not fathom why anyone would go that far out on a limb for me. My career had practically ended. I was clinging to one last straw: that some kid who liked me when he was growing up would turn into a filmmaker and give me a job. Sometimes that happens. Sometimes artists hand out favors the size of which cannot be exaggerated. Sometimes and forever they change the landscape of lives. Jack's essay about Quentin gives insight into this crafter of stories.

When writing about the great Ray Charles, Jack tells us that Fathead Newman credits *his* career to Charles. It *does* happen sometimes; it's one of the things artists do for others. Artists are good people. It isn't art if it isn't good – that's my take on it. The artist is there to enhance understanding with every action he or she creates. That, in itself, is a good thing.

And as long as we're talking about singers: Actors all want to be singers. Me too! The great Ray tells us in Jack's piece that "soul" is making the song part of you. It's a little like that for an actor, too; you need to internalize the material, make it into who you are. Unlike a singer, though, who may sing the song many times over a career, the actor takes each new scene, starting always at zero, and hopes to deliver a 10 before the shot is finished. Each shot is a new card trick to master.

And as long as we're talking about guys named Ray (what a segue): I got one of my best acting lessons from one, the painter Ramon Santiago (Jack knew him). Ramon picked up a stretched canvas one soft afternoon in his studio, primed the surface of the canvas, selected a long-handled brush from among hundreds, worked the bristles, found two colors he liked, loaded the brush and stood facing the canvas on its easel. After some seconds he started at the upper right, drew a strong line toward the lower left and finished that first stroke with a tiny flourish. You couldn't tell till later what that line or that flourish would mean in the final composition. But it serves to remind the actor that on the first day of a shoot, when he is least ready to do so, he must deliver a confident stroke that serves the needs of the final composition and must include detail (that little flourish). He will never address that film moment again. The actor needs to be all-in on every shot.

Ramon claimed that he picked up some bad habits from me, though I'm sure I picked them up from someone else. Gene Parrotta, for instance, who tipped pretty good. Gene reminded me that guys who worked for tips always hope some sport will walk in and treat them nicely. Whenever I had dough, I figured I was supposed to be that sport. Gene told a story about Frank Sinatra: it seems he was waiting for his car, peeled off a c-note, and asked the valet what was the biggest tip he'd ever gotten. The valet replied, "A hundred dollars, sir." Sinatra then peeled off a second hundred and handed the deuce to the valet. Just before pulling out, Sinatra inquired, "Who was it gave you that hundred?" The valet replied, "Why, you did, sir!" Ramon couldn't outdo Sinatra, but he tried.

Jack's appreciation for Sinatra, Ray Charles, Gregory Peck, Philip Seymour Hoffman and others he writes about in this book is further proof that we have much in common. In fact, we ought to be pals. So, why on this evening in 1986, was he getting ready to pan my little *Hollywood Harry*? Tick, tock.

And about Gregory Peck: till his passing we had warm contact, and he'd be first on my list of favorites. I did my second picture, *The Stalking Moon,* with him. He gave me my best example of what a movie star ought to be and, second only to my father, of what a man should be. And he sponsored me into the Academy. I lived in Rochester at the time and didn't know many people in Hollywood. Knowing I needed a second sponsor, he got his friend Macdonald Carey to usher me in. Before he passed, Greg established a readers' program at the Los Angeles Library. I've been privileged to read there, and since his death, I've continued to read for his wife, Veronique, who kept the program going. Artists also leave things behind that are good.

And so, dear reader (tick, tock), you're probably wondering what Jack's review of *Hollywood Harry* was actually like …

Truthfully, I don't remember. I hope someone is posting old clippings into the iCloud and that review will be found someday, or that one of my grandchildren will discover it on an archaeological dig through old things. What I do remember is that I was worried for nothing. Jack was generous and kind to me, as well as insightful – qualities that are well on display in this book. He has always been good at clarifying, and with understanding, and he has been generous to his readers. This, also, is the stuff of art.

A final note: Jack was not the first of my benefactors at Gannett. Hamilton Allen, an older newspaperman who retired maybe six or eight years into my career, was a supporter from the beginning. For a couple of years I had a press agent, John Springer, who is mentioned in this book, came from Rochester, was Elizabeth Taylor's press agent. By the time Jack came along, I'd skidded quite a ways and had begun my 13-year sojourn into playing bad guys. Jack, it is plain to see, has been good to me for a long time. He is much the reason I am, in some precincts, still well thought of in my hometown. Thank you, Jack.

PREFACE

SCOTT PITONIAK

THE YEAR IS 1950 AND THE SCENE IS A QUAINT MOVIE THEATER IN COLLINGSWOOD, N.J. There, on the edge of a cushiony seat, we see a 5-year-old boy, mouth agape, eyes as big as saucers as he stares at the big screen.

"Watching King Kong burst through those gates made quite an impression on me," Jack Garner recalls, more than 60 years after his first exposure to the power of the silver screen.

Jack didn't realize it at the time, but a seed had been planted in that old movie house. The Pennsylvania native found his life's passion in reviewing movies for the *Democrat and Chronicle* and Gannett News Service.

From *Star Wars* to *Hugo*, Jack has cultivated a legion of readers in more than three decades as a critic. Jack retired in 2007, but he has continued to write a weekly freelance column and weekly reviews of jazz CDs and classic movie DVDs.

Jack's contributions to the community would not be forgotten with his retirement. His work for the newspaper and his status as chief film critic for Gannett News Service lifted the profile of Rochester as a movie town, allowing more first-run films to be released here sooner.

And his passion for his work was honored when George Eastman House presented Jack with the Eastman Medal of Honor for his contribution to motion pictures and the community, and will rename his favorite seats at the Dryden Theatre after him and his wife. He was only the second to receive the prestigious medal, which honors people who advance the principles embodied by Eastman Kodak Co. founder George Eastman. The first was U.S. Rep. Louise Slaughter, D-Fairport.

"I know from my travels that he's valued by actors and directors and others in the industry because they know they can count on Jack to provide opinion that's based on ample knowledge and a sense of fairness," says Anthony Bannon, former director of George

Eastman House. "Jack is not a shoot-from-the-hip kind of critic. He's not looking for the excerpt-able phrase that will be quoted in the ads across the country. He'd rather write something that is well-reasoned, and that takes talent."

Indeed. "Jack is an icon for this paper and this community," said Michael G. Kane, president and publisher of the *Democrat and Chronicle*. "Looking ahead, I'm very pleased that his bylines will still be a part of what we deliver through his part-time writing assignments.

"What I love most about Jack is how he translates his passion about the cinema and the arts in such lucid ways," Kane said. "It literally comes through in his writing voice – so intelligent, but easy to understand."

Those sentiments were echoed by Karen Magnuson, vice president for news and editor of the *Democrat and Chronicle:* "The newspaper wouldn't be the same without his byline."

Now, he and Bonnie, who was once his college sweetheart and is now his wife of 42 years, hope to do a little traveling and spend more time with their three grown children and four grandchildren, and explore a few book ideas.

Jack's voice has also been heard on Rochester area TV and radio. For several years, he appeared regularly on Brother Wease's former morning radio show on WCMF-FM (96.5).

"He's the kind of guy who can carry on an intelligent conversation about anything," says Brother Wease. "I think that's why his reviews are so meaty and respected. He sees how a particular movie relates to the bigger picture. The thing I also like about Jack is his sense of humor. You can definitely bust on him, and he doesn't take offense. He's just a wonderful, big-hearted, bear of a guy."

For a boy who spent his formative years in the small central Pennsylvania town of Williamsport, the movies provided a glimpse of worlds he never knew existed.

"They enabled me to expand my horizons," Jack says. "Here I am, going to a school where there isn't a single black kid, and I go to the movies and I see people of color on that screen. That's one of the things I've always loved about movies. They expose you to people and places you didn't know about. They can broaden your perspective."

He developed a similar fascination with music. With a weekly allowance of $1, Garner was often faced with a tough choice. "I could either go to the movies, which meant 60 cents for the ticket and another 40 for popcorn, or buy the latest 45 rpm record, which usually was a buck," he says. "There were weeks when it was a very difficult decision."

Garner also grew up with a passion for sports, playing both football and basketball in high school. American University offered the 6-foot-9, 260-pound Garner an opportunity to earn a hoops scholarship as a walk-on.

Garner opted instead for St. Bonaventure University, the college that nine of his relatives had attended. Blessed with a deep baritone, Garner believed broadcasting would be his future, but at Bonaventure, he developed a love for the written word and decided on a career in newspaper journalism.

After graduating in 1967, he spent a year as a general assignment reporter before pursuing his master's degree at Syracuse University. It was there that a mutual friend introduced him to Bonnie, who was pursing her graduate degree in education.

Garner joined the Rochester *Times-Union* as a "rewrite man" in 1970 and rose quickly through the ranks. He was part of the team that won a Pulitzer Prize for covering the Attica prison uprisings. One of Garner's most vivid memories of that national story was of taking dictation over the phone from a reporter on the scene and hearing gunshots in the background.

In 1973, Garner became city editor of the *Democrat and Chronicle,* and shortly thereafter became features editor. He also doubled as a concert reviewer. He recalls covering a young Bruce Springsteen at the Auditorium Theater and a Rolling Stones concert in Toronto that still ranks as his all-time favorite.

Then in 1977, he decided he wanted to go back to full-time writing and found his journalistic niche in movie reviewing. Through the years, he's interviewed the biggest names in Hollywood. Among them: Robert De Niro, whom Garner considers the best actor of his generation, Meryl Streep, Robert Redford, Spike Lee, and Martin Scorsese.

Garner remembers having unprecedented access to Woody Allen on the movie set and attempting to interview Bill Murray when the comedian was more interested in mixing Bloody Marys for reporters.

Garner's biggest thrills included meeting two of his heroes beyond the movie world – Muhammad Ali and John Lennon. "The job has been really, really great," he says. "I feel blessed that I got paid to go to the movies."

Scott Pitoniak is a former Rochester Democrat & Chronicle *sportswriter and author of books on the Buffalo Bills,* The Hickok Belt, *baseball great Johnny Antonelli, and Syracuse basketball coach Jim Boeheim. He worked alongside Jack Garner for several years.*

INTRODUCTION

JACK GARNER

THIS IS A BOOK ABOUT ONE MAN'S JOURNEY THROUGH THE MOVIES, AND ABOUT A passion he fostered to spend his life watching films and, hopefully to help others discover the rewards to be found on the screen.

I was fortunate to be the film critic of the Rochester *Democrat & Chronicle* from 1977 to 2007, when I retired. For 20 of those 30 years I was the chief national film critic for the hundred or so newspapers and outlets of Gannett. I used to say, "People pay me to go to the movies." I wasn't joking.

For a lifelong movie lover, the job was absolute heaven. Not only did I see every movie of any artistic or commercial interest, but I also often had chances to talk with people who appeared in the films or who made the movies. This only enhanced my knowledge and appreciation for the films I was watching, and I hope it had the same effect on my readers.

Like most things for most people, my passion for film began when I was a youngster.

I haven't been in the movie theaters of my youth for nearly a half century, yet I remember them fondly, the way some people remember a great Christmas Day, or visits from favorite relatives, or the big game. They were the three theaters of Williamsport, Pennsylvania, in the 1950s and early '60s. I grew up across the Susquehanna River in South Williamsport. For me, it was a Huck Finn sort of childhood, swimming in the river and nearby Loyalsock Creek in the summer, ice skating on Tiny Luppert's pond in Mosquito Valley in the winter, playing Little League and Pony League baseball (with little success), and going to lots of movies. Lots and lots of movies.

I would ride my Raleigh three-speed bike across the Market Street Bridge every Saturday, with a dollar allowance burning a hole in my pocket. Occasionally I'd use it to buy the latest 45 rpm record that had caught my ear. Mostly, though, I went to the movies. Sometimes, friends or my brother joined me. Often, I went alone. Nobody I knew was as passionate about the movies as I was.

The Capitol on Fourth Street was the most elegant and largest of the theaters, with a full-sized balcony and a big screen. I remember being at the Capitol in 1953 for the 3-D French and Indian War film, *Fort Ti.* We ducked when French soldiers aimed a cannon at "us" and fired it. After the film, we exited the theater into bright sunlight and saw that a car had crashed in front of the theater. It was a crumpled mess. My witty brother said, "Look, a direct hit!"

Later that year, after the 3-D boom had gone bust, I saw the first Cinemascope film, *The Robe,* at the Capitol. I remember thinking, *Wow, the new widescreen is big,* but I was disappointed because it was not the second coming of 3-D, as had been advertised. It was big – and 2-D.

The Keystone (later, the State) on Third Street was the least elegant of the three theaters, a large, high-ceilinged box with no balcony. It was a favorite for Saturday matinee B movies, and they still ran serials and cartoons with the features into the 1950s. That's where I saw *House on Haunted Hill* in 1959 from schlocky horror maven William Castle. It was filmed in "Emergo," which meant an inflatable glow-in-the-dark skeleton attached to a wire floated over the audience during the final moments, echoing a scene in which a skeleton arose from a vat of acid and chased Vincent Price's villainous wife. As you can imagine, it was far more laughable than frightening.

I wasn't laughing a year later when I was at the Keystone for Alfred Hitchcock's *Psycho.* That was the film that turned horror into art – and scared the bejeezus out of me like no film before or since.

The third theatre, the Rialto, on Market Street, may have been my favorite; a long, narrow brick building, it had a small balcony with two side portions that jutted out over the orchestra. It offered a neat, semi-private place to sit (and, I must confess, to occasionally bomb downstairs patrons with Jujubes).

Funny enough, I remember the theater more than many of the films I saw there, although the lackluster *Swingin' Along* in 1961 is a fond memory only because my favorite performer, the great Ray Charles, sang "What'd I Say" and "Sticks and Stones" in it.

It's not easy to pinpoint exactly why and when I became passionate about films. I think I was always drawn to the way movies efficiently told stories, generated emotions, and exposed you to people and places and things around the world (and even beyond the world).

The first movie I can remember seeing wasn't a typical childhood Disney film, though, Lord knows, I eventually saw and loved plenty of those. No, I remember going to celebrate the birthday of a fellow four-year-old and being taken with the party gang of boys to the movies. (The idea of watching a movie at home was only a pipe dream in 1949.) The movie we saw, as strange as it may seem, was *Sands of Iwo Jima* with John Wayne. In those days, parents would think nothing of taking young kids to any movie, within reason. If anything, it gave us ideas for when we played "war" in the backyard.

Television also fed my movie passion, but not until we got cable TV in 1952. In those days, you got cable just so you could watch two or three network stations. Williamsport is in a valley, surrounded by the foothills of the Allegheny Mountains, and we couldn't get any TV stations, no matter how many wires or pieces of aluminum foil we spread through the attic. Finally, cable became available. Since our house was in the southernmost part of the borough and the cable came down from Bald Eagle Mountain, just to our south, I've often thought our house might have been the first house in America to get cable. That's a cool distinction, right?

At any rate, we started getting CBS, NBC, and Mutual channels, out of Wilkes-Barre/Scranton, as I recall. At least one of those channels broadcast a nightly "Million Dollar Movie." On many a non-school night I'd stay up, fighting sleep, to watch those films. Two I especially remember seeing a few times each – and loving – were Victor Fleming's 1941 version of *Dr. Jekyll and Mr. Hyde*, with Spencer Tracy and Ingrid Bergman, and Mervyn LeRoy's 1944 *Thirty Seconds Over Tokyo,* again with Spencer Tracy.

A lot of the films on TV in the '50s were from Warner Bros. because that was the only studio smart enough to realize the riches to be gained by unloading old movies on TV. (The other studios saw television as "the enemy"; Warners saw it as a lucrative partner.) If you ever wondered why Humphrey Bogart and James Cagney had a secondary push to their careers, it was because of all those Warner films on TV.

I also think it helped that I had a mother who also loved the arts. My dad was more of a sports and meat-and-potatoes guy, but he was devoted to my mother, and what she said or wanted to do regarding the arts was fine with him. Only by doing the math have I come to realize I saw *High Noon* at age seven and *On the Waterfront* at age 9. I'm proud of my parents for letting that happen, and proud of myself for honestly understanding and enjoying such films at such a young age. (Of course, I was also a *Davy Crockett* and *Peter Pan* fanatic and religiously watched *The Mickey Mouse Club* every afternoon after school, at least until I graduated to *American Bandstand*.)

Mother also made sure we drove the two hours east to Scranton to see the limited road show engagement of *Lawrence of Arabia* in 1962. I'm so impressed that in those pre-Internet days, Mom knew the film was there, and that it was essential viewing.

I knew in high school that journalism was my future. I loved history and English and geography, so I figured journalism was the perfect blend. You use English to record history (whether on a large scale or a small one).

My initial interest was sports reporting, because I loved sports nearly as much as films. (I don't think at that young age I could even *imagine* having an opportunity to review and write about movies.) My high school mentor and basketball coach, Bill Byham, was a major influence. He also worked at a Williamsport area radio station as a sports commentator and broadcaster, and he was kind and patient enough to take me along for the broadcasts. That's how I ended up being a 16-year-old color commentator for broadcasts of high school football games on WMPT-AM.

However, when I went to St. Bonaventure University, I shifted gears in two important ways: I decided I'd rather write than broadcast, and I decided I was interested in straight-ahead reporting, or what we call "hard news." I worked a summer at the *Pittsburgh Post-*

Gazette, and then a full year upon graduation.

Then I went to Syracuse University for a graduate degree and two important things happened: I met my future wife, and I started aiming my life (without really realizing it) at film. I volunteered to write film reviews for a community advertiser weekly, for which I was paid the price of admission to a movie. (That meant a lot to a money-strapped grad student.) Then, after I met Bonnie, I insisted they double my "salary" so she could join me at the movies. She's been my movie-going partner and chief sounding board ever since.

After getting my master's, I was hired by the *Times-Union,* then Gannett's evening newspaper in Rochester, NY I was a rewrite man, which is a position newspaper don't have anymore. (Think of all those old movies in which somebody yells "Get me rewrite, sweetheart!") That job, and for that matter, that newspaper, are gone.

The job was to take information over the telephone (usually a pay phone) from the reporter on the scene, and then convert those notes into a story for the newspapers. The job was *essential* in the era before cell phones, before laptops, and especially at an evening newspaper, which had deadlines scattered through the day for a paper that was on the streets at different times from midday to evening.

At the *Times-Union,* I was the rewrite man for reports of the nearby Attica Prison rebellion of 1971. One of the stories that I helped write as a rewrite man won the Pulitzer Prize for two of our reporters, though the newspaper stressed that all of us on "the Attica Prison reporting staff" shared in the honor.

These events elevated me, and I was hired away in 1972 from the evening *Times-Union* to Gannett's morning *Democrat & Chronicle,* where I stayed until my retirement in 2007, and for whom I continue to write a weekly film and entertainment commentary column as of this writing.

After a few years of editing, I finally knew what I wanted, and I knew the newspaper was ready for its own film critic. So, in May of 1977, I reviewed the opening of the year's sensation, *Star Wars,* and I'm glad I at least had enough sense to suggest the film called out for a sequel.

I continued to write film reviews and interviews for Rochester until 1987, when I was elevated to the role of chief film critic for all the Gannett newspapers, so readers were likely to find my copy from Westchester-Rockland to Fort Myers to Palm Springs and beyond. And, of course, in Rochester. Despite a brief temptation to move to Westchester County, where Gannett had newspapers and I could be closer to New York City, I decided to stay in Rochester. It was a town my family and I loved, despite the need for me to make many trips to New York and to film festivals around the world.

Rochester is also home to one of the great film archives of the world, the Eastman House, and that has also provided hours of film-watching and research pleasure over the decades. Also many of Hollywood's greats made pilgrimages here to receive honors, which provided many interview opportunities for me. I would not have met Lillian Gish or Audrey Hepburn were it not for the Eastman House.

Because of the impetus of my national title and the impact of writing for scores of newspapers (potentially as many as 100), I suddenly had increased access to numerous stars, directors, advance screenings, and other things that fall into the bailiwick of film critic.

And that's what I was doing until my retirement in July of 2007.

This book, then, is a collection, a sampling, of the sorts of things I was writing about the film world, mostly for the Gannett newspapers, from the '70s through the first years of the new millennium. Two longer essays were written for other projects and are so marked. Everything else is from the archives of the Rochester *Democrat & Chronicle*.

I've arranged this book to accommodate three kinds of writing: interviews (Chapter One – Talking about the Movies), essays (Chapter Two – Thinking about the Movies), and reviews (Chapter Three – A Review Sampler). Then I got a bit more personal with my favorite sessions with film actors or directors (Chapter Four – Memorable Encounters) and with essays that I specifically wrote to appraise noteworthy filmmakers when they died (Chapter Five – The Final Curtain).

I concluded with an Afterword, in which I wrote about what makes a good film, what a critic looks for in a film, and why movies matter in our lives. And then, just to start arguments, I included an appendix with my list of the 200 most essential films, plus a short piece on my choices for the greatest and most essential Oscar winners over the decades.

Like most anthologies, *From My Seat on the Aisle* will hopefully be enjoyed either in bits and pieces, perhaps as you come across an actor or film of interest, or as a whole. Either way, I hope it is enjoyed.

Mostly, I hope I convey to you, friend reader, my deep sense of passion for the arts, and especially for the motion pictures that have given me so much pleasure over the decades.

CHAPTER ONE

TALKING ABOUT THE MOVIES

One of the great pleasures of my life covering the world of film has been the chance to talk with people who made the movies I've loved, or starred in them. To me, it is always a question of learning more about the process of the director or the actor, and about where their art comes from, their roots and their sources of inspiration. I very seldom get personal; I have little interest in their off-screen lives and romances and private worlds, except when it influences the work.

AUDREY HEPBURN

THE VOICE ON THE PHONE, CALLING FROM SWITZERLAND, WAS INSTANTLY RECOGNIZABLE. It had the refinement required to properly enunciate "the rain in Spain falls mainly on the plain." But the voice also had the spunk and still-unaffected innocence to belong to the aptly named Holly Golightly.

It was as recognizable as the speaker's large, sparkling almond eyes, or stylishly short dark hair, and her trademark — that astonishingly long and elegant neck. The speaker was clearly Audrey Hepburn.

It was the fall of 1992, and she was talking about her pride in being named the recipient of the prestigious George Eastman award at Rochester's Eastman House, and her special excitement about being able to travel soon to accept the award in person, in what for her had become a family town. The love of Hepburn's life for more than a decade was a tall, handsome former actor named Robert Wolders, whose mother and two sisters lived in the Rochester suburb of Irondequoit.

"I am very impressed and very honored to be named by the Eastman House," Hepburn said, "and I know that in receiving this award, I'm in extraordinary company." Coming back to Rochester was an added bonus.

Hepburn said she enjoyed the Rochester area. "There is a sense of constancy there that I admire. I've been in so many strange places that it's nice to see the tree-lined streets, the peacefulness and coziness. There is a sense of tranquility there."

Those "strange places" include a lot of the less fortunate corners of the Third World where Hepburn traveled as a goodwill ambassador for the United Nations Children's Fund. UNICEF and the fight against world hunger are causes that caught the 63-year-old actor's passion, much more than films in her last years.

She and Wolders, for example, had returned just one month before our conversation from a tour of starvation-wracked Somalia. The pair had traveled there with the hope that her presence might help draw attention to the tragedy unfolding there daily.

"It's frustrating for everybody. You feel you can't do anything," Hepburn said, "but I've been told that there's something I can do, which is to draw attention to things.

"Obviously, when you go to these places, you see the work of thousands of dedicated people who are having wonderful results, and it makes you feel terribly small and unimportant, and full of admiration. We plunge wholeheartedly into these missions, which is what you can call it."

Hepburn believed the most challenging impediment to solving the world hunger problem is war. "Civil war and the fighting is what impedes reconstructing. You can seed and develop, and it all gets destroyed by war. All people must put their weight behind the goal of stopping warfare. We do not want to just help children survive — we want to give them a future.

"We are very responsible for a lot of the suffering in Africa, because we didn't do much about these populations when they were colonies," Hepburn said. "We didn't help where education is concerned, and now we are paying the price. We enriched ourselves on the backs of these people, and now we must pay the price. Drought is a tragedy of nature, but famine is not."

Though Hepburn's UNICEF activities most certainly deserved praise, the Eastman House Award was more specifically given in recognition of an important, sustained career as a motion picture artist.

Looking back on her career, Hepburn said, "Everything happened in a wonderful way. I expected nothing. I wanted to be a dancer, and found myself little by little making movies, with this array of genius directors.

"My career was my working life but it also was the fun in my life. I was always terribly happy on the set. Going to work was always something I looked forward to. Though, of course, I worried a lot, because I tried to get things right."

The actress was born Audrey Kathleen Ruston on an estate near Brussels, Belgium, on May 4, 1929. She was the daughter of a wealthy English banker and a Dutch baroness, and spent her childhood in the Netherlands, during the Nazi occupation. Indeed, she traced her devotion to UNICEF to her gratitude toward the relief agencies that helped refugees in the Netherlands during and after the war.

As an adolescent, Hepburn was first trained for the ballet. To this day, she sees her film career as a big, happy accident.

It began when she was cast as a dancer in the musical *High Button Shoes in* London's West End, a role that was followed by dancing parts and other London reviews and musicals. But she began to be noticed for her distinctive look and singular qualities, beyond her dancing, and found herself cast in small roles in a few films in England and France. Most notable among these is a one-scene appearance near the beginning of *The Lavender Hill Mob,* starring Alec Guinness.

Hepburn's big break came, though, from a haphazard meeting with the French writer Colette on the set of a film in Monte Carlo. Colette was captivated by Hepburn and selected her for the title role in *Gigi,* a play being readied for the Broadway stage.

In that same year, 1953, Hepburn was also cast, surprisingly, as an unknown lead in *Roman Holiday* and contributed a performance opposite Gregory Peck that earned her an Oscar for her first major film role.

Roman Holiday was a project originally developed by Frank Capra as a European-style remake of *It Happened One Night.* He passed the project onto director William Wyler. In it, Hepburn played an English princess who longs for freedom on a visit to Rome. She escapes her entourage, poses as a commoner, and meets a U.S. newspaperman played by Gregory Peck. He knows her identity, though, and works on what he hopes will be a major scoop. Everything changes when he realizes he's falling in love with her.

Roman Holiday introduced to film audiences everywhere a type of actress that hadn't often been seen. Fine-boned and boyishly slim, she didn't meet the buxom standard of the day, typified by Marilyn Monroe and Jane Russell. But she displayed an aura of sophistication combined with a spunky vulnerability. Hepburn also had a gorgeous face and knew how best to present herself on screen.

Her image and impact were not unlike that of another Hepburn a generation earlier. Katharine Hepburn, however, presented a strength that came from Yankee New England stock; Audrey Hepburn's style came from Europe.

It was a case not only of her looks and her restrained acting, but also of her soft, eloquent, almost imperceptibly accented voice. Not only did no one look like Audrey Hepburn — no one sounded like her either.

Thanks to *Roman Holiday,* Hepburn's stock soared, and she went on to star during the '50s in such films as *Sabrina,* opposite Humphrey Bogart; *Funny Face,* opposite Fred Astaire; *The Nun's Story;* and the iconic *Breakfast at Tiffany's.* At one point, she was second only to Elizabeth Taylor among the best paid actresses in Hollywood, and she graced fashion magazines by the score.

In 1963, she fell into the only Hollywood controversy of her career when she was chosen over Broadway star Julie Andrews for the film version of *My Fair Lady.* Hepburn turned in a memorable performance as Eliza Doolittle, but Julie Andrews won the Oscar for *Mary Poppins,* so it all ended well.

Hepburn's other '60s films included the highly regarded *Two for the Road,* with Albert Finney, and the frightening thriller *Wait Until Dark,* in which she played a blind woman tormented by a psychotic drug dealer (Alan Arkin). But then, at the peak of her career and at only 38 years of age, Hepburn quit the screen to live quietly in Switzerland and raise her children.

Though there was no reason to doubt her stated motive—to be with her family—Hepburn also avoided one of the most challenging times in an actress's career: the point between the ages of 40 and 60, when opportunities for roles dwindle until the performer is old enough to play grandmothers and other character parts.

Hepburn had a son, Sean, in 1960 with her first husband, actor Mel Ferrer, and a second son, Luca, in 1970, with her second husband, psychiatrist Andrea Dotti. Both marriages ended in divorce.

"I just didn't work as long as some other actresses," Hepburn said. "I removed myself in the middle of my career, because I had a young son at the age where I could not travel anymore. I wanted this child all my life, and I felt miserable away from him. Some people can manage children and a career, but it was difficult for me at that time because movies were being made all over the world."

Though she returned to occasional film acting in the late 1970s, she still had only about 25 films to her credit (60 or 70 films are more typical of a long, successful movie career). "But I've never regretted it," she assured me; "that was one of my better decisions, to know my sons and see them grow up."

Her few later films included the marvelous *Robin and Marian*, in which she and Sean Connery co-star as Maid Marian and Robin Hood in their later years; Sidney Sheldon's potboiler *Bloodline*; Peter Bogdanovich's *They All Laughed*; and finally, a Steven Spielberg's romance *Always*.

Asked to name her favorites from her films, Hepburn begged off.

"That's very difficult for me to answer. I didn't make 99 movies; I only made 25 or so. Each picture was very important in my life. They were all very happy ones, exciting but also very hard. Most pictures were either too hot or too cold, or I was in every scene. It was a long, hard job.

"But I loved every minute of it."

I was especially proud of this interview, not only because of my respect for the actress, but also because I suspect it may have been the last interview of any depth she ever gave.

Though we talked on the phone, we also spoke together informally when she came to the Eastman House ceremony. She was gracious and lovely, of course, but didn't stay long, begging off from the post-award reception. Only later did we learn the real reason. About four months after her Rochester appearance, Hepburn died, on Jan. 20, 1993, at her Swiss home, at 63. She had appendiceal cancer.

GREGORY PECK

A CONVERSATION WITH GREGORY PECK WAS A TALK WITH A CONTENTED MAN.

The veteran star was not one to rail on about the public or critics not supporting one of his pictures. Nor would you ever catch him bad-mouthing the old studio days in Hollywood.

Asked whether any of his more than 50 films had ever been unjustly overlooked, for example, Peck said with a laugh, "No, but several have been justly overlooked. I've always believed the public is usually right about a film, and it may surprise you to hear that I think the critics are generally right as well. Sam Goldwyn had a great way of putting it: 'If the public won't go to the box office, you can't stop 'em.'"

Much more often than not, over Peck's 43-year career, we flocked to the box office for his films. From his Oscar-winning performance in *To Kill a Mockingbird* to his romancing of Audrey Hepburn in *Roman Holiday*, Gregory Peck has been one of our most admired stars.

It is that impressive film career — including five Oscar nominations — that was honored in 1987 when he came to Rochester to receive the prestigious George Eastman Award, given for lifetime achievement. He also introduced a screening of his 1947 classic western, *Duel in the Sun*. "We don't get honors like that every other day," Peck told me at that time.

He said he had been eager to see Rochester because he had roots there. "As it happens, my father was born in Rochester, in either 1884 or 1886; he was never sure which. His name also was Gregory Peck. He didn't stay there very long though. His mother was an Irish immigrant and married an American who I assume was also a Rochesterian. He died rather abruptly from diphtheria, so my grandmother took my father back to Ireland. They came back to America a few years later, but I don't know where they settled."

By 1916, they were in La Jolla, CA. That's where Gregory Peck was born. He studied pre-med at Berkeley, but found himself drawn to acting through experiences with college theatrics.

A summer tour in George Bernard Shaw's *The Doctor's Dilemma* led to Broadway stage work, and theatrical success brought Peck to Hollywood. His first picture was *Days of Glory,* and he won his first Oscar nomination for his second picture — as a missionary priest in *The Keys of the Kingdom.*

Peck's lanky, dark-haired good looks and the suggestion of quiet strength and integrity made him a favorite with producer David O. Selznick, directors Alfred Hitchcock, Henry King and William Wyler, and the public in general.

And though many stars of his generation are quick to condemn the strict contract and mass production aspects of the old studio days, Peck said the system helped make him a star. "The studios turned out so many pictures that you were seeing maybe three a year," Peck said. "Carole Lombard used to say it takes 10 pictures to make a star, and she was right." In those days, it didn't take long to rack up 10 pictures.

Peck also came to realize how much easier it was to act in a picture when he was directed by someone he considered a friend. That's why William Wyler and Henry King were Peck's two favorite directors.

"It's important to have a real friend on the other side of the camera, because that's who you play to. You don't play to the electrician and technicians on the set — that's all a myth. They are busy doing their own jobs. You'd play to one fellow — the director. And you are willing to take chances and make a fool out of yourself when you know the guy on the other side of the camera will catch up, and protect you."

If there was a major disappointment in Gregory Peck's career, the actor would have considered it to be his much-debated casting as Captain Ahab in John Huston's 1956 version of *Moby Dick.* Peck said his age at the time — 39 — made it difficult for him to portray Ahab convincingly. "I may have been too young," he acknowledged, adding, "I think I could play it better now, because I've been through the ups and downs of life a good deal more, and I'd play it differently."

Peck also had a personal reason for wanting to forget *Moby Dick:* "I almost got killed on that picture," he said. For Ahab's final scene, Peck was strapped, wooden leg and all, onto the side of a giant artificial wheel that rolled along in the Irish Sea (simulating Ahab's being entangled in ropes on the struggling giant whale). "It was on a rotating device, and it would sometimes rotate me under the ocean," Peck explained. At one point, divers had to rescue him after he remained submerged.

"I think John Huston rather enjoyed the struggles," said Peck, describing his theory about Huston's attitude toward actors. "I don't think John was really fond of actors. I think he had a bit of a father complex and spent his life trying to outdo his father." John Huston's father, Walter Huston, was, according to Peck, "such a beloved figure and a well-loved actor, and I think there was some kind of competition on John's part. Whether he knew it or not, I think John Huston was out to top his father."

The highlight of Peck's career, of course, was his performance as the father and attorney Atticus Finch in Robert Mulligan's 1962 film *To Kill a Mockingbird.* The movie earned Peck his long-awaited Oscar, in one of the greatest competitions in Oscar history, against Peter

O'Toole's *Lawrence of Arabia. Mockingbird* has continued to survive as a classic literary adaptation.

"I think we were all riding the wave when I made that picture," Peck reported. "It was like being swept along the river. It was emotional. I feel we came very close to those characters. And the author, Harper Lee, felt the same way."

Asked to name his favorite co-stars over the years, Peck said he always lists four names: "Audrey Hepburn, with whom I made *Roman Holiday*. The results were special; it was an old-fashioned love story and we made a great sacrifice for love. Sophia Loren, who is such great fun. She's a terrific woman, which everybody knows. And Ingrid Bergman and Ava Gardner. I worked with Ava three times, and we have a special understanding, maybe because we each had our beginnings in small towns. It was like we were cousins. Ava Gardner was also one of the most beautiful women to ever appear on screen. I worked with her when she was 23, and people got weak in the knees just looking at her."

Peck continued to act — though sparingly — in his later years. He played the president, for example, in 1987's *Amazing Grace and Chuck*, a heart-tugging drama about a little boy's campaign to stop the nuclear arms race. He also starred in *Old Gringo* in 1989, and he had a cameo in Martin Scorsese's *Cape Fear* remake (because he had been the star of the original 1962 film noir).

Peck was one of Hollywood's most active citizens for social and political causes, having served on the National Council on the Arts, as national chairman of the American Cancer Society, and as a director of the American Film Institute, the Academy of Motion Picture Arts and Sciences, and the Salk Institute. Peck's many honors also included the Jean Hersholt Humanitarian Award and the Medal of Freedom.

And, of course, the George Eastman Award.

MICHAEL CAINE

One of my favorite actors over the years has been Michael Caine; he's always interesting, no matter how large or small the role, or even how good or bad the film. He's also always been an entertaining interview subject; he's smart, friendly, witty and forthcoming, and very knowledgeable on film history (elements that are also evident in his two published autobiographies).

He's also a perceptive film viewer. He once listed for rottentomatoes.com his five favorite films of all time, and I'd be hard-pressed to argue with him: Casablanca, The Third Man, The Treasure of the Sierra Madre, Charade, *and* The Maltese Falcon.

Here are excerpts of stories I did after three interviews with Caine, in 1998, 2002, and 2003, in connection with Little Voice, Austin Powers, *and the superb* The Quiet American, *respectively.*

IN HIS BREAKTHROUGH ROLE IN *ALFIE*, IN 1966, MICHAEL CAINE DEMONSTRATED A peculiar talent that would stay with him: even when he's a "dirty rotten scoundrel" or a randy rogue, we enjoy his company.

He proved it again in 1998 as the self-serving, low-life show-biz promoter Ray Say in *Little Voice* — it's Caine's best performance in a decade, a piece of colorful acting that's already earned the actor his third Golden Globe, at age 65.

What's Caine's secret to making a slimeball lovable?

"No man is a scoundrel to himself," Caine said. "I'm sure even Hitler thought he was a wonderful guy. He loved little children and animals, and he painted pretty pictures. No man is a villain to himself, and you have to play him that way.

"When I analyze myself as an actor," Caine continued, "I think part of my appeal is that I am not an obvious winner. I have the air of a loser. I spent a large part of my life being a loser, which I think adds an interesting dimension to my personality."

Ray Say is such a loser, you feel sorry for him, no matter how sleazy he is.

"He's a disaster. He's a would-be promoter who's gone out to the boondocks and become more and more disastrous," Caine said. "It's a lovely character to play."

Caine said he also identified with the role because "there, but for the grace of God, go I." He explained that for "everybody who starts in show business, failure is 90 percent of your vision. Failure to get the job, failure to do it right, failure of the entire show, because a lot depends on other people as well."

Little Voice marks Caine's return to films after a brief lull. "There's a metamorphosis when you're in acting in which you stop being the leading man, and you become Dad. So you have to go away for a little while, and then return under a new guise. I'm now officially not a leading man." He's quick to add that he's not complaining. As an older character actor, Caine said, "you get marvelous parts."

Next up was *The Cider House Rules*, from the John Irving novel of the same name. Caine plays a physician who runs an abortion clinic and an orphanage in the 1940s. "It's an incredible way of addressing the abortion issue, and Irving is a great writer," he stated, adding, "It's a gut-wrenching story."

Caine said he remains busy reading scripts, but the days when he would say yes to anything and everything (including such stinkers as *Jaws 4* and *The Swarm*) are behind him. "I used to think: *If I'm good, even in a bad movie, it'll be OK.* But I've learned. I've been burned too many times. That's why everybody else matters when you pick a project. If I'm the only guy hoeing my row in the field, it makes for bad farming."

In 2002, Michael Caine told me he wasn't just a good choice to play Austin Powers' father in the latest '60s spy spoof. He was the only choice. The veteran wasn't being cocky — just realistic. Mike Myers, the star and creator of the *Austin Powers* film franchise, told Caine he was inspired by Caine's films of the 1960s, especially the Harry Palmer spy stories, *The Ipcress File* and *Funeral in Berlin*, as well as *Alfie*, the memorable portrait of a womanizing English cad in the swingin' '60s.

"Austin has (Harry's) glasses and Alfie's libido," Caine said. He added that Myers sent "a nice letter about his father and how I was one of his father's favorite actors, and how much he loved the Harry Palmer movies." But despite nearly a half-century of performances and two Oscars, Caine admitted, "I was a bit scared of it at first." *Austin Powers in Goldmember* is the third installment in the campy series, and being the new guy is never easy. "Everyone else has worked together on two other projects," Caine noted, adding, "but they were really welcoming."

Caine said he also wasn't used to being quite so silly. "I think I'm known as an actor who's generally restrained in my performances. In *Austin Powers*, the actors are anything but restrained. I asked director Jay Roach if he thought maybe I was acting a bit over the top. He said you can't be too over the top in an Austin Powers movie."

Caine said the other challenge was acting like Myers, because he had to make it believable that Myers was his son. "But since Mike had been acting like me, that wasn't much of a problem."

Caine said he was comfortable with the film's sophomoric style of humor. "It's a British type of humor. It's a humor I've known since I was a kid. All the pratfalls and fart jokes that the kids love, and then the sexual double entendres for the adults that go over the heads of the kids."

A legendary cockney, Caine was born Maurice Mickelwhite to a fish-market porter and a cleaning woman in London. A school dropout at 15, he took various working-class jobs and joined the British Army to serve in Korea. After returning, he began thinking about an acting career, but started as an assistant stage manager for a small company. On the advice of an agent, he took a stage name, inspired by the marquee advertising *The Caine Mutiny*, a film that stars his favorite actor, Humphrey Bogart.

Despite such inauspicious beginnings, Caine has gone on to be one of the most popular and successful actors in movie history. He was knighted by Queen Elizabeth in June 2000. Such a turn-around in life leaves Caine feeling blessed. "I do believe in God," Caine said. "If you had my life, you'd believe in God, too."

I asked Caine to list the films he'd most like to be remembered for. Caine included *Alfie* and *The Ipcress File*, along with *Zulu, Hannah and Her Sisters, The Cider House Rules, The Man Who Would Be King* and *Educating Rita* ("which I think includes my best performance"). It's a list with which I concur, though I'd also add the hilarious comedy *Dirty Rotten Scoundrels.*

Caine also believed his next film, *The Quiet American*, would end up on that list (and he was right). Based on Graham Greene's novel, the dark, serious drama stars Caine as an opium-addicted British reporter in Southeast Asia in the '50s who vies with a young American (Brendan Fraser) for the affections of a Vietnamese woman.

"If we were talking about that film instead of *Austin Powers*, this would be quite a different interview," Caine said, with a laugh.

And now, here's that interview, from 2003...

After nearly a half-century in films, many at the very top of his profession, Michael Caine knows about being a star. Lord knows, he's enjoyed the trappings of stardom — the lavish homes and restaurants he's owned all over the globe, the country gardens he tends, the two Academy Awards on his shelf and knighthood from his queen.

But he's happiest when you don't notice the star on the screen, but buy into the character. That's why, he told me, *The Quiet American* was his most satisfying film experience. With no false modesty, he said, "I felt I was getting it absolutely right. I'm carrying the picture — and I disappear. It's a great part for a man my age." Caine looks a robust 60 but would turn 70 on March 14, 2003. Academy voters agree: He was nominated as best actor (an award he eventually would lose to Adrien Brody for *The Pianist*).

The Quiet American combines romance and intrigue in Vietnam under the French in

1952. Caine is Thomas Fowler, a cynical *London Times* correspondent having an affair with a much younger Vietnamese woman. A newly arrived brash young American (Brendan Fraser) with a hidden agenda becomes Fowler's competition for her affection. The young man also becomes a metaphor for the United States' growing involvement in Southeast Asia. But if the film is a cautionary tale, Caine jokes, "The caution is this: Don't try to take a 20-year-old girl away from a 69-year-old man."

Graham Greene wrote the book on which the film is based — and Caine believes Fowler is based on Greene's life: He too was a British newspaperman in Saigon, and Caine believes he also did part-time intelligence work for the British Foreign Service.

Caine met Greene around the time he shot another film based on the author's work, *The Honorary Consul.* Caine plays the title character, who becomes involved with a physician (Richard Gere) as revolution foments in a Latin American country. Caine said, "He told me he didn't like that film, but he liked me in it. Through knowing Greene, I thought I knew Fowler."

The Quiet American was the first major Western production filmed in post-war Vietnam. "It was great because I was in a situation where I knew nothing," Caine explained. "I'd never been there before. It's a very pervasive place. It gets under your skin. It's quite easy to be absorbed by the place."

The film was shot in the spring of 2001, but the release was delayed by Miramax because of the volatile political mood in America in the wake of Sept. 11, 2001. "They were worried the film would be seen as anti-American," Caine recalled "But it's really only anti-the people-who-took-America-into-the-Vietnam-War. And as I remember it, 90 percent of the other Americans are anti-them, too."

The Quiet American was a high-water mark in what has been a fruitful latter-day portion of Caine's long film career. The actor had slowed down in the early 1990s — taking the occasional made-for-TV movie, writing his memoirs, and running his restaurants in London, Miami and elsewhere. But he was tempted back by great character parts in *Blood and Wine,* offered by co-star Jack Nicholson; and in *Little Voice, The Cider House Rules* and *The Quiet American.*

In the latter years of his career, Caine said he's interested only in challenging roles. "I don't need to work for money anymore. I only do what I really, really want to do. I'm not going to get up at 6 a.m., put on makeup and learn six pages of dialogue unless I'm having a really good time."

MERYL STREEP

EVERYONE TALKS ABOUT MERYL STREEP'S FACILITY WITH ACCENTS — the halting accuracy of her Polish immigrant in *Sophie's Choice*, for example. It's as if being an audio sponge makes her special.

But here's the real reason we treasure the film, the reason Streep won an Oscar for the role: we believe Sophie's story, her painful memory of the day a Nazi made her choose which of her two children would die.

We believe Meryl Streep.

She finds the hooks to lure her audience into her films, like Sophie's accent, or Karen's blue-collar playfulness in *Silkwood*, or Francesca's emotional hunger in *The Bridges of Madison County*, or Gail's buffed-up body in *The River Wild,* or the violin teacher's prowess in the forthcoming *Music of the Heart,* or the sternness and haunting dementia as Margaret Thatcher in *The Iron Lady*, the 2011 film for which she won her third Academy Award.

But if Streep doesn't get the whole package right, the character won't come to life. And we won't care enough to go on her journey with her. That's what acting is all about, and Meryl Streep is among the best ever to do it.

I talked with Streep a handful of times in my career, most recently when the actress came to Rochester in 1999 to be honored with a lifetime achievement award at the Eastman House. "In our 50th anniversary year," said Eastman House director Anthony Bannon, "we've selected one of the most important artists of the century to receive our George Eastman Award."

Streep had just turned 50 the summer we talked, and hoped she was only at the midway point in her career. Of course, she was right. Over the next dozen years, she earned acclaim for performances in *Adaptation, The Hours, The Devil Wore Prada, Doubt, Julie & Julia* (as Julia Child), and *The Iron Lady*. And she shows no signs of slowing down.

Streep may be among the greatest of all stars, but she seldom acts like one. She's "the last great Hollywood diva," said Eastman House senior film curator Paolo Cherchi-Usai, "but without a Hollywood mentality." Streep lives in rural Connecticut with her sculptor husband, Donald Gummer, and their four children. She seldom goes to parties, isn't a regular on David Letterman, and limits her interviews. "I stay away from the gargantuan events, because if you go to too many of those, you feel gargantuan yourself," she said. "I feel like who I am."

Granted, Streep sees the plus side of celebrity. "I often get the first look at a lot of scripts. But then again, some things don't come my way because they want to attach a new face to the project. So that's hard."

But she doesn't want to complain. "It's not really a problem. Life is good. Besides, I really don't go to too many big events because I just don't want to get dressed up."

She also isn't one to choose a movie just for fame and mass appeal. So while her films generally earn critical plaudits, they don't always top box office lists. One exception was 1994's *The River Wild,* in which Streep proved she could hold her own in a popcorn thriller and combat the glass ceiling for actresses over 40. She hit the gym, developed a taut body and whitewater rafting skills, and was right at home in the adventure.

But even with *The River Wild*, she had a distinctly Streep moment: She was asked to pose holding a gun for a promotional poster. She refused. That's because Streep is worried about the rise in violence in America and believes Hollywood plays a role. "I just felt as an industry, nothing happens," she told me. "But as an individual, you can say, 'No, I can't do that.' You don't have to be pointing a gun in your lingerie. If more people felt that way, there'd be less glamorization of weapons. I don't know what the industry can do, but if everyone followed their conscience, it would help."

Born into a comfortable New Jersey family as Mary Louise Streep, she first wanted to sing opera. But by the end of high school, acting had become her passion. She studied drama at Vassar and went on to advanced studies at the venerable Yale School of Drama. She came to Broadway in *27 Wagons Full of Cotton*, earned a Tony nomination, and secured a supporting role in the 1977 film *Julia*, alongside Vanessa Redgrave and Jane Fonda. Within a year, she was the talk of the film industry.

Since then, she's had a career that's placed her opposite some of the most formidable talents of the '80s and '90s, including Kevin Kline, Woody Allen and Jack Nicholson. On the screen, Robert De Niro has been her lover, Cher her friend, Leonardo DiCaprio her son. Dustin Hoffman has divorced her and Kevin Bacon has tried to kill her. Asked to name her most memorable co-star, she diplomatically declined. "Think of who I've worked with. They've all been so different and so wonderful, in different ways. It's the same with directors."

But she's willing to help us assemble a make-believe Meryl Streep Film Festival of the movies she most wants to be remembered for: "I'd pick a few of the more obscure ones first, like *Cry in the Dark* and *Plenty*, both directed by Fred Schepisi, a very underrated filmmaker; *Ironweed*, which we shot up in Albany; and the Irish film, *Dancing at Lughnasa*." Her other, better-known favorites include *Sophie's Choice, Silkwood, Out of Africa* and *The*

Bridges of Madison County. "I also love *Postcards from the Edge* and *Heartburn*," she added.

Of course, she also speaks fondly of *Music of the Heart*, which was due to open a few weeks after our conversation. Streep plays a real-life music teacher, Roberta Guaspari, who leads her class of violin-playing East Harlem youngsters to the stage of Carnegie Hall. True to form, Streep plunged into her character by learning to play the violin. "Faking it" apparently isn't in her lexicon.

"Well, I couldn't fake it, because I'm sawing away on the strings," she said, adding that actors can use a "dead" piano with dubbed music, but a violin is out in the open for everyone to see. Director Wes Craven planned to record the film's grand-finale violin concert live, with Streep's character sharing a stage with several music legends, including Isaac Stern and Itzhak Perlman. "When you heard it on stage — I'm in there. I really had to keep up. Fear is a great motivator. I was so terrified. We mostly shot in continuity, so at least the concert scene was at the end of the schedule."

Streep sees the film as a *Mother Courage* for the '90s. Her character, she said, "is financially strapped and needy, but she wants to make her life meaningful and is trying to give something back." But is it intimidating to play a living person who's around to watch you work and see the movie? "Oh, yeah," Streep said, with a laugh. "I was apologizing every day. But she's very happy with it, and she's a tough character." Streep said she watched Guaspari teach one day and studied videotapes of her classes; "but once I started working, I didn't pay any attention to any of that. First I look and listen. Then I shut up and go to work."

Asked if she has any advice for the young who wish to follow her into acting, Streep hesitates. "There are different ways to pursue this profession, depending on what you want. A hit series? To play all of Shakespeare's heroines? To move among all sorts of media?"

But after a pause, Streep has the answer. And it sounds like an appropriate motto for a great actor: "Don't limit yourself or be limited by others."

CLINT EASTWOOD

WHAT WERE ROWDY YATES, DIRTY HARRY AND THE MAN WITH NO NAME DOING IN A place like Savannah, making a movie about a gay antiques dealer and a drag queen?

"Am I wearing lip gloss?" Clint Eastwood asked with a sly smile, talking later in a Manhattan hotel. "I've always considered myself very tolerant of other lifestyles. But it's also interesting to tell a story about things you don't know about."

He hadn't read John Berendt's book *Midnight in the Garden of Good and Evil* when the screenplay, by John Lee Hancock, crossed his desk. Hancock had written Eastwood's *A Perfect World* and wanted the veteran actor-director's opinion on his new adaptation. Instead, he got an enthusiastic Eastwood asking to direct it.

"I was drawn to the individuality of the characters," Eastwood said during our 1997 interview. "I've always done stories about individuals. Think of *Bronco Billy*, who says, 'I am who I want to be.' I'm at that stage in life where I don't want to repeat myself. But storytelling is storytelling, and I'm a storyteller."

Sixty-seven at the time of this interview — with 42 years in the business and 50 features behind him — Eastwood wasn't worried about others' expectations. "A friend of mine said that the good thing about being in your 60s is: What can they do to you? You become very philosophical. Heck, even if they say good things, they can be wrong."

When I entered his suite, I had to step around a baby car seat on the floor. This, too, seemed unusual in the world of Eastwood — unless you happen to know that he and his 30-something wife, Dina Ruiz, were the parents of a girl who was 2 at the time of this interview. "Being a father again is great," Eastwood said. "I have a friend who says, 'You should always have a 5-year-old around the house. It keeps the old vitality going.'"

Eastwood fell for Ruiz, a television newscaster, during an interview. "This is my second — and last — marriage," he said forcefully. "I finally found the woman I'm nuts about. It just came upon me."

Meanwhile, a daughter from his first marriage, Alison, played the romantic lead in *Midnight in the Garden of Good and Evil* at age 27. Lest anyone accuse Eastwood of nepotism, both father and daughter insist the casting went through normal channels. "My agent told me I had an audition," Alison said. "I read several times. It was very professional."

Eastwood's only nagging fear, he said, was, "What would happen if she wasn't good and I had to fire her? That's why I insisted on the complete audition process."

Once she was hired, Dad was in the awkward position of directing a love scene between his daughter and John Cusack. Though the scene eventually was cut, it was filmed. "It was nice to be there as a chaperone," Eastwood said with a smile. But the actors said he insisted the scene be done in one take. "That's part of the chaperoning," he added.

Alison and Cusack play the only conventional people amid a city of bizarre characters. "It's the oddities that make Savannah unique," Eastwood said. "But there's a certain tolerance for it all — and that's also refreshing at this time."

In the middle of *Midnight*, a young man is killed — and the antiques dealer (played by Kevin Spacey) is charged with murder. But the film never resolves the case. "I don't know what happened," Eastwood said. "What I'm expressing is that nobody will ever know." That ambiguity, he added, is precisely what attracted him to the project. But one thing he knows: *Midnight* is just as much a "Clint Eastwood film" as *Play Misty for Me, The Outlaw Josey Wales, Bird, The Bridges of Madison County* and the Oscar-winning *Unforgiven*. "I don't seek out any specific kinds of themes," he said. "I grew up liking all kinds of things — heavy dramas to Abbott and Costello."

The only shift in his thinking is away from the violence of his earlier work.

"As you go along, you'll see a good violent film that says something — that was my argument with *Unforgiven*. But bad violent movies are ruining it for everyone today."

Midnight in the Garden of Good and Evil also registers as an Eastwood film because of its use of jazz and standards associated with Savannah native Johnny Mercer for the film soundtrack. The film even includes a glimpse of Mercer's tombstone there. Eastwood is an acknowledged fan of great American jazz; he is a moderately skilled pianist and a film composer. He also used Johnny Hartman jazz ballads in *The Bridges of Madison County*, filmed *Bird* (a biopic about Charlie Parker), and made a documentary segment on piano blues for the PBS series *The Blues.*

Still robust, Eastwood showed no sign of slowing down. "I like both acting and directing," he told me, "though directing is more satisfying as I go down the line. But I still enjoy working — and I'll do it forever."

He spoke the truth. In the years following this interview, as he moved into his 70s, he made such important work as *Million Dollar Baby, Gran Torino, Invictus, J. Edgar,* and a film I believe is his masterpiece, *Mystic River.* And, in 2006, at the age of 76, he made *two* World War II epics about Iwo Jima, *Flags of Our Fathers* and *Letters from Iwo Jima* (the latter in Japanese!).

PHILIP SEYMOUR HOFFMAN

YOUNG FOLKS WHO ATTEND SPECIALTY SUMMER CAMPS — FOR BASKETBALL, DRAMA, dance or whatever — have every right to dream, even if such aspirations seldom come true. For a future actor, director and writer, those dreams were realized.

Philip Seymour Hoffman has gone on to earn a substantial reputation as one of the great actors of his generation, in film and on stage. But years ago, between his junior and senior years at Fairport (NY) High School, Hoffman met Westchester natives Bennett Miller and Dan Futterman at a state drama camp in Saratoga Springs, Saratoga County. The boys dreamed of someday working together.

Check the credits on *Capote*, the highly praised, Oscar-winning 2005 film, and you'll see their summer camp aspirations bore fruit. Miller directed. Futterman wrote. And Hoffman starred as eccentric writer Truman Capote. All three earned Oscar nominations. And Hoffman won.

"It's not enough to be friends," Hoffman said during the lead-up to the film's release. "It can be dangerous. But the script was really strong. I didn't know (Capote's) story, per se. It led me to read the biography. And I was compelled. Then Danny sent me a nice letter about 'What else are we to do on this planet but make this film with old friends?'"

Actually, Hoffman said, he wasn't worried about the relatively untested abilities of his old friends. He was worried about himself. Was he right to play the famously odd and troubled Capote? "I wasn't sure I could pull it off," Hoffman said.

Ah, but he did. Reviews proclaimed it the performance of the year.

Capote chronicles five key years in the writer's life as he crafts the landmark book *In Cold Blood*. He pursues the stories of the murder of a family of four in a Kansas farmhouse and of the two men charged with the crime. Along the way, he grows perilously close to one of those murderers, Perry Smith, because he identifies with Smith's troubled childhood.

Some even suggest Capote fell in love with Smith. Yet Capote needed Smith to be executed so he could have a potent finale for his all-important book. Once it happened, Capote was never again the same, and he never finished another book.

"I didn't have a lot of knowledge (about Capote)," Hoffman said. "But I think that was a huge plus. I had the layman's knowledge. I didn't have a basic take or a judgment on him. I could make choices that were naive and innocent and nonjudgment[al]. That helped me have the courage to play him. If I was a big fan, or knew a lot about him, it might have been different."

Hoffman has made a career out of playing oddballs and eccentrics on the fringes of society. He has "a remarkable face," wrote *Interview* magazine several years ago. "One look at it and you know that, contrary to rumor, movies haven't lost their genius for discovering actors who are capable of being themselves while occupying the spirit of another person and mirroring the secrets and desires of everyone watching in the dark."

Hoffman's mother, Marilyn O'Connor, a retired family court judge, proudly put it another way. After watching her son's performance of the painful loner in *Happiness*, she told him, "You know, Philip, you give a voice to the voiceless."

Hoffman has built his reputation, in part, by embracing difficult roles that a more vain actor might reject. From the pathetic, lovesick Scotty J. in *Boogie Nights* to the masturbating loser in *Happiness*, Hoffman has brought insight and humanity to people we might otherwise avoid.

"People who have these really difficult feelings and moments never get themselves seen," O'Connor said. "You don't understand their inner torment. Philip makes you feel a person — not just see their actions."

Hoffman said such roles are "the ones people notice because the emotions are really laid bare. I think people really appreciate that." And to make such characters live and breathe, Hoffman must take risks, opening himself to raw, painful emotions. "I know that the leap of faith is my job. Directors have a lot of control, but I know that at the end of the day, it's my job to make it work, to make people believe me."

But, Hoffman quickly points out, he likes to play all sorts of characters, not just life's losers. He is the very definition of a character actor.

"Along with George Eastman, Rochester can claim Philip as a true genius," said Joel Schumacher, the veteran director who guided Hoffman through *Flawless*, co-starring Robert De Niro. In it, Hoffman played a cross-dressing man who desperately wants to be a woman. "Phil can do anything," the director said. "Just look at the range he's played. His research and attention to detail are amazing. Philip could do *Richard III* one day and *Hellzapoppin'* the next day. He could go from *A Balm in Gilead* to a cops-and-robbers show on TV. I feel about Philip the way I do about Kevin Spacey — they're truly great character actors. The bad news is they may not earn $25 million a movie, but they'll work forever."

Talking about *Capote*, the film that would eventually bring him the Oscar, Hoffman said, "The character stands for more than just himself. This tale is a classic American tragedy." It could be anybody in the media or the corporate world who empowers himself with self-promotion, Hoffman said, adding, "The big cities are filled with people like that. Ultimately, *Capote* stands in for that classic American archetype. This story gives voice to that idea — ambition — as an obsession that has to be seen through."

Hoffman sees *Capote* as a Faustian tale. "Whether he sold his soul to the devil, once he saw Perry Smith, it was inevitable that two men were going to die, one literally, one figuratively. It wasn't a choice Capote could make. It chose him."

As for those famous mannerisms, Hoffman said they involved five months of work and didn't really come together until he had an understanding of who Capote was.

"You can't work on the external stuff till you start working on the internal," he explained. "Everything has to be at the same time. That's the awful truth. Sometimes things get held up on the set. You're trying to figure out what makes him tick."

But, as we talked, he was already aware of a lot of Oscar talk for *Capote*. "What I really want is for a lot of people to see the movie," Hoffman said. "The response so far is strong. My dream is that *Capote* is in the theaters for six-plus months. An Oscar nomination would help that. And so would a Golden Globe."

Hoffman and I talked once more, only a few days before the actor would attend the Oscars, where those who made *Capote* would celebrate five nominations — for Hoffman, Futterman, Miller, co-star Catherine Keener, and the film itself. To augment this second conversation, I also talked with Hoffman's two *Capote* collaborators, Futterman and Miller.

Knowing that he would share the night with friends has almost been enough to free Hoffman from his nervousness as Oscar night approaches. "Maybe this will be fun and not as stressful as I had imagined it would be," he said.

Hoffman talked between bites of a ham and cheese crêpe at Cafe Rafaella, a favorite lunch place near his home in New York City's Greenwich Village. It's also only two blocks from New York University, where Hoffman and Miller studied theater at the famed Tisch School of the Arts. (In those days, Futterman was uptown at Columbia University.)

Hoffman recalled where the three met: at the Saratoga Springs summer camp, sponsored by the state and run by the Circle Repertory Theatre in Saratoga Springs. Hoffman came from Fairport High School, where he'd already developed a reputation as a student actor after an injury curtailed his wrestling career. Miller and Futterman were from Mamaroneck High School and had been friends since they were 12.

"Phil had charisma," the 39-year-old Miller said of those Saratoga days. "I recognized sociability in him. And he said the same thing about me. I noted that people liked Phil. He has a sincerity and a lack of vanity, and it's disarming, even to adolescents who are easily uptight."

Futterman, who has appeared on TV's *Will & Grace* and *Judging Amy*, said he first connected with Hoffman's athletic side. "First thing we did was go to the gym and lift weights. Phil had been a good athlete but had just recently tried acting. Later, in class, doing improvisations, it was apparent that Phil 'got it' in a way that nobody else did. He had a direct channel to his emotional life. I felt I better get serious, because 'This guy gets something I don't get.'"

For Hoffman, the emergence of the trio with *Capote* isn't as much a reunion as a continuation: "We've been friends all along. These are two really talented, bright men who happened to grow up together."

Capote got its start with Futterman, who had the script in incubation for six years.

"I got interested in the idea of a relationship between a journalist and a subject. Then I happened to read Gerald Clarke's biography of Capote — and it seemed like a great way to get at the subject. And there's a huge bonus: Capote is a fascinating character."

Futterman, married to screenwriter Anya Epstein, eventually sent his script to Miller, who saw the potential for a film "that would delve into an individual and peel back the layers and get to a private place. It was a public figure, but a story that was private." But both men knew the project would stand or fall on the actor cast as Capote. And they thought of their old friend.

"'But what happens if Phil doesn't do it?'" Futterman, 38, said the two friends wondered. "So we made a list. Phil was the only person on the list. 'If he'll do it, we'll do it. If not, we won't do it.'"

All three admitted that it took some convincing. Hoffman had two major concerns. First, would he be doing the film for the right reasons and not just because it was brought to him by old friends? "When I decided to do it," he recalled, "I knew it was right. But that didn't mean I was confident I would do it well. I was confident that it was a good script and a good story, and I knew Bennett was going to do a great job. And what a great opportunity to work with two old friends."

Then there was the second issue — portraying an extreme character, and yet giving him substance, reality and pain. Then there was losing 40 pounds, making yourself seem a half-foot shorter and speaking with a high-pitched voice that seems generated by helium. Hoffman was frightened of the fine line between genius and a joke. "If I wasn't completely, absolutely, with clarity and precision, on point with what (Capote) was doing and why, then the way that he behaved and walked and talked would go out the window. It would be awful."

The actor said yes, but he told me the first two weeks of the six-week shoot were pure anguish as he struggled to find his way into the character. "It was awful. Bennett is the director; he's not getting what he wants. I'm not giving what I want. But he's allowing the events to play out, be they ugly or nasty or whatever. I felt floundering and failing in front of everybody."

Miller, who had directed *The Cruise*, a documentary about an eccentric, semi-homeless Manhattan tour guide, said all he could do with Hoffman was be honest with him until he got to where he needed to be with Capote. "When he makes a commitment to a role or a character," the director explained, "there is nowhere he won't go. It gives him the appearance of being fearless. The vanity is gone; there's so much there that is truthful. He's an enormously sensitive person."

Hoffman's purported lack of vanity often comes up in reviews and interviews, demonstrated by the often-disturbing characters he has been willing to play on film and by the rumpled way he shows up in plaid shirts and khakis for Jay Leno and David Letterman. But

Hoffman believes he has as much vanity as the next man. "It's just I'm not one for putting on airs or whatever," he said. "I like being comfortable. I like being in my own skin."

It must have been a challenge for him to remain comfortable through the intensity of the *Capote* media frenzy. Hoffman went through "literally hundreds" of interviews as he has launched the film in markets in London, Berlin, Japan and elsewhere. Then came the promotion of the film's next stage: its DVD release.

Hoffman also made dutiful appearances at the Critics' Choice, Golden Globe, Screen Actors Guild and Independent Spirit award shows and at the British Academy Awards. (He won in all five cases.)

But he insisted that all of the celebrity and interviews haven't changed him. "I don't think it's changing who I am in any way. I think there are lessons that are learned. The circumstances in your life are changing a bit. I learn about myself and what I'll need to do if I have to go through this again."

His biggest concern, he said, is opening up about his private life. His reticence is not because of any selfish reason but because openness could interfere with his ability to be convincing as an actor. The less we know about Phil Hoffman, he thinks, the more we can believe he's somebody else on the screen or the stage.

Hoffman said this briefly became an issue after a *60 Minutes* interview, when he revealed that 16 years ago he went into rehab to curb a youthful hunger for alcohol and drugs. "I was a little worried about (the rehab thing). I'm not that private about that in my life. I don't care if people know. It's something I did when I was 22. It's not something I keep close to my chest. But was it something I wanted to talk about on *60 Minutes*? That's what it's about. Then I realized there was a way to talk about it without divulging too much information. You give the simple, basic truths of it without getting into the wacky, dirty intricacies. And it was fine."

Hoffman said the "why" of rehab was simple: "I got panicked for my life."

He hasn't been an overnight success. He's satisfied that his career has had a gradual buildup over many years. "These young celebrities who become famous and rich right away — if I was one of them, I'd be dead now."

Instead, Philip Seymour Hoffman is a father, a man who calls Greenwich Village home, and an actor determined to continue doing theater in New York and taking on intriguing roles — big and small — in worthwhile films.

And, a few days after this conversation, Hoffman also became an Oscar winner.

TOM HANKS and STEVEN SPIELBERG

People often ask me who was the most genuinely nice person I've ever interviewed. Fortunately, there are several candidates, but I believe the nicest was Tom Hanks. Put it this way: In a handful of interviews over the years, Tom Hanks has always struck me as coming the closest to what you would expect or want him to be. He and his public persona seem pretty much the same.

Of my Hanks interviews, my favorites are the two that follow.

The first finds us talking at NASA's Johnson Space Center in Houston, TX. We met there in 1995 to discuss Ron Howard's 1995 film, Apollo 13, *in which Hanks played courageous astronaut Jim Lovell. Catching Hanks at the location was like talking with a kid in a candy store. Hanks is, he readily admits, a space junkie.*

In the second case, I talked with both Hanks and his director, Steven Spielberg, in Washington, D.C., in 1998, after they worked together on the impassioned and gut-wrenching Saving Private Ryan.

WINNING TWO OSCARS IN TWO YEARS HAS PUT TOM HANKS IN A RAREFIED CLASS WITH Spencer Tracy. But around the Hanks household, it just means he finally has something to put on the family trophy shelf.

"Yep, they're on a little shelf, next to my son's soccer plaque and my daughter's riding ribbons and my youngest boy's swimming trophies. It's the Hanks family Wall of Shame."

He's proud of his Oscars and the astronomical success he's experienced, from *Big* to *Philadelphia* to *Forrest Gump*. These days, he reportedly earns $15 million a picture. But with his latest film, *Apollo 13*, the 38-year-old actor received another reward: the chance to fulfill a boyhood dream. He got to play one of the most respected heroes of America's space program. He wore the uniforms, went through some of the training, experienced weight-lessness, hung out with astronauts.

Hanks was 13 at the time of the 1969 Apollo 11 mission that put Neil Armstrong on the moon. "I knew all the Apollo flights. I knew what they did," he said. "I had the models; I watched what I could. I felt lucky to be alive when man was going to walk on the moon. It was history. And I always felt *Apollo 13* would make a fabulous story."

He was still excited as he sat for an interview in an office at the Johnson Space Center in Houston.

During filming, Hanks would show up for work already wearing his olive-drab NASA jumpsuit. "I had Jim Lovell patches all over it," he said. "I was so gung-ho, I embarrassed people." With many actors, such innocent enthusiasm would seem like so much guff. But with Hanks, it's believable. And the fact that it is believable may just be why he's among the most successful of actors.

"He is that person you see on the screen," said *Apollo 13* co-star Gary Sinise.

Sinise also co-starred with Hanks in *Forrest Gump* and remembers an incident when the two were on the road doing publicity for the film. "We were in a limo passing by some sweaty guys in hard hats, digging a ditch along the side of the road," Sinise recalled. "Tom looked at them and then looked over at me and asked, in all seriousness, 'Why are we in here and they're out there?' But those are the cards he's been dealt. And Tom's worked a long time to achieve what he has."

Apollo 13 reunites Hanks with Ron Howard, who directed him in *Splash* 11 years ago. "Directing Hanks now, at this stage in his career, is like managing Mickey Mantle in 1956, the year he won baseball's triple crown," Howard said in a separate interview. And yet, the director added, Hanks insisted that *Apollo 13* not become a showcase for himself.

"This story wouldn't have survived as a cheesy star vehicle," Hanks said. "That wouldn't be fair to any aspect of the story. My own knowledge of the space program said to me that it would be such a disservice to absolutely everything. It wasn't just one guy who figured out how to do something."

In fact, Hanks wanted the film's final credits to list all the NASA employees and contractors involved in the Apollo 13 mission — until he realized the list would go on forever. "When we make a movie about a true story, it's our responsibility to be as authentic to the reality as is possible," Hanks said.

Still, he pointed out another reality to the man he plays, astronaut Jim Lovell. "I told him, 'Jim, whether you like it or not, from here on out I'm the definitive celluloid version of you.' And I apologized to him. 'That's the bad news. The good news is: you'll never have to sign an autograph again. I'll have to do it.'"

Hanks was drawn to *Apollo 13* because it's a tale in which failure and potential tragedy are overcome. "There is triumph through struggle," Hanks said. "The great victory is that these guys got home. At a time when all that matters is who's first and who wins, the cumulative effort of these guys getting back is worthy of a human undertaking.

"You learn as much through failure as through success. You can qualify your life just as much through trying your absolute best — even though you don't achieve — than achieving some goal that you probably didn't set for yourself anyway."

Yet Hanks admitted he's not much for goal setting. "I've never thought much about the long range," he said. "I think that's what the Communists did, and look where their five-year plans got them! Your next choice should always be instinctive and something you have to do. I hoped Penny (Marshall) would let me play the broken-down old ballplayer in *A League of Their Own*. I hoped Nora (Ephron) would accept me as this guy whose wife just died for *Sleepless in Seattle*. If you're trying to accomplish something or prove something or satisfy some goal, then emotion and instinct get taken out of the mix. The decision is tainted."

That's why, for example, Hollywood's most acclaimed "nice guy" isn't especially eager to play a bad guy just so he can strut his diversity. "There's nothing to be gained for me to play a psycho killer just because I'm tired of being a nice guy," he explained, "or because I want the audience to see some other side of my personality. That's horseshit. That's not the artistic undertaking that making movies should be. I played a bad guy in *Punchline*. The movie didn't do well, but I think it's the best work I've ever done. Was he a bad guy? He didn't kill anybody, but he was totally unredeemable and unpleasant. But unless I understand how my countenance can fit into a bad guy, I'm not interested in playing it. Would I play Iago in *Othello*? You bet I would. In the meantime, I'll let somebody else blow up buildings."

I next met Tom Hanks with director Steven Spielberg in Washington, D.C., where we talked about a project very near and dear to their hearts, the just-completed Saving Private Ryan.

Saving Private Ryan is set during World War II. But Steven Spielberg says the decision to make it painfully violent was a product of another era. "If it weren't for Vietnam, I wouldn't have made *Private Ryan* as graphically realistic as I did," he said.

"I began to resent the misconception among Americans that Vietnam was the most painful war, simply because we saw it regularly in color and on TV. So people think Vietnam was a cruel, blatantly horrific war, while World War II was that black-and-white war starring John Wayne. In fact, a war is a war, and World War II and Korea and the First World War and Vietnam were all chambers of horrors. I never felt the World War II veteran had his story told the way it happened to them."

Though it was a hot summer day, Spielberg wore a sweater vest over his open-collar shirt, topped by a tweed sports coat. The one-time wunderkind of Hollywood sported graying hair and looked more and more professorial as he moved through his 50s.

And with age, Spielberg said he's become more interested in serious topics. This may explain why the former champion of childhood fantasies moved on to the Holocaust horrors of *Schindler's List* and the searing slavery of *Amistad*.

With *Saving Private Ryan*, that dark odyssey continued. "It was different when I was in my 40s. I was still hanging on to Peter Pan," he said. "And I still have Pan." But, he said, with age, he thinks more of his seven children than of the child within himself.

"Now, when I make a picture, I want it to be of value for them. If not now, because they're too young, then in the future. Part of why I decide to tell a story is because I want to leave it behind for them. Certainly, I want to leave behind *E.T.* and some of the lighter films, but there are also things I want them to know that are tougher."

With *Saving Private Ryan*, it's the legacy of the everyday heroes of World War II. One of them was his father, now 81, who served in Burma during that war. "He never waved the flag in front of me," Spielberg added, "but he's always been so proud of being an American.

"When Vietnam came along, and I was in college, I resented people who said they were proud to be American, because I felt what the government was doing to the soldiers in that war was criminal. Only when I became older did I begin to understand my dad's generation. I went from resenting the American flag to thanking it. In a sense, this movie is a memorial to those combat veterans of the Normandy invasion, and a way for me to say thank you to my dad and to a lot of people like him."

The key thing Spielberg learned from the veterans, and from historians like Stephen Ambrose, was that previous World War II movies had never captured the terror of warfare. Therefore, Spielberg decided to begin his film with 25 minutes of the most harrowing action ever seen in a mainstream film.

"I knew what I was getting into when I chose to tell the story from the veterans' point of view, not from a filmmaker's point of view. I don't know war, because I never fought in a war. But I honor the veterans by letting them inform me, and through the documentaries I watched, and Robert Capa's eight surviving D-Day photographs. They all helped me determine how I wanted the film to look."

Ambrose, the late author of *Citizen Soldiers*, had high praise for Spielberg's *Saving Private Ryan,* along with *Schindler's List* and *Amistad.* "The guy who made *E.T.* and *Jaws* and *Raiders* has now become America's historian," Ambrose said. "As a storyteller, he has the biggest audience. In recent years, his stories have been American history."

We talked in a hotel in Washington, D.C., a week before the film was to open. After a half-hour with Spielberg and a few minutes with Ambrose, I moved down the hall for another conversation with Spielberg's star, Tom Hanks.

Spielberg is the most successful filmmaker in history, having made seven of the 20 top-grossing films ever. So two-time Academy Award winner Tom Hanks was happy to discover that he and Spielberg were interested in the same project.

"The story was always great — and the philosophical question was there," Hanks said. "But the captain I was supposed to play originally was a cigar-chomping Medal of Honor winner. However, Steven said he wanted to make the most realistic war movie ever made. I told him that meant changing every line. He said, 'Yeah.' I said, 'Can I help?'"

Hanks said the tone of *Saving Private Ryan* — realistic and devoid of John Wayne bravado — was established as soon as they staged the Omaha Beach invasion at the start of production. "After we had shot it," he recalled, "there were so many times later that we'd see that certain scenes or lines were stupid, and we'd cut the lines."

Spielberg and Hanks were nervous about working together because they're close friends.

"Our families are joined at the hip," Spielberg had told me. But they needn't have worried. "At least a dozen times" during the shooting, Hanks reported, the two men came up with similar ideas to maintain the integrity of the project.

And working alongside Spielberg, Hanks got a firsthand look at why his friend is Hollywood's top director. "He never censors his instincts or gets precious about what he's doing," Hanks said. "He sees it, he wants it, he gets it, and he gets it as fast as he can. He's got the artistry and expertise to make it all first-rate, so none of it is slapdash or haphazard unless he wants it to look that way. In the time it takes me to set up one shot, Steven would have seven shots under his belt and be working on the next 14. That speed and momentum and clarity — and not questioning his instincts — that's why he's who he is."

The film, Hanks added, was special for all the actors. "We all felt it. We know actors will come up to us for the rest of our lives, wanting to know what it was like to make *Saving Private Ryan*."

SPIKE LEE

I've followed Spike Lee's film career from the beginning. I can remember walking into a press conference at the 1986 Toronto Film Festival for his first feature, She's Gotta Have It, *and finding only a handful of folks there. Lee was reading a newspaper in the corner, waiting for the questioning to start.*

He wouldn't have to wait long, career-wise. By his third feature, 1989's brilliant and explosive Do the Right Thing, *Lee had become a major and controversial figure in film and American culture. His directorial star continued to ascend through* Mo' Better Blues, Jungle Fever, *the great* Malcolm X, Clockers, *the painful and insightful documentary* 4 Little Girls, *and more.*

We talked several times over the years. However, to me, the most entertaining interview took place in 1998, because we were talking about his latest movie, He Got Game, *and a passion we share for basketball. It was also fun to try to catch and hold Lee's attention, because while we talked, the filmmaker was watching his beloved New York Knicks play the game.*

SPIKE LEE FIGURES HE HAD MORE PREPARATION FOR *HE GOT GAME* THAN FOR ANY other film he could have made.

"My father introduced me to basketball when I was 4 years old," he said. "So I've been doing research on the game for nearly 40 years." For Lee, basketball is a passion eclipsed only by his love for his wife and children, and for making movies.

That's why, as we talk, we're in front of a television set, watching Lee's beloved New York Knicks in game two of their playoff series with the Miami Heat in May of 1998. It was a Sunday and the Knicks were in Miami, and Lee was in Rochester, being honored with a career retrospective at the George Eastman House. So he had to settle for a borrowed TV set in an

Eastman House office, not quite as exclusive as his Madison Square Garden courtside seats.

Lee tried to focus on my questions, but clearly it wasn't easy. At one point, while framing an answer, he pointed to the screen and yelled, "That's a walk!"

Fortunately, halftime arrived, and Lee hit the mute button. Now I had his attention. It was only fair. He got my attention with *He Got Game*, a film that targets young athletes, as basketball becomes increasingly big business. And as he has with his other works on racism, on the life of Malcolm X, on the Million Man March, he makes his points with gritty conviction.

Lee believes sports deserve scrutiny because they've become such a big part of our culture. "Nowadays, you can't relegate sports just to the playing field," he said. "They're part of entertainment. But we have too many young men — boys — banking their entire lives on a million-to-one shot, trying to get into professional sports."

Lee said his goal in *He Got Game* was to explore two aspects of sports: the pressures on talented young players, and the relationships between fathers and sons. He depicts colleges, family members, girlfriends and agents all trying to get a piece of a hot prospect named Jesus Shuttlesworth (played by Ray Allen, then of the Milwaukee Bucks). And he explores the volatile feelings between the young man and his father, a convict named Jake (Denzel Washington).

"We wanted to show the extreme pressure on an athlete of Jesus' ability; how these guys who are 17 or 18 years old are asked to make decisions that a lot of mature men would have trouble making. Also, we show how these guys are exploited."

Lee added that the parallel narrative about fathers and sons was a natural.

"Sports are handed down from father to son," he said. "In this age, we can also say father to daughter or mother to son or daughter, but when I was growing up, it was father to son. You can't explain away that a father is going to put a ball in a son's crib when he's two days old. To me, a father and son throwing a football or baseball back and forth is an act or exchange that can't be topped. We felt this father-son relationship would be key. In a lot of cases, guys have made it to a high level because of their fathers."

Lee added, though, that some fathers are frustrated because they didn't get as far in sports as they would have liked. "With these crushed dreams, they transfer them to their sons," he said. "That's both good and bad. All children need to be pushed by their parents. But there comes a time you have to hold back. In this film, Jake goes overboard."

Lee wanted the basketball in his film to be as realistic as the emotions. "We felt we had to cast real ballplayers in the basketball roles," he told me. "It'd be a bigger risk to try to find an actor to display the skills we needed. It was a more sensible choice to go into the NBA and find guys who could act, but who just don't know it yet. We didn't want to film scenes where you'd see the guy shoot, the ball leaves his hand, there's a cut, and then a separate shot at the basket, when the ball goes in. That's terrible."

Lee rounded up several NBA players young enough to look like high school seniors. Allen earned the lead role because he was convincing, on and off the court.

"He had to work," Lee said. "He had eight weeks of coaching by a great acting instructor."

One of the other candidates for the lead role, Toronto Raptor John Wallace (the former Syracuse University star), plays one of Shuttlesworth's high school teammates. Other real-life ballplayers to appear include Boston Celtic Walter McCarty, Los Angeles Laker Rick Fox, and Indiana Pacer Travis Best. Lee said Allen, Wallace and the other ballplayers "took direction really well. I think it's because they've had years of coaching."

Lee's efforts toward realism extended to frank portrayals of sex in *He Got Game.* It's depicted as part of high school romance, and as conducted by hookers, and as a cynical college recruiting tool. The result is his raunchiest film to date.

Lee made no apologies. "It's basketball," he said, laughing. "It's just part of basketball. On campuses, in high school, in the NBA."

He Got Game is Lee's 12th film in 12 years, following his Oscar-nominated HBO documentary, *4 Little Girls.*

We were talking at Eastman House because the 42-year-old filmmaker had come to conclude a two-month retrospective of his works. He also announced his decision to store all his features in the archive here, including the only 70-millimeter print of his epic, *Malcolm X.* His films now sit alongside Martin Scorsese's movies.

"I'm very honored," Lee said. "I think I'm on the right track with what I wanted to do, which is build a body of work. Right now I'm just crossing my fingers for good box office numbers (for *He Got Game*) this Friday, Saturday and Sunday. Nowadays, if you don't have good numbers the first weekend, you're out."

Like his beloved Knicks, Lee needed to score.

MARTIN SCORSESE

I'm among the many who consider Martin Scorsese America's greatest living filmmaker. And I've been fortunate to talk with Scorsese in person on several occasions. However, the most all-encompassing interview took place over the phone in 1994, when Scorsese was in Las Vegas, diligently working on what would become the film Casino. *I was granted the opportunity for an in-depth interview because Scorsese had been named recipient of the prestigious George Eastman Award for achievement in filmmaking.*

MARTIN SCORSESE SAID HE'D LIKE NOTHING BETTER THAN TO BE IN ROCHESTER TO receive the George Eastman Award. After all, the director has long been a friend of the Eastman House because of the museum's extensive contribution to film preservation. Indeed, Scorsese has entrusted his extensive collection of some 8,000 films to the Eastman House since 1991; he'd love to visit the depository.

"I'm so disappointed that I can't be there to receive the award, because I haven't yet seen the place," Scorsese said over the phone. "I've seen photographs and talked (with Eastman House officials) a great deal. It was originally my plan to come up for a few days, receive my award and maybe see some films. But instead, I'm here with this sideline of mine, as a movie director."

In other words, Scorsese is too busy doing what he's being honored for. He's knee-deep in making a movie called *Casino* and has dispatched actor Griffin Dunne to appear in his place at the black-tie gala here Saturday night.

Dunne starred in an inventive Scorsese comedy called *After Hours* in 1985; it's being screened at 2 p.m. Sunday as part of the weekend of activities at the Eastman House. In addition to his appearance Saturday night, Dunne, 39, will introduce the film Sunday and answer questions.

Meanwhile, the 52-year-old Scorsese will stay in Las Vegas, where he's about halfway through filming *Casino* with his favorite actor, Robert De Niro. Sharon Stone co-stars in the crime drama. "I don't know what they want from me," Scorsese said with a jittery little laugh. "Can't this film shoot itself?"

For more than 30 years, Scorsese has been making films that couldn't shoot themselves. His personal, incisive, visceral films — *Mean Streets, Taxi Driver, Raging Bull, GoodFellas* and many others — are among the most important by any director of his generation. His range is unequaled: from dark comedy (*After Hours, The King of Comedy*) to musical drama (*New York, New York*), from a controversial biblical epic (*The Last Temptation of Christ)* to a high-toned literary adaptation (*The Age of Innocence)* to a concert film (*The Last Waltz*).

A lifelong New Yorker, Scorsese was raised on the "mean streets" of Little Italy. He entered the seminary to become a Roman Catholic priest, but soon shifted to film studies at New York University, where he became an instructor. His student films led to acclaimed work as an editor and independent filmmaker. His film career shifted into high gear with *Mean Streets* (1973) and *Taxi Driver* (1976).

Though he had not yet won an Academy Award at this point, actors such as Robert De Niro and Joe Pesci have won Oscars under his direction, and most critics and serious students of film list Scorsese as the most important American director of the modern era. His 1980 film *Raging Bull* was named the greatest film of that decade in a major critics' poll. And now the Eastman House adds its highest honor to his accolades.

Scorsese "represents the ideal synthesis of the qualities we regard as paramount in our activities," said Eastman House film curator Paolo Cherchi Usai. "He's first of all an artist, acting within the Hollywood context, but he's uncompromising and has always taken risks for the sake of art." Also, Scorsese "is deeply committed to the mission of preserving, restoring and making accessible our film heritage."

Scorsese is grateful. "Naturally, I'm greatly honored by the Eastman House distinction," he said. He has a cold, but his voice and rapid, clipped delivery would be familiar to those who've seen his cameos in films ranging from his own *Taxi Driver* to Robert Redford's recent *Quiz Show*. He continued, "My main interest (in accepting the award) is to draw attention to the preservation work at the Eastman House as much as possible."

He credits the Eastman House not only with transferring films from unstable nitrate to celluloid, but also with collecting and preserving thousands of production stills and other materials. "Hopefully, this (ceremony) will help them continue preservation, because more than half our film heritage is rapidly disappearing," the director noted.

Scorsese's ties with the Eastman House were forged in October 1991, when he chose the archive as the storage facility for his private film collection. It includes not only his own films, but also some 2,000 other features, including a broad range of Hollywood films, B-movies and foreign titles, mostly from the 1940s through the '70s.

Scorsese's contributions definitely fill a gap in the Eastman House's collections, said Cherchi Usai. The museum is strong in silent films and in Hollywood movies from the

1930s and '40s, and it has begun to collect contemporary films. But it was short on films from the postwar period to the 1970s. Scorsese's collection covers that period, in addition to "areas, movements and tendencies not represented" in the collection. Scorsese's collection, for example, is strong in B-movies, which "have been neglected so much and are now receiving due attention. We can now legitimately claim that the Eastman House's collection covers the entire history of cinema," said Cherchi Usai. And more films will be coming from Scorsese in the future. The Eastman House gets to show the films and make them available for research, and will continue to keep them after the director's death.

Scorsese frequently asks the Eastman House to ship him movies that he needs to screen for inspiration or technical insight for his actors and crew on current films. "If I need a print for research, I get it right away," he said. "My cameraman looks at things in case he wants to supplement his work with ideas from earlier cinematographers." On the set of *Casino*, for example, the director has screened such films as Allan Dwan's *Slightly Scarlet*, Anthony Mann's *Reign of Terror*, and Vincente Minnelli's *The Bad and the Beautiful*.

When Scorsese screened *Reign of Terror*, he brought a special guest: director Quentin Tarantino, whose violent *Pulp Fiction* had recently made him the hot new kid in Hollywood. Tarantino, in fact, was then often called "a young Scorsese," though the veteran director thinks Tarantino has more in common with Brian De Palma.

"I really enjoy and admire his work," Scorsese said. "I've only just met the boy; he came to my set a few weeks ago and had dinner in my trailer. We talked about old films and new films. It really does look good for the future of film, because Tarantino and a few other young directors aren't just good people — they have something to say and they're learning how to say it with the lens. And with words, too."

Scorsese said he's reminded of the early '70s, when he and Francis Coppola were among the *enfants terribles* of the day. In some ways, Scorsese's *Mean Streets* was the *Pulp Fiction* of 1973. It divided audiences into two camps: one group considered it brilliant, provocative moviemaking, while the other thought it gratuitously violent and exploitative.

But unlike Tarantino's pulp fantasy, Scorsese's *Mean Streets* is a semi-autobiographical work, set in a real world. And Scorsese said *Mean Street's* themes of alienation and loneliness continue to dominate much of his work — and his life. Scorsese, who is currently single with two grown daughters, has been in and out of four marriages.

"I was very interested in religion and Catholicism at the time of *Mean Streets*," said Scorsese. "The question I found myself asking in the film is: how does a person live a good, honest life in the world in which we find ourselves? In the phrase of the street: how do you do the right thing in a world that is primally dangerous? — I'm beginning to sound like Jeremiah," he said, laughing. "I've got to be careful."

Scorsese said *Casino* explores similar themes. "It's about people who are allegedly associated with the mob in Las Vegas in the '70s. It's also about the undoing of people because of pride and greed, and it takes place at an exciting time in Vegas."

His work on *Casino* finds Scorsese once again dealing with another Rochester institution: Eastman Kodak Co., with which he's had an up-and-down relationship. Having used many of its products, Scorsese challenged the company in 1979 when certain Kodak color film stocks began to fade drastically. The director led a highly vocal campaign to push Kodak to create a better product. "By 1983-84, they introduced the new stock — and at no extra cost," he said. "I can't say enough how it's turned around. They're the best."

When he's not making movies, Scorsese is a fierce advocate for preserving them. But the cause took a harsh blow recently when the National Endowment for the Arts dropped its annual $1.3 million commitment to the Eastman House and America's four other major film archives.

"We've been struggling to get the government to accept film as an art form that's worthy of preservation," Scorsese said. "Especially since it's the American art form, and we're approaching the 100th anniversary of film (in 1995). Film is something to cherish and preserve for future generations. My fascination with motion pictures isn't just with feature films and all sorts of underground films, but also newsreels. I feel the moving image is such an important and powerful persuader and informer."

PETER WEIR

In the late '70s and early '80s, cinema from Australia became an international sensation, with films by directors like Fred Schepisi, Bruce Beresford, Gillian Armstrong, and George Miller finding global audiences. And I was among their most enthusiastic advocates. The most successful of the Aussie filmmakers of that period, and perhaps the greatest, was Peter Weir. I was fortunate to interview Weir in connection with The Truman Show *(1998) and* Master and Commander: The Far Side of the World *(2003).*

PETER WEIR WAS WELL INTO PRODUCTION OF *THE TRUMAN SHOW* WHEN PRINCESS Diana was killed in a car crash last summer. But the tragedy and its aftermath reassured him that his movie really hits its mark.

The film is a parable about the encroachment of the media on our lives. In the film, Jim Carrey plays a man who is the unwitting prisoner of a TV show for 24 hours each day, seven days a week. When Truman discovers that all the other people he knows are actors and that his life is bogus, he tries to escape.

"I love the idea that the millions of fans of Truman's TV show begin to root for him to escape," Weir said. "I thought of the Lady Diana tragedy and the way the public turned against the paparazzi, who were, after all, working for them. They didn't make the connection that their lust for her life in print or on television was somehow responsible."

The Truman Show may seem like offbeat stuff for Jim Carrey, but it's perfect for Weir. Over more than 20 years, the Australian-born filmmaker has created an impressive body of films that explore complex themes while remembering to entertain and enrich filmgoers.

In particular, Weir seems fascinated by characters who must survive in hostile environments — whether it's the Aussie reporter in Indonesia in *The Year of Living Dangerously*

(1983), the tough city cop on an Amish farm in *Witness* (1985), or the free-spirited teacher at a tradition-bound school in *Dead Poets Society* (1989). In *The Truman Show*, Truman lives in sunny environs that seem perfect — except they aren't real.

Weir believes his fascination with alien environments comes from his own sense of being a wanderer on planet Earth. "Australia is a very young country. Sometimes I think some Australians are rather rootless," he said. "My background is Scottish, but I went to Scotland and didn't fit in there. So now we're wandering, putting up our tents anywhere we can."

The 53-year-old filmmaker was the first of several directors to make an international reputation out of the powerful wave of Australian films in the mid-1970s. Such films as *Picnic at Hanging Rock* (1975), *The Last Wave* (1977), and *Gallipoli* (1981) brought Weir to the attention of American filmgoers — and Hollywood producers.

Weir has a justified reputation for picking offbeat projects that match his passions. He's less concerned with how well a film might perform at the box office than with what it means to him. "Peter cares what's being done," said *Truman* star Ed Harris. "A Weir movie is about finding out where the truth is. He's not just stamping something onto film."

Because Weir works from the heart, he sometimes takes time off between projects. *The Truman Show* is his first movie in five years, following *Fearless*, a difficult saga about a man's near-death experience in an airplane crash.

Weir said a lot of people advised him to find something more commercial for his next film after *Fearless*. "But I decided I'd keep going over the edge," he added, with a laugh. "I told people to send me things that were considered different or difficult." That kind of attitude, he explained, "keeps you alive."

Five years later, we talked again . . .

One of Peter Weir's tricks as a director, he said, is to cast his movies from the dead, especially if he's stuck for ideas. He considers all the actors of the past and then picks his ideal for a role. Then he considers who's a close match today.

"For Captain Jack Aubrey (in *Master and Commander*), I cast Richard Burton," he said. "And that led to Russell Crowe." Indeed, the late Welsh actor with the booming voice was adept at the period characters and larger-than-life heroics of *The Robe* and *Becket*, but could also play the stark drama of a *Who's Afraid of Virginia Woolf.* Crowe is among very few actors today with similar skills. (Witness *Gladiator* and *A Beautiful Mind*.)

"Russell has his own remarkable range," Weir said. "He's a rare figure in the world of movie stars. Without the movie star quality, whatever that is, he'd be one of the actors of his generation anyway. To combine the two is exceptional."

Weir said he especially likes Crowe's unpredictability. "I think that is a building block of a movie. In that lies tension, especially in a predictable story like this. You're never quite sure what he might do or say in any situation. It takes such dexterity."

Weir, a respected veteran of such gems as *The Year of Living Dangerously*, *Witness* and *The Truman Show*, has always been a fan of Patrick O'Brian's seagoing adventure stories. But he knows they also present challenges for filmmakers.

"You have to inhabit that world (of early 19th-century naval life)," Weir said. He pretended his film company was "the admiralty film unit. We imagined we were making a recruiting film. I didn't want to patronize the past, or to instruct or admonish. It's a unique way to revisit the past."

Weir was also determined to structure his film so he could make almost all of it on soundstages (interiors) and in a controllable water tank (most of the exteriors). He researched Steven Spielberg's experiences on *Jaws* and John Huston's on *Moby Dick* and heard too many horror stories of folks trying to make big-budget movies on the open sea. The few days the cast and crew did work on the ocean — with many getting sick — convinced him he was right.

Even though O'Brian wrote 20 Jack Aubrey novels, Weir isn't convinced there will be other *Master and Commander* films. "It would have to be phenomenally successful, given its cost ($135 million). I don't think I'd sign on for another."

As for what's next for Weir, he said, "They have a phrase in the Navy when you return your ship: you're on the beach, waiting for the admiralty to reassign you. Well, now I'm on the beach."

RUSSELL CROWE and GUY PEARCE

It's always interesting to look back on a moment in time when a star is made. That was my sense during the interviews in 1997 for the nouveau noir film L.A. Confidential. *The film was an international launching pad for Russell Crowe and, to a lesser extent, Guy Pearce, and is an apt demonstration of why directors sometimes cast unknown actors. Also, the film is one of my favorite movies of the '90s, as you can read in this book's review sampler.*

THREE COPS STAND AT THE CENTER OF *L.A. CONFIDENTIAL*, CURTIS HANSON'S FABULOUS new detective saga adapted from James Ellroy's hard-boiled novel. In casting one of the cops, Hanson took no chances: He chose the much-respected recent Oscar winner Kevin Spacey. But to play the other two leads, Hanson selected two actors who, at this point, were relative unknowns: Russell Crowe, 33, and Guy Pearce, 27. From Australia, no less.

"This picture works, to the degree that it does, because I was able to cast those two actors," asserted Hanson. "I wanted actors who would bring a clean slate to the film — audiences have no history with them. Audiences have complicated emotional involvement with James Ellroy's characters. I wanted these actors to generate that."

Hanson confided that Warner Bros. tried to get him to ditch the little-known Australians in favor of two big Hollywood stars. "But I said no, and because of my success with *The Hand That Rocks the Cradle* and *The River Wild,* they let me make the movie I wanted to make."

Hanson and his actors talked about *L.A. Confidential* at the Toronto International Film Festival in September 1997, where the film tied for the top prize as the favorite among the more than 700 journalists there. It would later go on to earn nine Oscar nominations, including one for best picture. It was *L.A. Confidential's* misfortune to compete in the year of the Oscar King, *Titanic*, though, in my opinion, *Confidential* is the better film.

By 1997, Crowe and Pearce had substantial reputations in Australia, but they'd only begun to be recognized in America. (That soon changed with their superb work in *L.A. Confidential*.) Crowe, who was born in New Zealand but raised in Australia, has co-starred in *Romper Stomper, The Quick and the Dead* and *Virtuosity*, while Pearce made a strong impression in the Aussie drag comedy *The Adventures of Priscilla, Queen of the Desert*.

"In Australia, I'm top of the pile. Here, I'm the parking lot valet," Crowe said, with a laugh. "I've made five movies before I had the chance to make a really good movie. My intentions were always good, but I only get the good roles when other actors are distracted."

The incredibly handsome Pearce says *Priscilla* gave him good exposure in America, but a drag comedy doesn't necessarily lead to a lot of other parts. "Since people have begun seeing *L.A. Confidential*, I've been getting film offers. It's just that I haven't seen anything I like yet," Pearce reported.

Once Hanson had selected his actors, he had to begin the process of turning the two 1990s Aussies into 1950s L.A. cops. "I brought Russell and Guy to America seven weeks early to work on accents and to get to know L.A. They each had a thousand questions," Hanson remembered. "I also put together 15 photographs of the L.A. of the period: crime-scene photos, salacious covers of *Confidential* magazine, (the famous photo of) Robert Mitchum getting out of jail, et cetera. I also showed them LAPD training films from the period and organized a mini-festival of Hollywood film noir, like *The Bad and the Beautiful, In a Lonely Place, Kiss Me Deadly* and *The Line-Up*. I wanted them to get to the point that they could be true to the period, and then ignore it."

Crowe, in fact, discovered a prototype for what he wanted to convey as tough cop Bud White. "It was Sterling Hayden. He had a certain manner and a telegraphed weight in everything he did. I watched him in *The Killing*. What a movie!"

Both actors said the American accent wasn't particularly challenging, though Crowe kept a dialogue coach nearby to make sure he stayed on track. Ultimately, the only way people could tell the two stars were Australian was when they threw a party for the cast and crew. "Guy and I flew in special stuff from Australia," Crowe recounted. "Shark steaks, meat pies, and, of course, Vegemite."

RICHARD WIDMARK

IN THE 1954 WESTERN *GARDEN OF EVIL*, RICHARD WIDMARK PLAYED A GAMBLER WHO tells an ex-sheriff (Gary Cooper), "You're made out of leather."

"What about you?" replies Cooper.

"Words and flesh," Widmark replies. "I think I'm the only human being here."

Widmark made a career out of finding the human being within a range of characters, from evil film-noir thugs, pickpockets and killers to tough cops, naval officers and Western heroes. As a result, Widmark is remembered as one of Hollywood's most dependable and memorable performers, with the skills of a great character actor and the handsome, rugged blond looks of a leading man.

That's why one of the few surviving veterans of Hollywood's Golden Age was honored on Aug. 24, 2002, with the George Eastman Honorary Scholar Award. Widmark appeared before a showing of his 1953 classic, Sam Fuller's *Pickup on South Street.*

Widmark, a surprisingly youthful 87, said he's been bemused to discover that some of his early films have become known as dark, disturbing, hardboiled film-noir classics, because "at that time they were just B pictures."

A native of Sunrise, Minn., Widmark grew up in Princeton, IL, and discovered acting at Lake Forest (IL) College, where he planned to study law. Instead, a friend encouraged him to audition for a play. Widmark came under the influence of a drama professor who liked his work so much, he hired him after graduation to teach drama. Soon Widmark moved to New York City, where he worked on the stage and in the then-important medium of radio.

Widmark's film break came in his first picture, *Kiss of Death* (1947). As Tommy Udo, a thug with a cackling laugh, he famously pushed the wheelchair-bound Mildred Dunnock down a flight of stairs. The good news was an Oscar nomination; the bad news was having to overcome a bad-guy stereotype.

"Well, it's nice to be remembered for something," Widmark said. "But (studio boss) Darryl Zanuck knew I couldn't keep playing the same thing. To protect his studio's investment, he finally put me in different things. We made two or three pictures a year."

Widmark's films included *Night and the City, Judgment at Nuremberg, Cheyenne Autumn* and *Madigan*. Along the way he worked with many legends, including Spencer Tracy, Marilyn Monroe and director John Ford.

"Tracy was my idol from long before, when I was a kid. He was the kind of actor I wanted to be. He's the definitive screen actor. He had total concentration … and he was the best listener in the business. Listening is the trick for movie actors.

"I also loved John Ford. I got him in his late years (for *Cheyenne Autumn*). I found him very funny. He was a tough, mean, sadistic autocrat, but we got along great. Nobody could figure him out. He was a great paradox."

About Monroe, his co-star in *Don't Bother to Knock,* Widmark said, "I liked her a lot, but she was miserable to work with. She was a wounded bird and frightened to death, yet she had a powerful presence on the screen."

Off-screen, Widmark was known as a quiet man who was married for 55 years to screenwriter Jean Hazlewood until her death in 1997. "I never mixed it up with the big parties," he said. "We just went our way, did the work and went home." Asked the secret of a successful marriage in the Hollywood pressure cooker, he replied, "We liked each other."

In 1999, widower Widmark married Susan Blanchard, third wife of the late Henry Fonda. They lived in Connecticut until his death at 93 in 2008.

Widmark said truth is an actor's greatest trait. "You believe him, whatever he does. You always believed Spencer Tracy."

As for his own legacy, Widmark said, "That's up to the people who've watched my movies. I hope I'll be remembered as somebody who did his job."

DENNIS HOPPER

MOVIE FANS OFTEN CONFUSE HOLLYWOOD STARS WITH THE PEOPLE THEY PLAY ON screen. But Dennis Hopper may be the first star to admit that he once made the same mistake, and it nearly killed him. In the 1960s and '70s, Hopper was the wild man of Hollywood. No one else was even a close second.

How wild was he?

He once was found naked, running through the jungles of Mexico, without a clue about who he was or how he got there.

"I think I'm a pretty shy person," a sober, reflective Hopper said when we talked in 1998. "But after *Easy Rider* (1969), everyone thought I was a drug dealer, like Billy. So, I tried to look up to that character; I tried to emulate him."

The same thing happened with his crazy, drugged-up character in *Apocalypse Now* (1979). "I thought that's what people wanted me to be," Hopper explained. "After a bottle of cognac and an ounce of cocaine, it got easier. It's difficult to think about that guy now. I feel like I don't even know him. I've been sober for 18 years."

The famous turning point in his career came in 1985, when the now-straight Hopper turned in great performances in three movies that came out in one year: *Blue Velvet, Hoosiers* and *The River's Edge.* His was the comeback of the year, perhaps the decade. From then until his death in 2010, Hopper had a strong, latter-day career as a character actor, usually playing heavies, in such films as *Speed* and *Waterworld.* The *Easy Rider* director also got his directing career back on track, making *Colors, The Hot Spot* and *Chasers* during the 1990s.

All that, plus his early performances in *Rebel Without a Cause, Giant* and some classic Westerns, adds up to an impressive and extensive body of work — and prompted Rochester's George Eastman House to honor Hopper with a two-month retrospective of his films in 1988. The retrospective concluded with Hopper's sold-out appearance.

Hopper said Eastman House "is terrific." Hopper even selected the Eastman House to store his films, following the lead of filmmakers Martin Scorsese and Spike Lee.

"Mr. Hopper is important to me," said Eastman House senior curator Paolo Cherchi Usai, "because he represents the kind of artist who matches a personal vision with a need to come to terms with the Hollywood industry. Like Scorsese, he's been one of the few who's managed to make this seemingly impossible compromise in a way that's aesthetically pleasing." He added that Hopper is rare among contemporary filmmakers because he's knowledgeable about the films and filmmakers who have come before him, and builds upon their ideas and innovations.

"Too many filmmakers today think they can reinvent cinema, but they have a very short memory," said Cherchi Usai. "That's not true of Hopper." The curator noted that he expects the museum's relationship with Hopper to expand, encompassing the filmmaker's latter-day passion for still photography. "Because we're dedicated to both film and photography, this is the ideal place for an artist like Hopper," he explained.

A native of Dodge City, Hopper came to Hollywood in his late teens and worked in two landmark films with the legendary James Dean: *Rebel Without a Cause* and *Giant.* His other early films included the Westerns *Gunfight at the O.K. Corral, From Hell to Texas* and *The Sons of Katie Elder.*

But by the late '60s, Hopper had begun working with a group of young film rebels, including the then-unknown Jack Nicholson and Peter Fonda, and low-budget producer Roger Corman. Eventually, Hopper directed *Easy Rider,* a touchstone film of the '60s — and, many believe, the nail in the coffin of the so-called Golden Age of old Hollywood.

By then, Hopper was going through alcohol, cocaine and wives with wild abandon. The fog didn't clear until 1980. Ironically, those famous comeback roles found the sober Hopper playing a drugged-up psycho (in *Blue Velvet*) and a drunk (in *Hoosiers*).

"Life — everything — is a lot easier for me today," reported Hopper, 62. "I wish I'd gotten sober a lot earlier. It's great living in a world without paranoia and schizophrenia. It's also a lot easier to perform. Because I had relied on the booze so much, I was scared I wouldn't be able to get the big emotions." But he went back to techniques he had learned as a Method actor and to "the basics of acting, and everything was a lot easier and cleaner." And — thank goodness — he was no longer interested in trying to be like the guys he plays on screen.

Before his death in 2010, he also turned to shooting and exhibiting photographs, and publishing photo essay books. He also kept in touch with his grown family from earlier marriages and enjoying playing with his youngest child, Henry, who was 8 when we talked.

Heck, Hollywood's one-time hellion had even been known to play a round of golf.

ROBERT FORSTER

I've known Robert Forster for decades. He's a native of Rochester, the place I've called home for more than 40 years, where he's a much-admired favorite son. But even before I too had Rochester connections, I admired Forster for his lead performance in a seminal '60s film, Medium Cool. *Then in the early '70s, before I'd had a chance to meet him, I loved a short-lived TV detective he played in* Banyon.

That show, set in the '30s, made me realize that Forster's cool, slightly cynical aura may have been better served by the gangster flicks and melodramas from Warner Brothers in the '30s. I could see him working alongside Bogart, Cagney, Muni and those guys.

For whatever reason, Forster's star never quite got into the ascendency it deserved in the '70s and '80s, and he went into a 25-year slump. But he never lost interest or ambition, and he kept at his craft, whether in classroom lectures or playing villains in B movies.

Finally, Forster's star came into alignment with public taste when Quentin Tarantino picked him for Jackie Brown, *the director's follow-up to* Pulp Fiction. *Forster's portrayal of a bail bondsman with a big heart led to an Oscar nomination and a rejuvenated career. In 2011, he earned more plaudits as George Clooney's two-fisted father-in-law in* The Descendants.

But I'm getting ahead of things. Let's go back to a breakfast in Santa Monica in December 1997, shortly after Jackie Brown *catapulted Forster back onto casting directors' A list.*

ROBERT FORSTER WAS EATING BREAKFAST ON THE PATIO OF A SANTA MONICA Boulevard diner when he had what he calls "a life-changing experience": Quentin Tarantino — arguably the hottest director in Hollywood — stopped by Forster's table and offered him a lead role in his eagerly anticipated motion picture, *Jackie Brown*.

Breakfasting a year later at the same café, Forster recalled how stunning the offer was after a 25-year career slide. The Rochester-born actor had a promising career for five hot years in the late '60s and early '70s. But after making movies with the likes of Marlon Brando, Elizabeth Taylor and Gregory Peck, he'd become a character actor, bit player and all-around heavy in a slew of often-forgettable B movies.

Tarantino was one of the people who noticed something interesting: even in the midst of garbage, Forster managed to do work that ranged from credible to very good. When the writer-director was putting together his follow-up to *Pulp Fiction*, he remembered Forster's work.

At 56, Forster called his down years "the long second act" of his life, but he said he never got discouraged. "I told myself, Bob, you can still win it in the late innings," Forster said, demonstrating his penchant for upbeat philosophy. "It ain't over till it's over."

Now Tarantino was giving him a chance to bat clean-up for a team that included Robert De Niro and Samuel L. Jackson, along with another '70s comeback star, Pam Grier.

And, at the time we had breakfast, it looked as if Forster had hit at least a triple — maybe even a home run. Critic Roger Ebert told a national television audience recently that Forster deserved an Oscar nomination.

"Oh, I don't know about that," Forster said, shifting uneasily in his seat at the very idea. "But maybe I can start getting good jobs." (The predictions were right: he got an Oscar nomination.)

Luckily for Forster, Tarantino had long been a fan of the actor's good work in some not-so-good jobs: for instance, *Alligator*, the campy horror flick Forster made in 1980. Tarantino (and I) also admired *Banyon*, the cult-favorite TV series from the early '70s in which Forster played a '30s Hollywood detective, and *Delta Force,* the 1986 Chuck Norris actioner, elevated by Forster's portrait of a villainous Arab hijacker.

The actor was born Robert Foster in the Dutchtown neighborhood on Rochester's west side, but changed his name to Forster in Hollywood after discovering another Robert Foster was already listed in the Screen Actors Guild. Forster graduated from Madison High School and the University of Rochester, where he originally took pre-law courses. But in his junior year at UR, he discovered acting — mostly because he was interested in an attractive young woman, June, who was appearing in plays; she later became his wife.

Instead of law school, Forster headed for the Manhattan stage and, with an agent's help, to Hollywood in 1966. He co-starred as a handsome young soldier who comes between husband and wife (Brando and Taylor) in *Reflections in a Golden Eye*.

Then came the lead in Haskell Wexler's seminal '60s film *Medium Cool*, playing a TV newsman caught up in his coverage of the Democratic convention in Chicago in 1968. Famously, the film was shot at the actual convention and featured Forster on the streets, acting in front of real rioting. Next was a key role in *The Stalking Moon* opposite Gregory Peck. Then came TV's *Banyon* and a few other respectable jobs, and Forster's successful first act was over.

"Over the last five years or so I haven't had any job that paid more than scale," he said at our 1997 breakfast.

The actor said he then hated all the publicity and hoopla that were part of being a movie star. "I didn't feel comfortable self-promoting. What the hell did I know? I didn't like what was coming out of my mouth (in interviews)," Forster said. "So I put myself up in Rochester and didn't come down to enter the fray. I decided if I ever made it again, I better have more to say."

Forster eventually moved back to Los Angeles. To fill the time — and help pay the rent — Forster opened a small acting studio where he helped young actors hone their craft. And he began putting his upbeat philosophy into a series of free lectures that he'd give to any group who wanted to listen. Forster said he also learned to make parenting a number-one priority along the way. He now has four grown children.

"I tell them that an artist uses life experience to learn with and understand with, and to use each creative act to deliver that understanding. If you do that, you have a really rich life. I decided I was not going to languish."

Forster picked at a bit of fruit left on his plate. His face brightened when he saw a friend walk in the door. It was Tarantino, coming for breakfast with his then-love, actress Mira Sorvino. Friendly greetings were exchanged, just as they had been in this same restaurant more than a year earlier, on that day when Forster's life was changed.

The next time I talked professionally with Bob was three years later...

In the three years leading up to his 1997 Oscar nomination for *Jackie Brown*, Rochester native Robert Forster had mostly small roles in nine insignificant projects. It was the end of a two-decade slide for the once-hot actor. He had fallen victim to bad choices and near misses, such as the aptly named *The Black Hole*. His restrained acting style also fell into disfavor with some critics who mistook Forster's close-to-the-vest method for stiffness. (Now they call it subtle, which is much more accurate.)

Forster proved them wrong, as modern audiences embraced his deep talent when Quentin Tarantino cast him as bail bondsman Max Cherry, who falls for Pam Grier's title character in *Jackie Brown*.

In the three years since his Oscar nomination, Forster has been involved in 22 projects. He says this bump "has been an unqualified return to action." After *Jackie Brown*, Forster was in two Hitchcock remakes, Gus Van Sant's *Psycho* and a new *Rear Window* with Christopher Reeve, and, quite amusingly, opposite Jim Carrey in *Me, Myself and Irene*. He also co-starred opposite Mary Tyler Moore in CBS-TV's dark docudrama *Like Mother, Like Son*. Additionally, he received some of the best reviews of his career in 2000 for his touching portrayal of a sailor in *Lakeboat*, which marked his first stab at the precisely modulated dialogue of writer David Mamet.

"Mamet's stuff usually bothers me," he admitted. "In order for it to be natural, you have to give the actor some license to play it. Mamet wants it played precisely the way he puts it on paper. But I thought, *Maybe if you do it right, it'll work.* He reported that the movie "was an exercise in discipline for myself, and a lot more work than I ever imagined."

A.O. Scott of the *New York Times* called Forster the "bass note of melancholy soul under the scrappy bluff of *Lakeboat.*" Amy Taubin of the *Village Voice* and Peter Travers of *Rolling Stone* seconded the praise. *Lakeboat* had only limited success in movie theaters, but is available on DVD and well worth watching.

When Forster's career went into its tailspin in the late '70s, he began giving motivational speeches, and he still gives them. Clearly, he believes what he says, especially his "rules for success": "No. 1 is to have a good attitude. No. 2 is to accept all things, deliver excellence to whatever is offered, give it your best shot. And rule No. 3 is never quit. It's not over till it's over."

That has proved true in his life. "I always thought it'd be nice to work enough to save some dough and be comfortable, and to get creative choices and feel some satisfaction. For many years, those things eluded me. But since *Jackie Brown*, things have been great."

If you're ever lucky enough to hear Bob lecture, I hope he tells you his stories from his debut film, *Reflections in a Golden Eye.* Forster was a 26-year-old film novice when he walked onto the set for a film with three legends: Marlon Brando, Elizabeth Taylor and director John Huston.

"But I wasn't intimidated," he says. "I figured they must be scared about me because they know what they're doing. I'm the one who's never done it before."

The film is a challenging drama about desire and repressed homosexuality. Though it met with mixed reviews, Huston considered it one of his best films, and it's since achieved cult-classic status. In *Reflections*, Forster played an Army soldier whose bare-naked, bareback horse riding triggers the repressed homosexuality of his commanding officer (Brando).

When Forster got to the set one chilly morning, he saw an extra riding around and "realized it was supposed to be me. So I ran to Huston and said, 'I can do that.' In truth, my only horseback riding experience was around a circle for a dime when I was a kid in Rochester."

Huston and Brando taught numerous lessons to the novice. The director told Forster that he'd explain everything the actor needed to know before filming began. So, during pre-production, Forster kept asking questions. Huston would say, "Not now, Bobby." Finally, on his first day on the set, he heard Huston say, "Now's the time, Bobby." The great director had Forster look through the lens and pointed out the lines of the frame. "Now ask yourself this, Bobby: what needs to be in there?"

"That says it all," Forster affirmed. "The actor has to do the detective work to know what the writer needs. You have to figure out what's needed and provide it."

And Forster learned about power while visiting in Brando's elaborate trailer. Brando was berating production assistants. "I'm very, very upset," Forster recalled Brando saying to one fellow. "There are too many folks around here, and I need some tranquilizers. Oh, and I need music to soothe myself." Forster recalled, "The guy was back in 20 minutes with a stereo, a bunch of classical music albums and some pills. After the guy left, Brando looked at me and said, 'If you don't scare them, they'll never respect you.'"

QUENTIN TARANTINO

BOY, IF QUENTIN TARANTINO'S FORMER CO-WORKERS AT THE VIDEO STORE COULD SEE him now.

With the opening of *Pulp Fiction*, Tarantino, who supported himself by recommending titles at a Southern California video store in the mid-'80s, achieved a movie buff's dream. After swallowing all sorts of videotaped pop culture, especially crime films and movies by favorite directors from Sergio Leone to Brian De Palma, he's burped it back up in some of the most intense and outrageous movies of the 1990s.

Besides writing and directing *Pulp Fiction* and his first independent film, *Reservoir Dogs,* now a cult classic, he wrote the screenplay for Tony Scott's *True Romance.* (He was the original writer for Oliver Stone's *Natural Born Killers,* but after Stone's drastic rewrite, Tarantino asked that his credit be reduced to "story by.")

As we talked, he was sitting in a Manhattan hotel suite on the eve of the opening night of the 1994 New York Film Festival, where *Pulp Fiction* was showcased. Then 31, Tarantino was as intense as his movies, though not nearly as ominous. A tall, thin man with black, receding hair, he spoke in quick bursts of energy, punctuating the conversation with swirling hand gestures and by rattling the ice in his club soda. He became especially animated when I mentioned his surprise casting of John Travolta. Travolta is, after all, an actor whose career had long been on the skids.

"When I was in junior high school, John Travolta was the biggest star on the planet," said Tarantino. "I know all that hype went away, but I never forgot that John's a terrific actor. Before I was ever in a position to do anything about it, I thought to myself: *what's wrong with those directors out there? Why aren't they using this really talented guy?* So, I put my money where my mouth was. And people have thanked me for bringing John back."

Though curiosity about a revived Travolta no doubt drew people to theaters, when they left, they were more likely to be talking about the violence, racist language and intensity of *Pulp Fiction*. "Gangster films are a violent genre," said Tarantino, declining to make any apology. "If you make a swashbuckler, you expect to show people sword-fighting. I'm dealing with the crime genre, and violence is part and parcel of it."

Tarantino, though, always seeks surprising ways to use violence.

"When violence enters the lives of most regular citizens," he told me, "it usually rears its ugly head out of nowhere, like some guy picking a fight with you in the street. Sometimes, the shoe's on the other foot. Some guy makes you so mad you want to beat him up. You don't normally go around feeling that way. *Hell, where'd this come from?* Or you're sitting in a restaurant and some guy four tables over smacks his wife, and — whoa! — we have to deal with it, in deed or thought. That's how I like to have it come into my films. And that's when it has the most impact, when it comes out of nowhere."

He also likes to mix humor and other unexpected elements to heighten the impact of the violence. Who can forget the scene in *Reservoir Dogs* when Michael Madsen cuts off a cop's ear? "I think the scene is so effective," he speculated, "because Michael Madsen does his little dance to that catchy tune on the radio. I defy people not to enjoy Michael doing his little dance. He's very enjoyable doing that dance. Then he cuts the cop in the face, and you go, 'Oh, whoa.'"

The characters in Tarantino films also have the filthiest, most racist mouths in mainstream movies. But, he said, that's also because of the type of people he's portraying — gangsters and thugs.

"These characters don't bite their tongues before they say something," he asserted. "They might bite their tongues about each other, but they're not worried about being polite. They have different standards. They're just rude guys. Still, they won't say 'f---' in front of their mother."

The black humor, violence and language would seem to make Tarantino a champion for those who oppose those calling for inoffensive entertainment. But "I'm not like Oliver Stone," he said. "I don't make movies to make points. That's kind of a fool's battle."

Tarantino considers himself a storyteller and nothing more. He added, "And my characters have the freedom to go this way or that way. If they go beyond the line, I'm not going to play God with them and tell them they can't do something, just because some people won't like it."

PENÉLOPE CRUZ

HOW CAN YOU IMPROVE PERFECTION? BY GIVING IT A BIGGER BUTT.

Yes, that sounds like an old joke, but it's what Spanish director Pedro Almodóvar thought he needed to do to the gorgeous Penélope Cruz for his fabulous 2006 film, *Volver*.

Of course, there's much more to the mother in *Volver*, and it all comes from Cruz. Her performance of moral complexity, wit and rich humanity has already earned her nominations for an Oscar and a Golden Globe.

Cruz has the central role of a mother facing many challenges. Almodóvar knew she'd be great in the role but was worried that Cruz was too slender at the hips. He wanted the actress to convey a rustic maternal look, not unlike Sophia Loren in her early Italian classics such as *Two Women* and *Yesterday, Today and Tomorrow*.

"We talked about it," Cruz remembered, "and we tried it in a costume fitting, and we liked the way it looked and the way it made me walk. It was very simple." And, she added with a laugh, despite the references to Sophia Loren, Dustin Hoffman's fake derriere in *Tootsie* was "a reference point."

By returning to her Spanish roots and to her favorite director, Cruz vaulted into the top echelon of international actors. She's no longer just the world-class beauty. "Now I can play a woman," she stated, "where before I played the girl."

Born in Madrid in 1974, Cruz studied dance throughout her childhood and early teen years. But then films beckoned. "When I was a teenager," Cruz explained, "I became interested in movies because I liked the way they made me feel. I decided to try to act, and I went to an audition, and I got the part I auditioned for." It was a major role in the 1992 sex comedy *Jamón, Jamón*, which became an international hit. "I went to the Venice Film Festival, and I was nominated for the Spanish version of the Oscar, and I was only 16."

Five years later, she made her first Almodóvar film, *Live Flesh*. Then she ran off a string of American films, including *The Hi-Lo Country, All the Pretty Horses, Blow, Captain Corel-li's Mandolin, Vanilla Sky* and *Sahara* — and had high-profile relationships with several of her leading men, including Tom Cruise, Matt Damon and Matthew McConaughey. Then came her triumphant return to Spain. (Coincidentally, *Volver* means "to return.")

After we talked about *Volver*, Cruz worked again in her homeland, co-starring in *Mano-lete*, the portrait of the famous Spanish matador, played by Adrien Brody, and then as one of the stars of Woody Allen's *Vicki Cristina Barcelona*. Though she didn't win the Oscar for *Volver*, she eventually took home the statuette for Allen's film.

Meanwhile *Manolete* made its debut at the Cannes Film Festival, but despite the presence of two Oscar-winning stars, the film failed to acquire distribution. After a long delay, it finally surfaced as a DVD release, re-titled *A Matador's Mistress*. More recently, Cruz starred again for Allen, rekindling thoughts once again of a young Sophia Loren, in *To Rome with Love*, and came on board the *Pirates of the Caribbean* ship for *On Stranger Tides*, the fourth in that lucrative franchise series.

But her constant goal is to get involved with whatever the next Almodóvar film happens to be. In late 2012, she was working on Almodóvar's *I'm So Excited*, co-starring Antonio Banderas, another international star who owes his career to Almodóvar.

"Pedro is very special to me, my favorite director," Cruz said. "We've known each other for 10 years, and that's made the trust easier."

She also loves Almodóvar's movies. "His films are a beautiful homage to life, to happiness, to pain, to everything in life, because he is so honest. You can see yourself in almost every character, and you won't feel judged by him."

ENNIO MORRICONE

Given my equal love of movies and music, talking to great film composers is always a treat. One of my favorite such conversations took place in 2001.

FEW PEOPLE ARE AS RESPONSIBLE FOR A MOVIE'S MOOD AS THE COMPOSER. And no one has created more moods for the movies than the Italian maestro Ennio Morricone.

His music made Clint Eastwood ominous in *A Fistful of Dollars* and heroic in *In the Line of Fire*. Morricone brought angelic choirs to *The Mission* and ennobled Kevin Costner in *The Untouchables*. His music made us feel the searing pain of *Casualties of War*, the terror of *The Thing* and the nostalgic glow of *Cinema Paradiso*.

In a career spanning four decades, Morricone has penned the music for an estimated 400 films. No other film composer is even close. And this output is from a man who didn't create his first film score until he was 34.

Morricone demurred when I expressed amazement during a phone interview. "No, it's not incredible. If you think, over 40 years, I made music for 400 films. But what Bach wrote in just 33 years, I haven't even approached."

Morricone's most recent score is for the nostalgic Italian period film *Malena*. It marks his seventh collaboration with *Cinema Paradiso* director Giuseppe Tornatore.

It's no coincidence that Morricone works repeatedly with certain directors. Besides Tornatore, they've included Sergio Leone, Roland Joffe and Brian De Palma. Morricone said the director is the first factor he attends to when he is offered a project. "I consider the name, the esteem I have for him and his work," he explained. "If you put a screenplay, whether it's good or not, in the hands of many different directors, you'll get many different films. Therefore, it's the style of the director that draws me."

Tornatore long ago passed the first test. Morricone said he was then drawn to the elements of *Malena* that he would accent with his music. "First, there's the comic element of the many characters who populated the town. Second, the sensuality of the protagonist. Third, the historical aspect of the film, during World War II — that period of Italian history. And, fourth, the sentimental part, the relationship between the wife and her husband, who's off to war."

In most cases, music is the last step in the movie-making process. For *Malena*, Tornatore and Morricone tried something different: Morricone composed his main themes before shooting began and recorded versions with a small orchestra. Tornatore then used the recordings to inspire his cast. After *Malena* was in the can, Morricone fine-tuned the themes and added other music.

Born in Rome in 1928, Morricone studied trumpet and composition before composing for radio, television, the screen and the concert hall. He was one of three men — the others being Eastwood and Leone — whose stars rose with the international success of the so-called spaghetti Westerns: *A Fistful of Dollars, For a Few Dollars More,* and *The Good, the Bad, and the Ugly.* He has since become one of the few film composers whose name has box-office appeal and whose scores are routinely found in music shops, with the Western scores, *The Mission,* and *Cinema Paradiso* being particularly popular.

However, when I ask Morricone why my favorite — the music for Bernardo Bertolucci's epic *1900* — wasn't (at that time) available on CD, he said, "I don't know why." After a pause, Morricone detected my disappointment and offered: "I tell you what: I'll hum it for you." And then, over the phone, he gave me my own solo concert, humming the complete main theme to *1900*.

That's what I call an accommodating interview subject.

ZHANG YIMOU

One of most talented directors of the modern age is China's Zhang Yimou, a cinema visionary who first attracted international attention with a series of sublime art-house films in the 1990s and the first few years of the 21st century. He moved into a different phase, the creation of gorgeous martial arts epics, with the release of Hero *and* House of Flying Daggers *in 2004 and '05, respectively.*

In 2009, Zhang made A Woman, a Gun and a Noodle Shop, *a noodle-bar parody of the Coen brothers'* Blood Simple, *and in 2011 he crafted his first English-language film,* The Flowers of War, *starring Christian Bale.*

I did the interviews with Zhang that follow. The first took place in 1995 as he wound down the first phase of his career; the second was in 2004 as he was launching his first martial arts film.

In the interest of full disclosure, I offer the information that my son, Matt Garner, a film editor, worked with Zhang on a few films, most notably Hero. *He admires Zhang as much as his father does, and considers working with him a highlight of his career. In addition to Zhang's highly regarded work in film and opera, the stunning opening and closing ceremonies of the 2008 Beijing Olympics are a credit to the director.*

THE 1990S HAVEN'T BEEN A GOOD DECADE FOR MOST FOREIGN FILMS ON U.S. SCREENS, but Chinese films have thrived. And the great champion of Chinese cinema in the West has been filmmaker Zhang Yimou, who was 45 when we first spoke in Montreal in 1995.

Before the late 1980s, most U.S. filmgoers would have been hard-pressed to name one Chinese film. By now, most thoughtful film buffs have seen (or at least heard of) *Raise the Red Lantern, Ju Dou, To Live,* all by Zhang, and *Farewell My Concubine* and *The Blue Kite,* by his contemporaries.

Now comes Zhang's lush look at the gangster tradition, *Shanghai Triad*.

Ironically, Zhang believes he has achieved success in this country by not emulating American films. He considers himself "pure Chinese" and thinks that's the key.

We talked through a translator in the lobby of a Montreal hotel. Zhang sat on the edge of a sofa, dressed in blue denim jacket and pants.

"I know very little about anything else but China," said Zhang. "I use Chinese techniques, imagery and symbolism in my films, and perhaps Western audiences like them because they're different."

He also suggested that people of other cultures can identify with his films "because there's a common humanity. It's the same when I see a good American film. I'm touched by it, even though I don't understand the culture."

With *Shanghai Triad*, Zhang admirably shows again how he rolls with China's political punches. He said he felt compelled to make *Shanghai* after his previous film, the overtly political *To Live,* was banned in China.

"*Shanghai Triad*, compared to *To Live*, is not very sensitive, politically," he said. "After *To Live*, I wanted to continue working. So I decided on a topic that would be acceptable. But I'm also interested in the (gangster) topic. It's a challenge for me, because I know viewers in the West really like films about gangsters. I wanted to make a film on that topic, but in a Chinese way. It was a challenge to make something different from American films like *The Godfather*. The Chinese have an aesthetic, a way of doing things, that means not presenting things in an outright manner. I present the gangster society in the background, not in a direct way."

But despite Zhang's protestations that his film is not politically sensitive, Western viewers still seek a political subtext. We've come to expect it in Chinese cinema.

"That doesn't disturb me," Zhang said. "In China, we live in a political world. Politics is part of our daily life. I understand why people read that into my films. And it is there."

It is especially prominent in *To Live*, a 30-year saga of one couple's efforts to survive the volatile political shifts in their country. Zhang said that the problem with *To Live* was that it had not been approved when it was filmed. "A film in China always needs an official approval before it is shown inside or outside of China," he explained. "*To Live* was shown at film festivals before it had that approval; that's why it ran into trouble."

"As for my next film I will make, I don't know if it'll be the same situation or not. In China, I will only know when I start making the film."

The most obvious change in Zhang's future work, though, will be the presumed absence of the stunning actress Gong Li. She has starred in all his films, from *Red Sorghum* to *Shanghai Triad,* and in his personal life as well. But the couple broke up earlier this year.

Asked if he considered the actress his alter ego on the screen, Zhang said, "I would disagree with you on that, if what you mean is that hers is the point of view I most agree with in my films." He said she plays characters: Some share his perspective, others don't.

"She's very intelligent," he observed. "She can adapt to each different role. Her face can portray many different emotions. She was predestined to be an actor."

For his next project, Zhang said, he's mulling over two ideas: One is a contemporary urban film, and the other is set among royalty in the Tang Dynasty.

"I like to have new challenges every time, as long as I don't repeat myself," he stated. "I wouldn't be interested in my own films if I kept repeating. But sometimes change is dangerous. There's a risk in that, because I may not know how to do it. But I like to live that way."

I caught up with Zhang Yimou again nine years later, when he released his first martial arts epic, Hero, *in the West.*

Chinese director Zhang Yimou had been a darling of the art house circuit in the '90s and beyond, creating such memorable films as *Raise the Red Lantern, Ju Dou* and *The Road Home*. But in 2004, with *Hero*, he turned to a mainstay of Asian popular cinema, the martial arts film.

Ang Lee's international hit *Crouching Tiger, Hidden Dragon* proved to him that art and action can go hand in hand. "I loved martial arts novels as a child," said the director, who was 52 when we spoke in August 2004. But after graduating from film school, as a leading member of China's famous Fifth Generation filmmakers — the first filmmakers to emerge since China's Cultural Revolution — he found people assumed such films were too commercial. "But *Crouching Tiger* gave me the freedom to move forward."

Zhang discovered that a martial arts film — especially an epic like *Hero* — offered distinct challenges. "The first requirement," he asserted, "is imagination. Imagination and creativity. These stories aren't true stories. They're legends. They aren't really real. You have to use creativity to make them believable. The other challenge is taking care of lots of things when you're doing such a big movie. So many things to coordinate and do."

Zhang also wanted his film to offer more depth. "Most of the time," he explained, "martial arts are entertaining. The characters are simple. I wanted to do something different and offer more depth of character. I think the theme of *Hero* relates to this world today. It's about a person using his heart to change others' feelings. It's not about fighting, fighting, fighting. Look at all the violence in the world. Today we have 10,000 reasons to kill a person; why not have one reason to not kill a person?"

Zhang apparently enjoyed the *Hero* experience. He went directly from the film (which he made three years before the U.S release) to another martial arts epic, *House of Flying Daggers*, which he'd just completed.

"I started writing *Flying Daggers* while I was finishing *Hero*," he reported. "I'd always planned to do two martial arts movies. The first would be about philosophy. The second is more about characters and the relationship between people. That's why there are two movies." He concluded, "But now I want to rest for a while and do something different. Someday, when I have a new script I like, maybe I'll do one again."

CHAPTER TWO

THINKING ABOUT MOVIES

I've labeled this chapter Thinking about Movies, because that's what these stories examine. They're essays about films and filmmakers, the influences they have and the way they challenge our thinking, or how they entertain us. Stories look at lighter topics, like the rise of profanity on screen (and in our culture), the resurgence of 3-D films, the qualities that make a great movie car chase, and other topics.

We start, though, with serious and recent concerns, about the influence of film violence on the rise of real-life violence.

A heavily armed gunman entered a crowded Aurora, CO, movie theater on June 20, 2012. He killed 12 people and wounded many others at a midnight showing of the Batman movie The Dark Knight Rises. *My editors at the Rochester* Democrat & Chronicle *asked me to write a column analyzing the relationship, if any, between films and the Colorado tragedy. Here is what I wrote:*

THE INFLUENCE OF MOVIES

MANY QUESTIONS REMAIN UNANSWERED IN THE TRAGEDY OF FRIDAY'S SHOOTINGS IN an Aurora, CO, movie theatre. It will be several days – or weeks – before authorities get a clear idea of the shooter's motivations and behavior. Or maybe they never will.

Will the new Batman movie figure into the equation? Or did the shooter pick the venue solely because he knew he'd have a lot of potential targets in a confined space? Does the fault lie in movies, or in the availability of deadly weapons, or in society's need to more efficiently recognize and help the demented people among us?

Yes, the tragedy happened in a theater, and, yes, the shooter reportedly exhibited certain garb and behavior that could, *could*, conceivably have been influenced by *The Dark Knight Rises*. That's the Batman movie that had begun unspooling when a man entered through an exit door and began firing.

So, of course, the possible influence of film and other media (like violent video games) has already become part of the discussion.

This is not a new phenomenon.

– In a dream sequence in *The Basketball Diaries*, the Leonardo DiCaprio character strolls into a classroom with a shotgun that he pulls out from under his long trench coat and starts shooting. It was a sequence thought to have inspired Eric Harris and Dylan Klebold, the Columbine killers, who reportedly had seen the film.

– John F. Hinckley Jr. was reportedly obsessed with Martin Scorsese's *Taxi Driver* (featuring a demented cabbie, a botched political assassination attempt, and a breakthrough performance by a young Jodie Foster). He reportedly watched it at least 15 times. Then, the idea of assassination and a growing obsession with Foster became irrationally entangled in his mind, leading to his attempt to kill President Ronald Reagan.

– *The Program,* a drama about a college football program, stirred controversy with a scene in which the team quarterback tries foolishly to show courage under pressure. He lies on the yellow line between opposing lanes on a busy highway. His teammates join him. When several real-life teenagers tried the stunt around the country, a few were killed or injured. The scene was quickly expunged from the film after its initial release. (The film resulted in my making a few brief national TV appearances, including a segment on *Good Morning, America,* because I had suggested in my review that the scene was irresponsible and I feared kids would emulate the action around the country. Sadly, I was prescient.)

However, as I said at the time of *The Program* controversy, I will defend the right of a filmmaker to address any topic, including, for example, the violent insanity of the *Taxi Driver.* That said, I do argue for a filmmaker's sense of discretion and responsibility. That's particularly true for films aimed at impressionable young audiences, *and* when a change won't dilute the filmmaker's justifiable artistic intent and integrity. It comes down to what's gratuitous or integral.

Surprisingly, a lesson in what I'm talking about can be found in a decision an artist made more than a century ago. James M. Barrie created the play *Peter Pan* in 1904 (with the second appearance of the character, previously found in *The Little White Bird* in 1902). For the play, Barrie included "pixie dust" as a prerequisite for flying.

In the play's dedication, Barrie describes the derivation of pixie dust. Apparently, some children who pretended to be Peter Pan injured themselves when they tried to fly. Parents requested that pixie dust be added as necessary for flying. This struck Barrie as a good idea, and he put it in the play.

That's an example of a prudent decision – and it even added a new element of creativity. But it makes no sense to eliminate any and all violent films or films with dangerous activity. After all, it's a matter of interpretation. Will a little girl drown by pretending to be *The Little Mermaid?* Will somebody crack up the family car after watching a race-car movie?

The movies are the messenger. They're a reflection of society. They're artistic outlets. Movies or books (or a play like *Peter Pan*) might influence behavior. Or perhaps a painting can. Can't you imagine a mentally ill man being triggered by Edvard Munch's *Scream,* or by the black crows over a cornfield in Van Gogh's painting? A demented prehistoric man may have been disturbed by a cave drawing. Or by the shadow of a tree.

The artist's ultimate responsibility is to his desire to create and to his sense of artistic integrity. An entertainer's goal is to entertain.

An *audience's* job is to help society determine what is worthwhile or helpful or amusing or moving or enlightening. We have a vote about what we want to see. It's cast in the act of buying tickets at a box office or making a purchase at a DVD store or online.

Ultimately, filmmakers and writers and performers can't be responsible for the insane behavior of a few disturbed individuals. It's impossible to determine what might trigger tragic actions performed by an irrational individual. Logic can't be applied to an illogical person, by definition.

JOHN HUSTON and ORSON WELLES

I've long considered John Huston and Orson Welles to be among the greatest of all filmmakers, and I always found great similarities in their attitudes and their artistry. Both were rebels, both were highly literate guys and both were consummate filmmakers. Yet, I couldn't help but notice that while Welles could never work comfortably with the Hollywood mainstream, Huston did. What was behind that?

When I mentioned this to a friend, Jim Healy, the former director of the George Eastman House's Dryden Theatre, he suggested I write about it for a book being assembled by an Italian film festival for which he was organizing a Huston retrospective. It is reprinted here with permission of Museo Nazionale del Cinema/Torino Film Festival.

WHEN THE AMERICAN FILM INSTITUTE HONORED JOHN HUSTON IN 1983, ORSON WELLES made a rare appearance because of his love and respect for the filmmaker.

"We've been friends since the world was young, and we have heard the chimes at midnight," Welles told the assemblage from the podium. "We've turned the moon to blood. I come before you as an expert witness." Welles described Huston as a Renaissance prince, a regency rake, and a gentleman cardsharp, as well as a "Mephistopheles to his own Faust."

But mostly, John Huston was among Welles' closest friends in the filmmaking community. And that's also how Huston felt about Orson Welles. Each was nearly as close to an alter ego for the other as one might get in the filmmaking community. Each recognized the artist in each other. And, I suspect, each knew a true rebel when he saw one.

Despite myriad similarities of interests and talent, there was, of course, one major difference. In spite of his rebellious nature and rugged streak of individualism, John Huston was able to work for his whole life in Hollywood's challenging studio system. Welles, just as famously, was not.

Still, Huston and Welles each recognized for most of their adult lives the kindred spirit in the other.

Huston cast Welles in roles in three of his films, roles for which Huston, the character actor, would also have been perfect. And then, for the last film Welles would ever attempt, the as-yet unreleased *The Other Side of the Wind*, Welles cast his old friend as the central character, a filmmaker named Hannaford who was attempting a comeback.

According to biographer Joseph McBride, Welles had decided against playing Hannaford "because he didn't want people to assume it was a self-portrait; he conceded that, despite having someone else in the role, people will still see it that way. When I asked whom he wanted for the part, he said, 'It's either John Huston or Peter O'Toole doing his imitation of John Huston.'" Huston was an apt choice for the role, not only because of his long personal and professional relationship with Welles, but also because of his public persona.

In Lawrence Grobel's *The Hustons*, the author recounts how Huston asked Welles what *The Other Side of the Wind* was about. "Well, John," Orson said, "it's a film about a bastard director who's full of himself, who catches people and creates and then destroys them. It's about us, John. It's a film about us."

Welles later called Huston's portrayal "one of the best I've ever seen." He told Grobel, "When I get to the Heavenly Gates, if I'm allowed in, it will be because I cast the best part I ever could have played myself with John Huston. He's better than I would have been – and I would have been great!"

Huston and Welles had much in common long before they met. They were born nine years apart, in mid-America: Huston in Missouri in 1906, Welles in Wisconsin in 1915. Both were raised unconventionally. (Welles lost his mother when he was nine, and his father succumbed to alcoholism when Orson was 12. Huston was the son of Walter Huston, a much-traveled vaudeville star and eventual great actor, and of Rhea Gore Huston, a newspaperwoman and restless traveler, and they had been separated since Huston was three.) So, both Huston and Welles developed the self-reliance to fend for themselves at early ages.

Both had sometimes-erratic, free-form educations and were largely self-taught (especially Huston), yet each was extremely literate. In truth, they were geniuses who far outstripped their formal educations. Both were teen *wunderkinds*. Welles wrote a book on Shakespeare, and faked his way onto the Irish stage at 16, and was on the New York stage before his 20th birthday. Huston was a boxer and a painter, acted in small roles in his father's plays before he was 20, and wrote a story accepted by H.L. Mencken for the American Mercury in his early 20s. Huston was writing scripts for Hollywood by the age of 24. Welles was making *Citizen Kane* by the age of 25.

Both lived rebellious lives and largely lived out strong impulses, yet they could be quite disciplined in their work, once they embraced it. However, Huston wasn't above chasing big game in Africa while making movies there; nor was Welles above pursuing his own version of "big game" on an intellectual level or among film producers and would-be financiers.

Both loved a good cigar.

Both were drawn to great literature and made the vast majority of their films based on great writing. In Huston's case, 31 of 37 features, discounting his wartime documentaries, were based on novels, short stories or plays. For Welles, nine of 13 completed features were based on literature. Huston focused strongly on American stories by American authors, with a handful of exceptions, such as those by Roman Gary (*The Roots of Heaven*), Rudyard Kipling (*The Man Who Would be King*), and James Joyce (*The Dead*). Welles was more European-oriented, favoring narratives from the classics of Shakespeare, Cervantes, Kafka, and Karen Blixen, though he embraced the fully American Booth Tarkington (*The Magnificent Ambersons*).

Of course, both also acted, though Welles did so more famously and consistently than Huston. Welles acted largely out of financial necessity; it was how he paid for his lifestyle and his work. And he was often brilliant, even in relatively brief cameos, including the ones in which he portrayed Father Mapple in Huston's *Moby Dick* and Cardinal Wolsey in Fred Zinneman's *A Man for All Seasons,* and, far more substantially and importantly, as Kane and Falstaff in his own *Citizen Kane* and *Chimes at Midnight,* respectively, and as the oh-so-memorable Harry Lime in Carol Reed's *The Third Man.*

For Huston, acting apparently was more of a whim, though that whim often resulted in brilliant work. His Noah Cross in *Chinatown* remains one of the cinema's most memorable and insidious villains.

Each man greatly admired the other, and they considered themselves good friends. Welles worked three times for Huston, most notably with that delightful cameo in *Moby Dick*; Huston was Welles' alter ego in the uncompleted *The Other Side of the Wind.*

Both were legendary raconteurs. And both took the air out of the room when they walked in. Anjelica Huston remembers: "Orson to me was just this huge, kind of blown-out figure of a man with an enormous voice and enormous laugh … and enormous body. I would feel faint to be in the same room as him."

James Agee, in his famous 1950 profile of Huston for *Life* magazine, described Huston as "one of the ranking grasshoppers of the Western Hemisphere." He added that Huston "has an indestructible kind of youthfulness, enjoys his enthusiasms with all his might and has the prompt appetite for new knowledge of a man whose intelligence has not been cloyed by much formal education." He reported that Huston "is wonderful company, almost anytime, for those who can stand the pace … he is particularly happy with animals, roughhousers and children."

Both men launched their directorial careers with great films, *The Maltese Falcon* for Huston and *Citizen Kane* for Welles; the films were released within five months of each other in 1941. However, only for Welles would the greatness of his debut film remain a curse as well as a blessing.

When you examine their films, you can imagine both men being capable of, or interested in, directing several of the other's movies. The films wouldn't be the same, of course, but I can see Huston making a *Kane* or *Ambersons* or *Touch of Evil* or *The Lady from Shanghai* or *Mr. Arkadin*. Likewise, I can imagine Wellesian versions of *The Maltese Falcon, Key Largo, The Asphalt Jungle, Moby Dick, The Man Who Would Be King,* and *The Dead*. However, in the Welles versions, the director's presence would most certainly be more strongly felt, as he would probably contribute a major performance or dub voices for other actors. For good or ill, Welles was far more of a one-man band than was Huston.

Both suffered at the hands of studio-controlled editing, Welles with *The Magnificent Ambersons* and Huston with *The Red Badge of Courage*. Yet, in the former case, the interference came close to killing Welles' career and gave him baggage that made it almost impossible for him to work again in the studio system. Not so for Huston. Why?

Before we suggest answers to that question, let's recall what happened with *Ambersons*. Welles' adaptation of the Booth Tarkington novel was the filmmaker's follow-up to *Citizen Kane*; it was shot in 1942. It starred Joseph Cotten, Dolores Costello, Anne Baxter, Tim Holt, Agnes Moorehead and Ray Collins. Though Welles did not appear, he acted as narrator.

When the film was completed, Welles went to South America to make a documentary on Carnival in Rio (released in fragmented form long after his death as part of the documentary *It's All True*). Welles' work was supposed to help cement relationships between North and South America during World War II. A disastrous test screening of *Ambersons* frightened RKO, and while Welles was away editors cut more than an hour of the footage and the studio tacked on a happy ending. And then, in an action considered one of the great tragedies of cinema history, the eliminated footage was destroyed. Thus, restoration is forever impossible.

Somehow, the incident reflected badly on Welles for most of his remaining career. He was labeled as the filmmaker who "abandoned" *Ambersons,* or, by amateur analysts (masquerading as writers), as suffering from an inability to complete a project.

In 1970, when another book once again placed the blame for the *Ambersons* debacle at Welles' feet, writer-filmmaker Peter Bogdanovich wrote a letter to the *New York Times*. "Far from 'abandoning' *The Magnificent Ambersons* (shooting just completed)," Bogdanovich wrote, "Welles made it a condition that his cutter join him in South America – but RKO never lived up to that agreement. One bad preview of *Ambersons* in Pomona (the audience had come to see a Dorothy Lamour musical) convinced the studio they had a disaster on their hands, and they decided to ignore Welles and perform their own surgery. And there was Welles, unable to return from Rio, desperately trying by long-distance phone calls, impassioned multi-page cables and reasoned, detailed letters to save his film, giving in on some beloved scenes in order to save others – ultimately losing everything."

And later, in his essential interview book, *This Is Orson Welles,* Bogdanovich quotes from a letter that Welles wrote to him about *Ambersons:* "I don't know of any more fun than making a movie, and the most fun of all comes in the cutting room when the shooting is over. How can it be thought that I'd deny myself so much of that joy with *Ambersons?* I felt then as I do now that it could have been a far better film than *Kane*. How can anyone seriously believe that I would jeopardize something I loved so much for the dubious project of shooting a documentary on the Carnival in Rio?"

Welles argued that he went to Brazil only at the strong insistence of John Hay Whitney and Nelson Rockefeller because it would be "a sorely needed contribution to inter-American affairs." Welles added that President Roosevelt himself helped to persuade him of the necessity of the South American project.

Ultimately, Welles added, the slashing of *Ambersons* not only cost him the two years he had spent on the film, but also "cost me many, many other pictures which I never made; and many years in which I couldn't work at all."

Welles also stressed that a key problem was a changing of the guard at RKO, where new studio bosses were less inclined to let Welles have his way with either *Ambersons* or the Rio documentary. "A truly merciless campaign was launched," Welles asserted, "and by the time I came back to America my image as a capricious and unstable wastrel was permanently fixed in the industry's mind."

In Huston's autobiography, *An Open Book*, he argues, "Orson has a wholly undeserved reputation for extravagance and unreliability. I think much of this dates from the time he went down to Rio de Janeiro some thirty years ago to get some second-unit material for a projected picture … This single incident was absurdly over-publicized. I have seen the way he works. He is a most economical filmmaker. Hollywood could well afford to imitate some of his methods."

Huston was right, of course. Consider what Welles did with scant money on *Othello* or *Touch of Evil* or other films, and then imagine what he could have done with the budget of *Avatar* or *Spider-Man* or a Harry Potter film.

In *An Open Book*, Huston also tells of the time he stood in for an absent Welles to accept his honorary Academy Award. "It was for his contributions to films over the years. It struck me that although he was being paid this tribute, none of the studios was offering him a picture to direct. Perhaps it can just be put down to fear. People are afraid of Orson. People who haven't his stamina, his force or his talent. Standing close to him, their own inadequacies show up all too clearly. They're afraid of being overwhelmed by him."

So, how did John Huston survive, nay, thrive in the studio system that so hard-heartedly rejected Orson Welles? In his biography of Welles, Joseph McBride writes, "The real problem with Welles was that though he functioned in a popular art form he was not the sort of ambidextrous popular artist who, as he once said of John Huston, 'can make a masterpiece or turn you out a blockbuster – or both.'"

But when Huston made *The Red Badge of Courage* in 1951, the studio apparently thought it neither a masterpiece nor a blockbuster. And Huston showed a pragmatic side by not arguing. He discussed the incident in a first-rate 1982 interview by Joseph Persico for *American Heritage* magazine, saying, "I never made anything so thoroughly disliked. The first time the picture was previewed, people walked out, not just in twos and threes but by the score … Before the picture was released I had to go to Africa to make *The African Queen*. I thought the *Red Badge* was safe, since I left it with two men who had championed it all along, Wolfgang Reinhardt and Dore Schary. But the studio decided the audience hadn't been sufficiently aware that they were watching a masterpiece. They had to be told. So they changed my opening … And they added a narration, too, that I hadn't wanted. They cut a 135-minute picture to 69 minutes. And it still failed. I don't blame the studio for its concern. I can understand their wanting to avoid an utter, ghastly failure. I believe that any picture, particularly an innovative picture, should pay for itself. If it doesn't, other innovators who follow you have to suffer. They aren't going to be given the opportunity to innovate. Still, I think *The Red Badge* was a good picture the way it was done originally. It's interesting, almost twenty-five years later, I got a cable from Metro wanting to know if by chance I had a print of the original. Of course I didn't. It's gone forever."

So, although the circumstances in the *Ambersons* and the *Red Badge* cases are similar, no blame landed at the feet of Huston. Perhaps it was because of the track record he had already amassed over the decade leading up to *Red Badge*. Or perhaps it was a certain conciliatory quality in Huston's makeup, a willingness to compromise.

Welles himself once suggested it might have been something as simple as Huston's legendary charisma. At that same AFI award dinner mentioned previously, Welles talked about the allure of Huston's charm and its effect not only on women, but also on studio bosses, "the grand panjandrums of the industry, from Stark to Spiegel; there is not one specimen of that ferocious breed whom John, when need arises, cannot most sweetly cause to lie down, roll over … and purr."

The answer also probably lies in Huston's ability to give the studios what they want so he can get what he wants. For clearly, not every movie John Huston ever made was a true and great "Huston picture." No one will ever put *Across the Pacific* or *Victory* or *Annie* on the same shelf as *The Maltese Falcon, The Treasure of the Sierra Madre, Fat City, Wise Blood* or *The Dead*. (I cut the great director some slack by not including *Phobia* in that "non-Huston" list; that rarely seen Canadian thriller was a case of taking the only job available at that time because medical issues made Huston uninsurable.)

Michael Caine once told me how, as an actor, he sometimes has to "do one for them, and then do one for me." I suspect Huston also realized that, especially in the latter stages of his career, as he negotiated with young studio honchos who weren't born when he made *The Maltese Falcon*.

Huston's son, actor Danny Huston, shed a positive light on his father's latter days in an interview with the BBC at Cannes in 2010. "He was able to work in the big studio setting and deliver larger Hollywood films, but also made smaller films, more independent films. There were two years in which he made *Under the Volcano, Annie, Wise Blood,* and *Victory.* Those are entirely different films with entirely different sensibilities."

John Huston also never had anything but positive things to say about the studio system. In a French interview in 1970, Huston said, "Warner gave great importance to the scriptwriter and that didn't exist at the other studios, except maybe at MGM, but in a completely different way. At Metro, they had to write for stars. At Warner, the scriptwriter came first and it was the story which counted because of the politics of this little group of men. (The old studios were) good for the scriptwriters. Warner was truly an extraordinary studio, and I have nothing but praise for it. But it was the studio system which was good."

Both Huston and Welles spent years abroad. Huston gave up his U.S. citizenship in the wake of McCarthyism and lived in Ireland, and then Mexico, for the last decades of his life. However, he remained primarily an American filmmaker, focusing on American themes and lost American souls (a favorite theme). There were exceptions, of course, including *The Man Who Would Be King* and *The Dead*.

Welles, on the other hand, became largely a European filmmaker, living and working abroad and raising funds as he moved like a nomad across Europe and North Africa. However, he never said embracing Europe was politically motivated. He also acted, a lot, to finance his own films.

So, never doubt Welles' ability to persevere to make films – and never believe that hokum that he had some sort of deep-seated psychological aversion to finishing films. He stayed with *Othello*, for example, for years, filming scenes where actors walked in a door in Venice and walked out of a door in Morocco. Famously, when Welles lacked cash or costumes, he even filmed a murder scene in a steam bath, with the actors covered only by towels.

Welles' affection for Europe was returned; it was a land where he gained far more respect than in his homeland. As astute Wellesian defender Jonathan Rosenbaum writes in his introduction to *This Is Orson Welles*, "It's a sad fact that when Orson Welles died in the fall of 1985, responses in the United States tended to differ sharply from those in the rest of the world. While the obituaries outside America devoted themselves almost exclusively to Welles' many accomplishments over more than half a century, the repeated refrains in his home country seemed to concentrate on his weight and on the specter of failure – almost as if these two fixed concepts seemed to 'explain' and justify each other. In a culture increasingly bent on defining success, history, and reality itself in terms of currently marketable items, Welles' artistic career seemed to consist of a spectacular debut followed by forty-odd years of inactivity."

In his *Biographical Dictionary of Film*, David Thomson put it this way in his entry on Welles: "He inhaled legend – and changed our air. It is the greatest career in film, the most tragic, and the one with most warnings for the rest of us."

For Welles, it all came down to the inescapable shadow of the *Ambersons* incident.

"It's an oddly comforting scenario for those who feel that both the marketplace and industry choices made on our behalf are always right," Rosenbaum continued. "But for those who have followed Welles' career more closely, his increasingly low visibility as a filmmaker during his lifetime suggests a highly troubling paradox – that the most universally revered of all American filmmakers found himself unable to make another studio picture over the last three decades of his life."

Rosenbaum addresses the reasons in detail in his knowledgeable book *Discovering Orson Welles*. However, he sums up the center of his arguments in his introduction to *This Is Orson Welles*, stating, "It is important to stress two factors: that the nature and proclivities of the film industry are every bit as pertinent to this 'failure' as Welles' own eccentricities, and that, far from being inactive, Welles continued to do creative work for the remainder of his life, even when he had to finance it himself. For these reasons, among others, Welles' work and career remain exemplary and highly subversive rebuttals to many received ideas about art and commerce that continue to circulate in this culture; they are ideological 'disturbances' in the best sense."

For Huston, especially in the last phase of his career, it was a case of remaining true to his goal of making the films he wanted to make, having made the films that others wanted him to make. So it was that the highly literate *Under the Volcano*, the rousing but dark *Prizzi's Honor*, and the sublime *The Dead* followed the Sylvester Stallone concentration camp soccer movie, *Victory*, and the musical *Annie*.

Huston made *The Dead* from a fine script by his son Tony, who adapted his father's beloved James Joyce. His health wouldn't allow Huston return to Ireland. So, except for a few moments of second-unit exteriors, *The Dead* was made in a warehouse in Valencia, California, where the filmmaker, attached to oxygen for his advanced emphysema, oversaw the performances of his Irish actors on video-direct monitors. Yet no artist ever made as appropriate a final statement as John Huston in his most eloquent final film.

Now we can only wish the same for Orson Welles: a glorious concluding statement. We must hope for the eventual completed assemblage and release of his final film, a movie that stars his good friend John Huston. It has long been whispered to be on the verge of some sort of release, pending the solving of financial complications. We must hope for the eventual release of *The Other Side of the Wind*.

THE ESSENTIAL JOHN HUSTON
The Maltese Falcon (1941)
The Battle of San Pietro (1945)
The Treasure of the Sierra Madre (1948)
Key Largo (1948)
The Asphalt Jungle (1950)
The African Queen (1951)
Moby Dick (1956)
The Misfits (1961)
Fat City (1972)
The Man Who Would Be King (1975)
Wise Blood (1979)
Prizzi's Honor (1985)
The Dead (1987)
As an actor: *The Cardinal* (1963), *Chinatown* (1974),
The Life and Times of Judge Roy Bean (1972), *The Wind and the Lion* (1975)

THE ESSENTIAL ORSON WELLES

Citizen Kane (1941)
The Magnificent Ambersons (1942)
The Stranger (1946)
The Lady from Shanghai (1947)
Othello (1952)
Touch of Evil (1958)
Chimes at Midnight (1965)
As an actor: *The Third Man* (1949), *Jane Eyre* (1944), *Prince of Foxes* (1949),
Moby Dick (1956), *Compulsion* (1959), *A Man for All Seasons* (1966)

ORSON WELLES: MOROCCAN MEMORIES

In 1992, I was one of a handful of international journalists, critics, filmmakers, and performers invited to participate as guests of the Moroccan government in a three-day celebration of the life and works of Orson Welles. For reasons that will soon become clear, the late Welles was an American director Moroccans adopted as their own.

STRANGE AS IT MAY SEEM, I WAS SITTING UNDER THE MOON IN A PUBLIC SQUARE IN A small town on the Atlantic coast of Africa, south of Casablanca, as black-and-white images of Orson Welles' film of Shakespeare's *Othello* flickered on a large outdoor screen.

I was among scores of guests in the center of the square. Thousands of townsfolk stood at barricades behind us. Three Arab children sneaked past the barriers and sat in rapt attention at my feet, while from rooftops in the distance a group of Arab women expressed their admiration as they have for centuries, with high-pitched trills.

Though it is unlikely that many of the French- and Arab-speaking Moroccans understood much of the English-language film, they were obviously thrilled to be watching. The biggest cheer went up when Othello kissed Desdemona. Some things need no translation. And the crowd became hushed at the tragic finale. The deaths, too, needed no translation.

At other times, though, murmurs could be heard among the thousands assembled in the square. It wasn't because of something Shakespeare wrote or Orson Welles performed. It was because the Moroccans had recognized another part of their hometown.

Forty years before, Orson Welles had shot much of *Othello* along the ancient ramparts and storm-tossed shores of this fishing town, then called Mogador. *Othello* was perhaps the best of the films Welles made more with passion than money throughout Europe and North

Africa, restocking his limited purse by taking time off to act in other people's movies.

Opening sequences were obviously shot in Mogador. So was the film's most famous scene: an improvised staging of the death of Roderigo. Welles filmed it in a makeshift Turkish bath because costumes had been delayed by a cash-flow problem. So, without the costumes, the brilliant Welles directed the actors, who were draped only in towels. And the Turkish bath? It was really a fish market in this harbor town, where sardines are still the mainstay of the economy.

Now, 40 years after the film's creation and seven years after Welles' death, *Othello* had come home.

The late-September screening was the centerpiece of a three-day symposium and celebration in honor of Welles, hosted by Prince Heritier Sidi Mohammed and the Moroccan government. The event was produced by Abdou Achouba, a Moroccan entrepreneur who conceived the idea while watching a screening of the recently restored Welles' *Othello* at the previous year's Cannes Film Festival.

Besides going to the screening, participants joined in panel discussions, watched a documentary about Welles, and observed a ceremony in which the Prince of Morocco renamed the town square after Welles.

Joining the Moroccans were several invited guests, including the late filmmaker's daughter, Beatrice Welles, and producer Julian Schlossberg, both of whom collaborated on the recent restoration of the film; Suzanne Cloutier, who played dumb Desdemona in the film; and George Fanto, one of three cinematographers used by Welles for *Othello*.

Also along for the festivities were actors who had worked with Welles on other projects, including Ruth Warrick (*Citizen Kane*), Keith Baxter (*Chimes at Midnight*), Dennis Hopper (from the never-released *The Other Side of the Wind*), and Gina Lollobrigida (who worked with Welles on a documentary), as well as various biographers and journalists.

"The idea that my little bit of work with Orson would get me to Morocco is far out," Hopper said whimsically while strolling with other dignitaries to the town square dedication. He wasn't alone in feeling excited and a little "far out" celebrating Orson Welles in an Arabian town in North Africa.

But for the Moroccans, a celebration of Welles made perfect sense. For, after Welles made *Othello* in Mogador, he took the film to the Cannes Film Festival. To enter it in competition, he had to declare a nationality for it. He said, "Moroccan." And that's how *Othello* came to be the only Moroccan film ever to win the top prize at the Cannes Film Festival.

Many filmmakers have turned to Morocco for timeless vistas, ancient settings and exotic locales. Parts of *Lawrence of Arabia*, *The Man Who Would Be King*, *Ishtar*, *Jesus of Nazareth*, and *The Last Temptation of Christ* were filmed within 100 km of where we were. But only Orson Welles declared his film to be Moroccan.

"*Othello* is a sort of trilogy for us," said the event organizer, Abdou Achouba. "It's part Shakespeare, part Orson Welles, and part Essaouria."

"And we hope the celebration will give new hope to Essaouria," he added.

The morning after the plaza screening, Beatrice Welles imagined her father's reaction.

"He would have been charmed by it all, and would have laughed so much from pure joy and from passion. Because that's what was there last night – his passion."

The presence of critics and journalists from France, England and Spain, as well as the United States, suggests that Morocco and America aren't the only countries to claim Welles. During the symposiums, Serge Toubiana, of France's prestigious *Les Cahiers du Cinéma,* quoted the late French director François Truffaut, who said, "Orson Welles was the most European of American filmmakers, and the most American of European filmmakers." Toubiana summed up: "So, obviously, everyone fights for him."

The Europeans respond to the Welles of anti-Hollywood legend, the man who was rejected by the major studios after *Citizen Kane* and *The Magnificent Ambersons,* but who continued to make movies his way – usually on the run and with considerable financial struggle, but with great creative impetus. "That was part of Welles' genius – the ability to make do with what you don't have," Toby said, "which is why his films remain so vibrant and enduring, because of his audaciousness and his passion."

Frank Brady, the author of the biography *Citizen Welles,* likened the Moroccan Welles celebration to a pilgrimage. "We come to see where he worked, and to pay tribute, and we can feel his presence here."

That presence took a bizarre twist later in the day, when a young Arab approached the scholarly looking Brady and said, "I want to thank you, Mr. Welles, for making your movie here."

"I didn't have the heart to destroy the illusion," said Brady, adding that being confused with Orson Welles was one of the greatest events of his life.

Brady also added his endorsement to the idea that more of Welles' released and unreleased movies call out "for continuing restoration." To that end, producer Julian Schlossberg and Beatrice Welles announced at the celebration the formation of Mogador productions, a company that will be devoted to additional restorations. The next goal, they said, was polishing the print and soundtrack of *Chimes at Midnight,* Welles' 1966 portrait of the character of Falstaff, adapted from several Shakespeare plays.

The restored *Othello,* meanwhile, went on to a significant theatrical distribution, and on to home video.

Beatrice Welles, however, objects to attempts by others to construct edited films from Welles' unfinished projects. "My father created his films in the editing room, and if he didn't edit it, it's not an Orson Welles film," she said firmly. Her comments were directed at a recent release of Welles' incomplete *Don Quixote* and an often-discussed plan to put together Welles' sprawling footage from the unreleased *The Other Side of the Wind,* which stars his old friend John Huston. She opposes both projects.

Actor-director Dennis Hopper said he understands Beatrice Welles' concerns, but added, "I'd love to see a foundation established solely for students and professionals so they could see the unreleased Welles material, even if it's not to be released in a commercial sense. His was a towering genius that we haven't yet begun to understand."

ELIA KAZAN and ARTHUR MILLER

A Bitter Past Echoes in Two Great Films

ARTHUR MILLER'S GREAT PLAY AND THE FILM *THE CRUCIBLE* IS A DRAMA ABOUT THE tragic hysteria of the Salem witch trials of the 17th century. Elia Kazan's *On the Waterfront* is a 42-year-old cinema classic about a former boxer who "coulda been a contender," but who now works as an errand boy for mobsters. Although the films seem separated by a lot more than time, they are, in fact, blood brothers – or, more accurately, contrary siblings.

On the Waterfront and *The Crucible* are opposing bookends to a dark period in 20th-century American history. And therein lies the story of two great American artists – Elia Kazan and Arthur Miller – and a friendship that was shattered.

The Crucible isn't just about witches, and *On the Waterfront* isn't just about dockworkers. Both films are about the so-called Joe McCarthy era, when the rabid Wisconsin senator led congressional committees to expose Communists and left-wing sympathizers in the military, in education – and in the arts. Scores of talented people lost their jobs and more, often on the flimsiest of testimony.

Elia Kazan was a Greek immigrant who had arrived in New York City in 1913, at age four. He rose to prominence in the American theater in the '30s and '40s, directing such stage landmarks as *A Streetcar Named Desire* and *Death of a Salesman*. The latter play is a masterpiece written by Arthur Miller, a New York City native six years younger than Kazan.

Like many people in the theater at that time, both men had socialist leanings and ties to left-wing organizations. But they took separate paths when called to testify before the House Un-American Activities Committee.

The committee wasn't content to get witnesses to tell just their own stories. They also insisted that the witnesses "name names." Witnesses were prodded – with the threat that they would never work again – into listing friends and associates who held similar beliefs.

Elia Kazan had become disenchanted with the Communist Party. He chose to testify against the party, and he named names. Miller, on the other hand, refused to testify or to name any names.

And so we come to the two great works of art.

In the early 1950s, as the HUAC hearings were beginning, Kazan and Miller had begun work on a film based on current newspaper stories about corruption in the Hoboken longshoreman's union, and about a courageous priest who fought the mob. But once the HUAC had driven a wedge between Kazan and Miller, Miller backed away from the project. Kazan turned to Budd Schulberg, another writer who, like Kazan, had been a friendly witness. Together, they fashioned *On the Waterfront*, which featured Marlon Brando's greatest performance. The film went on to win several Oscars, including best picture.

At the core of *On the Waterfront* is Terry Malloy (Brando), a character who becomes the hero of the film when he agrees to testify against his fellow mobsters. When chief hoodlum Johnny Friendly says, "You ratted on us, Terry," Malloy responds, "From where you stand, maybe. But I'm standing over here now. I was ratting on myself all them years and didn't know it, helping punks like you."

In his autobiography, Kazan wrote, "When critics say that I put my story and my feelings on the screen, to justify my informing, they are right."

At nearly the same time – in the early 1950s – Arthur Miller visited Salem, MA, to explore the roots of that community's notorious witch-hunts of the 17th century. From his research, Miller fashioned *The Crucible*, a play that opened on Broadway in 1953, won a Tony and is still performed around the world. And it finally made it to the screen in 1996, with a fine film directed by Nicholas Hytner and starring Daniel Day-Lewis. Its message remains as powerful and passionate as ever: to assume any role in a hysteria-fueled witch-hunt is to endorse it.

Near the end of the film, John Proctor (Day-Lewis) is accused of consorting with witches and is sentenced to be hanged. He is told he will live *only* if he agrees to sign a confession *and* name fellow villagers who joined him.

As Proctor waits in his cell, one of the interrogators argues with Proctor's good wife that even if such a confession is a lie, he should still give it. The wife replies, "I think that may be the Devil's argument." Moments later, upon threat of hanging, Proctor still refuses to sign his name, "because it is my name! Because I cannot have another in my life!"

In other words, Arthur Miller created a hero whose heroism is found in not testifying. Forty-two years after *On the Waterfront,* the opposing argument was finally on the screen. Those of us who appreciate superb films by true artists can only be grateful that both men created moving, eloquent masterpieces from their passion and pain. As Arthur Miller reportedly said to *Crucible* film director Nicholas Hytner, "You know, McCarthy is dust, and this play is still alive! It's the revenge of art."

WAR MOVIES

WAR IS HELL. BUT IT CAN ALSO MAKE A HELL OF A MOVIE.

Pioneering filmmaker D.W. Griffith knew it in 1914 when he made Hollywood's first great war epic, about the Civil War, only 50 years after Appomattox. In 1998, Steven Spielberg released another great film, also based on a war from a half-century earlier. From *Birth of a Nation* to *Saving Private Ryan*, filmmakers have turned to combat to ignite memorable movies.

War makes for great drama. Drama is based on conflict, and nothing offers such obvious conflict as war. It's sharply defined: life and death, good and evil. Except, perhaps, when the war itself is murky. In the '70s and '80s, most war movies addressed the nation's complex feelings about Vietnam. *The Deer Hunter, Platoon, Born on the Fourth of July* – such films wrestled with a morally ambiguous conflict waged without the support of many, a war that handed our nation its first conclusive military defeat.

Saving Private Ryan signaled a profound shift. Spielberg's 1998 D-Day drama was the crest of a wave of films that have returned the spotlight to our "good" war – to the righteous, heroic triumph of World War II. Terrence Malick's *The Thin Red Line*, a saga about the fight on Guadalcanal, and two superb HBO World War II series, *Band of Brothers*, about the Battle of the Bulge, and *The Pacific*, about the fight against Japan, followed. And Quentin Tarantino applied his potent, high-energy style to *Inglourious Basterds*, a hyper-tribute to earlier World War II action films like *The Dirty Dozen* and *Combat!*

More recent warfare in the Middle East has also prompted new films, including *Three Kings, The Messenger,* and the Oscar-winning *The Hurt Locker.*

Regarding *Saving Private Ryan*, Spielberg explained that he made it as a way to honor his father, a member of what newsman and author Tom Brokaw has labeled "the greatest generation." Spielberg explained, "My father, who is 81, fought in World War II. I wanted to do something for my dad and give him something back. Not unlike the stories he told me about his wartime experiences."

People need heroes.

Why now? Because World War II films "offer clear-cut victories over a clear-cut evil," notes Mark Betz, a programmer for the film archive at the George Eastman House. After all, the war was fought to save the world from totalitarianism.

Tom Hanks, the star of *Saving Private Ryan*, agrees. "World War II films require no editorializing about why we were there," he told me. "The Nazis were bad, the Japanese Empire was an evil thing, the world was at war. Period. The end."

For many younger viewers, the war also is brand new. Writes Dale Dye, a retired Marine captain who is Hollywood's preeminent military adviser: "It's not that they don't remember World War II; it's that these films will make them discover there *was* a World War II." (Dye has run boot camps for the casts of such films as *Platoon* and *Saving Private Ryan,* forcing actors such as Charlie Sheen and Hanks, the latter a two-time Oscar-winner, to crawl in the mud and eat out of a can.)

Historian Stephen E. Ambrose, author of the best-sellers *D-Day: June 6, 1944*, and *Citizen Soldiers*, said the time is right to re-examine the "Last Good War," which he called "the biggest event of the 20th century." He elaborated, "It had the most participants, which means it has a built-in audience. And it still does: There are still millions out there who were involved in World War II, one way or the other – many more than in Vietnam." The enlisted men who did most of the fighting were only 19 or 20 during the war. Now in their 80s, many want to revisit "their" war.

"There is a spurt in such films," Ambrose said when we talked in 1998. "The recent 50th anniversary (of D-Day and other key events) is one part of it. And I did a study of newspapers, magazines and books of 1913, 1914, 1915, and they devoted a lot of attention to the Civil War of 50 years earlier. More specifically, in 1998 we live in an age without any heroes. But people need heroes, and World War II gives us all kinds of heroes... ordinary guys caught up in extraordinary times. They met the demands placed on them, and that's genuine heroism."

What's more, Ambrose, who died in 2002, believed patriotism was back in fashion and had helped fuel the renewed interest in World War II. He said, "People are yearning for a national unity again."

"Film is like a battleground: love, hate, action, violence, death ... in a word, emotion," the late Sam Fuller, a hard-nosed filmmaker, told me in a 1980 interview for *The Big Red One*, his semi-autobiographical account of a squad of GIs.

Filmmakers also like the technical challenge of war. "War movies provide lots of opportunities for testing the range of sound and technology in film," says Betz, of the Eastman House. "Once sound came along (in 1927), they became a favorite movie form, along with other noise-generating genres, like musicals and gangster movies."

Such films also give free rein to man's worst impulses. "The battlefield is a world in which the laws, beliefs, behavior, and morality of civilization are suspended," writes John

Belton, author of *American Cinema/American Culture.* "It is not merely permitted for one man to kill another; it is imperative for him to do so." In *The Big Red One*, a foot soldier says, "I can't murder anyone." "We don't murder," answers his sergeant. "We kill."

Because war films stir emotions so powerfully, they've long been among Hollywood's most politicized dramas. Like soldiers, they seldom settle for the middle ground. During World War II, films became a form of propaganda supporting the war effort.

Hollywood filmmakers and stars felt obliged to do their part. Some enlisted; some pitched war bonds; some made patriotic movies. They depicted war as hard but gallant; Americans were in the right, and the Germans and Japanese were ignoble foes who deserved defeat.

For the next decade and more, movies continued to offer rousing adventures of wartime heroics. This was the era of John Wayne. He was tough, he was virtuous, he was uncomplicated. He was America. Wayne "personified the ideal soldier, sailor, or Marine," according to Lawrence H. Suid in the book *Guts and Glory: Great American War Movies*. In the decades after the actor starred in *Sands of Iwo Jima*, Wayne and his military image continued to be an influence. In Oliver Stone's anti-Vietnam drama *Born on the Fourth of July*, the film's real-life main character, Ron Kovic (Tom Cruise), is shown as enlisting out of a rah-rah conviction born, in part, of watching John Wayne movies.

By the mid-1960s, the political tone of war movies had turned. Thanks to the controversy surrounding Vietnam, patriotism fell out of favor, and war films all but disappeared from the screen. The only significant exception was John Wayne's gung-ho rant, *The Green Berets.*

After Americans fled Saigon, Hollywood tiptoed back to war films, but gave them a more negative slant. Soldiers were depicted as fodder for slaughter, pawns in a cynical game designed by politicians, generals and industrialists. "War films became a form of dissent," Betz says.

But with *Saving Private Ryan* and *Band of Brothers*, Hollywood returned to familiar ground – with a difference. *Saving Private Ryan* is remarkably bloody and painful, perhaps because its writers, directors, technicians and actors are products of the skepticism of the Vietnam era. The film pays homage to heroic sacrifice, but doesn't shrink from showing its incredibly high price. This isn't a film about romanticized adventure; it's about doing your duty despite a horrific cost.

That cost was further demonstrated in two World War II films by Clint Eastwood in 2006. With *Flag of Our Fathers* and *Letters from Iwo Jima,* the remarkable and seemingly ageless filmmaker (then 76) depicted the battle of Iwo Jima from the perspective of both countries, one in English, one in Japanese.

Though Spielberg's and Eastwood's films seem to approach perfection, filmmaker Fuller believed that the perfect war movie couldn't be made. "A war movie is just like a man doing an autopsy on his own body. It's impossible," he told me. "You can make a real love story. You can make a real mystery ... but you absolutely cannot make a real war movie. The closest I can think ... is to have a couple of riflemen behind the screen and during a firefight in the movie, people in the audience are shot at. Seeing that picture, going to it, you might get shot.

That's about the only way I can see you make a legitimate movie about war."

Nonetheless, Fuller tried. So have many other filmmakers. They may know they can't achieve perfection, but they feel a passion to try. War, after all, is the pinnacle of so many things: bravery, stupidity, violence, camaraderie, injustice, courage, cowardice. It is utterly glorious and utterly insane.

And of course, there's no end to it.

The Top WWII Films

Many of the greatest war movies have been about the Second World War. One Internet site currently lists 565 World War II feature films, from *A Bridge Too Far* to *You're in the Navy Now*. Most are forgettable, but the best are simply wonderful.

Here, in chronological order, are my choices of the most moving, artful and important World War II films. (We're focusing on films that depict combat, so war-related master-pieces such as *Casablanca, Schindler's List* and *The Best Years of Our Lives* aren't on the list.)

Wake Island (1942). Brian Donlevy stars in this stirring drama about U.S. efforts to hold a Pacific island. Directed by John Farrow.

In Which We Serve (1942). The most memorable of British wartime films, co-directed by David Lean and the film's writer and star, Noël Coward. Through flashbacks, it details the bravery and camaraderie of a naval crew.

Guadalcanal Diary (1943). Depicts the bloody struggle of the Marines for a key South Pacific island. Lewis Seiler directs, Preston Foster stars.

Thirty Seconds Over Tokyo (1944). Inspiring drama about an air strike against Japan that left several U.S. flyers stranded in China. Van Johnson and Spencer Tracy star for director Mervyn LeRoy.

The Sullivans (aka *The Fighting Sullivans*) (1944). A true-life drama based on the tragic combat deaths of five brothers, all serving on the same ship. The incident inspired the script for *Saving Private Ryan*.

The Story of G.I. Joe (1945). William Wellman's study of life among the grunts, from the experiences of fondly remembered war correspondent Ernie Pyle. Robert Mitchum stands out in an early performance as a soldier.

The Battle of San Pietro (1945). John Huston's documentary poignantly depicts one small battle in one small Italian village. This is the greatest of several fine wartime documentaries by Hollywood directors.

Twelve O'Clock High (1949). This classic study of U.S. flyers stationed in Britain features one of Gregory Peck's best performances. Dean Jagger won a supporting Oscar.

Battleground (1949).William Wellman's rugged drama about the Battle of the Bulge, starring Van Johnson and James Whitmore.

Sands of Iwo Jima (1949). Allan Dwan's drama about the Marines who raised the Stars and Stripes after a gruesome fight for a South Pacific island. John Wayne's performance earned him an Oscar nomination.

The Bridge on the River Kwai (1957). William Holden and Alec Guinness star in David Lean's Oscar-winning epic about wartime heroism and insanity.

The Enemy Below (1957). One of the best of the submarine dramas, this film by Dick Powell suspensefully portrays the deadly cat-and-mouse game between the skipper of a U.S. destroyer (Robert Mitchum) and a German U-boat captain (Curt Jurgens).

The Guns of Navarone (1961). An exciting fictional tale about a multinational team (Gregory Peck, Anthony Quinn, David Niven) sent to blow up a key German gun battery.

Two Women (1961). Vittorio DeSica's moving portrayal of the effects of war on two peasant women, a mother and her daughter, and the tragedy of rape in wartime. Sophia Loren won an Oscar as the mother.

The Longest Day (1962). Darryl F. Zanuck's masterful epic detailing the D-Day invasion. With its cast of thousands and dozens of star cameos, this is the best of several films – like *A Bridge Too Far* and *Midway* – that took the big-budget, big-movie approach to portraying the war.

The Great Escape (1963). One of the most rousing adventures to come out of World War II, this epic is about prisoners who escape from a German P.O.W. camp. Steve McQueen heads the all-star cast for director John Sturges.

Patton (1970). A fascinating portrait of the controversial warrior-general, stunningly played by George C. Scott. This Oscar winner, directed by Franklin J. Schaffner, was written by up-and-comer Francis Ford Coppola.

The Big Red One (1980). Sam Fuller's robust study of a squad on the European front is depicted entirely from the enlisted man's point of view. Loosely based on the director's own experiences, it stars Lee Marvin.

Das Boot (The Boat) (1981). A tense, intelligent German film that perfectly captures the bravery, fear and claustrophobia experienced by a U-boat crew. It's a masterpiece on both the emotional and the technical levels.

Saving Private Ryan (1998). Steven Spielberg's wrenching movie about D-Day is Hollywood's greatest portrayal of World War II valor and sacrifice.

Flag of Our Fathers and *Letters from Iwo Jima*, two companion films, made and released in 2006 by Clint Eastwood, depicting the battle of Iwo Jima. The former tells the story from the American perspective (in English), and the latter offers viewers the Japanese perspective (in Japanese).

THE GREATEST CAR CHASE

I WAS ASKED AT A PARTY TO NAME MY ALL-TIME FAVORITE CAR-CHASE FILM. My response was immediate and sure: "It's *The French Connection*. Anyone who says *Bullitt*, as good as it is, apparently doesn't know *The French Connection*."

If you've seen the 1971 police thriller, you'll recall how the cop, Popeye Doyle (Gene Hackman), pursues a French assassin through the streets of Brooklyn. The bad guy is on a subway, zooming along the elevated tracks. Popeye commandeers a car from an unlucky civilian and takes off along the crowded street on the roadway beneath the elevated railway.

It's hard to imagine a more imaginative setup, as director William Friedkin cuts between the assassin killing a train guard and threatening the engineer and passengers above, while Popeye sideswipes cars and almost kills a woman pushing a baby carriage as he tries to keep up with the swiftly moving train.

Keep in mind: This was all done before a computer could simulate all the dangerous driving for the filmmaker.

Friedkin has said he and his editor put the sequence together to the rhythms of Santana's "Black Magic Woman," although he was smart enough to put no music at all on the finished scene. (For one of the versions of the scene on YouTube, a fan has layered on the Santana music.)

Inspired by the party conversation, I also revisited the chase in Peter Yates' *Bullitt*, just to be sure I was right. Steve McQueen and two heavies chase each other, in overdrive, up and down the hills of San Francisco. Certainly, it's exciting, but it has less impact, at least for me, partly because it seems to peter out at the end. I'd still include it in any list of the top car-chase movies, along with John Frankenheimer's *Ronin*, George Miller's *Road Warrior*, Steven Spielberg's *Duel*, and Quentin Tarantino's *Death Proof*.

The late Frankenheimer was a particular genius of car films, creating not only *Ronin* but also *Grand Prix*. Ironically, the self-proclaimed car-chase junkie had to restrain himself when he was picked to direct the excellent sequel to *The French Connection*.

"I was in a bind," Frankenheimer told me. "Friedkin had already made the perfect car chase for the first film. So we decided to make the chase in our film a foot race." As a result, *The French Connection II* has, arguably, the greatest *foot race* in film history.

I also love the original *French Connection* for one of my favorite nonsense lines in all of film. My wife and I loved it so much, we'd often say it to each other. Popeye uses the sentence to mess with the minds of any thug he happens to be interrogating.

So, I'll ask you: "Did you ever pick your feet in Poughkeepsie?"

3-D FILMS LEAP OUT

EVERYONE HAS A HORROR FILM FROM THEIR CHILDHOOD THAT REMAINS ESPECIALLY frightening in the memory, even if they later revisit it and find it not nearly as scary as they remembered. That film earns its place in your personal experience because it allows you to discover how films not only excite you or make you laugh, but also can scare the daylights out of you.

For me, that film was the original *House of Wax,* with Vincent Price as the mad wax sculptor whose works are destroyed in a fire, and who seeks revenge by killing his antagonists and dipping their bodies in wax, like so many strawberries in melted chocolate.

I realize now that 1953's *House of Wax* was that film for me for two reasons. First, I was eight years old, for Pete's sake. Second, it was in 3-D, with the wax dripping on me and Vincent Price reaching out across the aisles for me! I'll never forget poor Carolyn Jones being pursued down a dank London alleyway by the villain. She even takes off her shoes to avoid making noise on the cobblestones and clutches them for dear life to her chest.

Gosh, I loved that original wave of 3-D films. I know now it was a desperate attempt by Hollywood to combat the arrival of television in American households. But for this eight-year-old, it was a remarkable technology that made the movies so real. I also embraced the fad because the initial 3-D films were almost all Westerns, adventure and sci-fi films, B-movie thrillers, and other Saturday matinee fodder, all beloved by an eight-year-old.

My 3-D experiences began with *Bwana Devil*, a saga of a great white hunter in Africa that featured lions leaping at you. The advertising line for the film was "A LION in your lap! A LOVER in your arms!" I didn't give a hoot about the latter, but the former sure excited me. My 3-D adventures continued with *Man in the Dark*, a 3-D thriller with a roller-coaster ride; *It Came from Outer Space*, with 3-D aliens; and *Fort Ti*, a French and Indian War drama, with arrows and cannonballs fired right at you.

The 3-D craze also took hold of movie shorts – I remember Mighty Mouse leaping out at us, and the Three Stooges trying to poke *my* eyes out. And Walt Disney released a 3-D Chip 'n' Dale cartoon.

The 3-D fad came *this* close to going legitimate: Alfred Hitchcock shot *Dial M for Murder* in 3-D, and the classy Hollywood musical *Kiss Me Kate* was also shot using the technology. However, a few sourpusses had begun to complain that 3-D gave them headaches, so studio executives got nervous and shelved the process. *Dial M for Murder* and *Kiss Me Kate* were released in conventional flat formats (and have been seen in 3-D only many years later at museums and revival houses).

All this 3-D reminiscing has been prompted by my seeing the 2008 movie *Journey to the Center of the Earth* in 3-D. The film is typical of the sorts of films in the first 3-D wave, a sometimes-silly adventure saga best enjoyed by youngsters or by older folks who, thankfully, have kept the youngsters alive within themselves. I was even reminded specifically of *House of Wax* during *Journey* when two characters play with a yo-yo. The purpose seems almost exclusively to employ something that'll fly out of the screen and back again, just like the rubber-band paddleball used by a London street busker in *House of Wax*.

Of course, today's 3-D craze shows no signs of fading; it is seen in more and more prestigious films, such as *Avatar* and reissues of *Star Wars* and *Titanic* (which employ modern technology to create 3-D where it previously did not exist). The new digital 3-D process is far more vivid, bright and exciting than the techniques filmmakers used during the '50s craze. And when modern 3-D is used to enhance complex or visually layered images, as in Martin Scorsese's brilliant *Hugo* or Ang Lee's breathtaking *Life of Pi*, its return is a blessing.

Most contemporary animated films also are in 3-D (as are some reissues, such as *Finding Nemo*). Nearly all these films have made box office waves in 3-D (and, typically, at a higher admission price). In addition, modern flat-screen TVs can be purchased with 3-D capability. (My television is a 3-D flat-screen, and I love watching my grandchildren react the way I did in the '50s.) So I think it is safe to say, more than a half-century after the first wave, that 3-D has finally got a grip on filmgoers.

And while I'm writing about that first wave of 3-D in the '50s, permit me one last remembrance: When my eight-year-old self had a nightmare prompted by *House of Wax*, my concerned dad rushed into my bedroom and asked what was troubling me. I told him, "It was that horror movie." I must have rushed my pronunciation of "horror," for Dad said, "Oh, you shouldn't be seeing movies about women like that." I didn't understand what he was talking about until years later.

THE F-BOMB

In Hollywood in the last three decades of the 20th century, the expletive that was once taboo was flourishing. That's why I decided to write about it in 1998.

THIS IS A STORY ABOUT A WORD I COULDN'T WRITE IN THE NEWSPAPER FOR WHICH I wrote it.

It starts with "F" and ends with "K" – and most people still think of it as the ultimate expletive in the English language. And now, since the column is in a book with more relaxed standards, there are no secrets. The word, of course, is "fuck."

For years it was strictly taboo, both in polite company and in the movies.

Clark Gable opened Hollywood's door to profanity in 1939 by declaring, "Frankly, my dear, I don't give a damn." But even after that, "fuck" wasn't heard in a mainstream movie for some 30 years.

Now, however, it's as commonplace in the cinema as any other obscenity. Maybe more so. And not just in gangster movies. It's become the offhand remark in action flicks, thrillers, dramas, coming-of-age movies – even romantic comedies.

Why? The answer used to be shock value. But for most regular filmgoers, the shock has worn off. Something else is going on.

Where profanity is concerned, there's a generation gap between young people and their elders. Teens and twenty-somethings frequently use language that their parents seldom used, except in private, or that their grandparents never used at all. The movies mirror this increasingly R-rated language culture, reflecting both the growing power of young audiences and the influence of young writers, directors and stars.

So Hollywood presents characters that speak the way many young people talk.

It uses the F-word as a sort of signal to attract the audience it wants: the 15- to 25-year-olds who rush out to opening weekends and put a movie on the map. If these films also attract older folks who like to think they're young, so much the better.

That's certainly the case with *Good Will Hunting,* the popular 1997 comedy-drama that received nine Oscar nominations, including one for best picture, as I wrote this. Made by, about and for young people, its screenplay includes "fuck" 85 times. Significantly, the film was co-produced by then-26-year-old Kevin Smith, who wrote and directed *Clerks,* the influential, foul-mouthed youth comedy of 1994.

Then there's *The Big Lebowski,* the wacky Coen brothers comedy (which is now a cult classic), in which the F-word shows up more than "the" or "and." From *Raising Arizona* to *Fargo,* younger viewers have long championed the inventive, edgy movies of the Coens. *Lebowski* goes a step further by poking fun at the profanity. As its cowboy narrator (Sam Elliott) pointedly asks star Jeff Bridges, "Why do you have to use so many cuss words?"

Sometimes, older directors and stars raise the profanity ante to grab a younger audience – perhaps alienating some of their older fans.

True, you don't hear the F-word in the titanically popular *Titanic.* But Kate Winslet's character offers the hand gesture version. When she gives somebody "the finger," older viewers see an anachronism for a character of 1912 – but young filmgoers readily identify with the young heroine.

"The F-bomb is out of the closet," says Monroe Community College professor Tom Proietti, who teaches about the media and culture. "We actually talked about it in class last week. Among college-aged students, it's not even an issue right now. All they've known is movies and video where the word is treated as normal discourse. It's no longer an issue among the audience that goes to most movies. That doesn't mean it's not an issue for other people who may sometimes go to movies."

"Fuck" has a long and, in recent years, studied history. "It's our worst word, at least of one syllable, and maybe our strongest," writes Roy Blount Jr. in his foreword to *The F Word,* a scholarly 1995 book by Jesse Sheidlower. "It's one of the best things we can do with someone, one of the worst to someone," Blount notes.

The word, which has German roots, first surfaced in the 15th century. But it was considered such a taboo that it "was never written down in the Middle Ages," writes Sheidlower. He and other scholars generally agree that the main purpose of the F-word in our culture is to shock.

"Taboo words draw their power and symbolic meaning largely from the fact that they are not supposed to be said," writes California State University professor Paul Martin Lester, in an essay on taboo language. "(Comedian) George Carlin's seven dirty words that couldn't be said on television in 1973 helped the process along. And since then, countless movies, comedians in clubs and on cable, and lyricists in their songs use the word to shock."

Ordinary men and women now say the F-word with increasing frequency, in conversations and public meetings, in literature and song; so its shock value is becoming increasingly passé. Even the once-staid *New Yorker* magazine has dropped its prohibition against the word.

Interestingly, ethnic slurs – particularly the N-word – have replaced profanity as the taboo words of today. Quentin Tarantino's use of "nigger" in *Pulp Fiction* and *Jackie Brown* drew far more complaints than his frequent use of "fuck."

Of course, the F-word isn't accepted by everyone. As a film critic, I hear more complaints about language in contemporary films than about any other element. Such complaints are usually, though not always, from older viewers. But most filmmakers and critics believe profanity, like sex and violence, is part of contemporary life.

The bottom line: We've raised a generation of free-thinking people. And now, like it or not, we have to listen to them.

Depending on your point of view, the following films are among those deserving a spot in a Profanity Hall of Fame (or Shame):

Gone With the Wind (1939), in which Rhett Butler delivers the memorable "Frankly, my dear, I don't give a damn." Producer David O. Selznick argued persuasively with censors that the line was the unforgettable final punch line from the very popular, highly regarded book, and that readers would miss it if it weren't in the film.

Who's Afraid of Virginia Woolf (1966), Mike Nichols' controversial, award-winning version of Edward Albee's scathing play, with Elizabeth Taylor and Richard Burton repeatedly shouting profanities at each other. But they stopped short of the F-word.

All the President's Men (1976), which detailed the *Washington Post's* coverage of Richard Nixon. The film is the first in the era of the rating system to not receive an R for including "fuck." The word appears once in the film, but the movie still earned a PG because of its serious, historic content. (The PG-13 rating wasn't instituted until 1984.) The film also gets away with Attorney General John Mitchell's warning to the *Washington Post*: "You tell your publisher, tell Katie Graham she's gonna get her tit caught in a big wringer if that's published."

Slap Shot (1977), a funny film about an incompetent hockey team, starring Paul Newman. The film's relentlessly foul mouth caused controversy at the time – it's a locker-room movie with locker-room language.

The Last Detail (1973), a military comedy-drama with a lot of profanity, which director Hal Ashby and writer Robert Towne argued was essential for this portrait of Navy sailors. While shooting, they made alternate scenes with less profanity for a TV version. However, there was so much profanity that they virtually shot the film twice.

Mean Streets (1973), *Raging Bull* (1980), *GoodFellas* (1990) and *Casino* (1995) – four Martin Scorsese films, set in the gangster milieu, all of which feature intense use of the F-word and other profanity. It could be argued that Scorsese and actors Robert De Niro and Joe Pesci turn profanity into poetry.

Richard Pryor – Live in Concert (1979), the first and best of the concert films by the brilliant Pryor. His clever, funny use of vulgar language led the way to other foul-mouthed comics on film who haven't been quite as inventive, including Eddie Murphy.

Clerks (1994), a youth-oriented comedy set in a convenience store and featuring, perhaps, the most vulgar language yet heard in a mainstream film. Writer-director Kevin Smith opened the door for rough language in much better young-adult comedies, including *Good Will Hunting*.

Pulp Fiction (1994), Quentin Tarantino's violent gangster cult hit with relentless profanity. Samuel L. Jackson, in this film and several others later, demonstrates a mastery of dramatically delivered cursing well beyond that of any other contemporary actor.

STAR WARS: A FAMILY AFFAIR

In May 2005, when the sixth Star Wars film had been released, I reflected on what these films meant to my family. After all, my film reviewing career began with the original Star Wars *in 1977.*

NONE OF THE STAR WARS TITLES WILL EVER SHOW UP ON A LIST I'D MAKE OF THE greatest films. (Well, to be truthful, I did put *The Empire Strikes Back*, the best of the lot, among my 200 essential films in the appendix of this book.)

Still, for 28 years the Star Wars movies have been like family. They've encircled the Garners like a squadron of Empire tie fighters surrounding the Millennium Falcon. Familiarity breeds affection, despite an awareness that some performances have been wooden and some of the dialogue clumsy.

Part of my affection stems from a pop culture affinity that George Lucas and I share. I felt that affinity even before *Star Wars,* with the 1973 release of his coming-of-age gem *American Graffiti.* I could have been a character in that film. Plus, I thought he stole my record collection to accompany the movie.

Much earlier, in the 1950s when I was 5 or 6, my first TV viewing included Saturday morning presentations of scratchy old *Flash Gordon* serials from the 1930s. Lucas apparently had the same source memory because I instantly recognized Flash Gordon elements in the initial *Star Wars.*

But that's just the beginning. *Star Wars* has loomed over the Garner family like Darth Vader's shadow. Consider:

– I've been reviewing movies for the *Democrat and Chronicle* as long as *Star Wars* has been in existence. My first review was of *Star Wars*, which I praised. I also had the foresight to suggest it would probably generate a sequel.

– My son Matt was three when *Star Wars* debuted, and it became a ritual film for us to watch together, along with the first two sequels. Some fathers and sons remember fishing together. We remember watching *Star Wars* together. Matt is now an editor in the movie business. Was *Star Wars* the first spark for his film career?

– And then there were Matt's Star Wars toys – the rather large Millennium Falcon and the little black suitcase jammed with small Star Wars figures. I still have the four McDonald's tie-in drinking glasses. Made of glass, not plastic, they represent what I suspect was the first big movie tie-in of the modern age. Then there's the 10-inch working model of R2-D2 still standing on a bookshelf in my den.

– Matt's younger sisters were not old enough to come under the influence of Vader and Skywalker, though they caught on in time to love the teddy bear qualities of the Ewoks in *Return of the Jedi*. But my wife and I noticed how the children's one-piece baby sleepers resembled the furry skin of a certain *Star Wars* character. To this day, we refer to such sleepwear as Wookies.

– I'll never forget the official *Star Wars* wallpaper. The toughest challenge my wife and I ever faced was putting it on a wall in Matt's childhood bedroom. Each sheet of wallpaper cut Obi-Wan Kenobi in half. Have you ever tried to exactly match the split nose and divided eyes of Obi-Wan Kenobi? I'd rather kiss a Wookie.

I felt a bit of sadness as the credits rolled on the *Revenge of the Sith* a few days ago. Lucas has said this sixth film will be the last. I take him at his word, so I felt the way I did when I realized there would never be another Beatles album.

No more would we sense the excitement in our children and hordes of other filmgoers as they cherished the phrase that began each adventure, words that now seem to convey a more personal meaning: "A long time ago, in a galaxy far, far away."

P.S. After this was written came the news that Disney had purchased Lucasfilm, including the *Star Wars* franchise, from George Lucas for $4 billion, and plans for make episodes seven, eight, and nine apparently are afoot. It seems I may be continuing the galactic trip with my grandchildren.

Audrey Hepburn. Courtesy of the Democrat & Chronicle Media Group.

Audrey Hepburn at the George Eastman House, 1992, Rochester, NY. Courtesy of the Democrat & Chronicle Media Group.

Audrey Hepburn displays her Eastman Award at the George Eastman House, 1992, Rochester, NY. ©2013 George Eastman House.

Lillian Gish, still vibrant at 92, at the George Eastman House to introduce a screening of her 1920 D.W. Griffith classic, *Way Down East.* Courtesy of the Democrat & Chronicle Media Group.

Lillian Gish, in *Way Down East* in 1920. Courtesy of the Democrat & Chronicle Media Group.

Louise Brooks, the legendary silent film star in photos from the early 1920s. Upper left photo, courtesy of Jack Garner. Remaining photos are ©2013 George Eastman House.

Jack Garner meets his cinematic love, Sophia Loren. Blame the sport coat on the era— the mid-1980s.
Photo courtesy of Jack Garner.

Robert Forster in 2012.
Courtesy of Robert Forster.

Meryl Streep at the Eastman House in 1999.
©2013 George Eastman House.

Michael Caine in 1997.
Courtesy of Jack Garner.

Oscar-winning actor, Philip Seymour Hoffman, returns to Rochester for an appearance, ca. 2005.
©2013 George Eastman House.

Jimmy Stewart greets an admirer when he is honored by the Eastman House in 1978. Courtesy of the Democrat & Chronicle Media Group.

Fred Astaire among the audience at the Dryden Theatre to receive his George Eastman Award in 1965. ©2013 George Eastman House.

Spike Lee being interviewed by Jack Garner in 1998. ©2013 George Eastman House.

Gregory Peck responds to a question as he receives his George Eastman Award in 1987.
He is surprised when his *Roman Holiday* co-star, Audrey Hepburn, appears at the ceremony.
Courtesy of the Democrat & Chronicle Media Group.

THE GEORGE EASTMAN HOUSE

It's a blessing for any film buff – and especially for a film commentator like me – to live within a few blocks of one of the world's great film archives within the mansion of the late George Eastman. I wrote this story in 1999 to honor the 50th anniversary of Rochester's Eastman House.

MOST FILMGOERS WHO WATCH CLASSIC FILMS IN THE DRYDEN THEATRE ARE USUALLY having too much fun to think about the world-class archive that supplied the film.

Yet, they're sitting almost on top of it. The Eastman House's basement archive – and its film preservation archive in nearby Chili – hold 23,000 titles. Among them are rare works, Hollywood collections and other gems that make the archive an international treasure – and the Eastman House one of the planet's great movie museums. And many Hollywood classics, such as *Gone With the Wind* and *Snow White and the Seven Dwarfs*, would be pale imitations if the archive had not restored them to visual splendor.

Fifty years after George Eastman's elegant colonial revival mansion at 900 East Ave. became a museum, its film archive remains a mecca for scholars, filmmakers and movie buffs, and a champion in the fight to preserve cinema's great history.

For great American filmmaker Martin Scorsese, the Eastman House film archive is the ideal place to store his beloved and ever-growing collection of American films. For director Spike Lee, it's also the archive of choice. For example, he gave the museum the only 70 mm print of *Malcolm X* in existence – a wide-screen version of his most personal film.

For Patrick Loughney of the Library of Congress, the Eastman House is a leader in the fight to save one of the world's visual records. "We've already lost forever half of all the movies produced before 1950," Loughney pointed out. "The Eastman House is an important force in preserving America's motion picture heritage. There are too few institutions doing that kind of work now."

For students who come to Rochester from around the world to study at the L. Jeffrey Selznick School of Film Preservation, the Eastman House is the only place to formally learn the art of saving films for future generations.

"That school is very important," Loughney says. "The process demands trained people, and no place offered that training before. In the past, preservation techniques could only be learned on the job."

As important as it is, the preservation campaign is waged largely unseen and unknown here at home. Local filmgoers who attend the Dryden Theatre think of it as a great place to see classic or offbeat movies on the big screen. Few stop to consider that they wouldn't have those films to watch if somebody didn't save them.

People in the movie business have always understood the importance of the Eastman House. That's why such stars as Jimmy Stewart, Gregory Peck, Audrey Hepburn, Lillian Gish and Isabella Rossellini have trekked here to pay homage – and be showcased – at benefit events.

While high-profile visitors grab attention for the Eastman House's link to movies, the Dryden programs merely hint at the film archive's riches. Only about 5 percent of the films in the collection are screened, says senior film curator Paolo Cherchi Usai.

Some films aren't shown because they haven't been requested by Dryden regulars or don't fit into program themes. In other cases, movies can't be shown because they're extremely rare and copies haven't been made. But, Cherchi Usai insists, they still must be saved. "When people ask me why, I respond with a question: why bother preserving the Mona Lisa? Same reason. A life without art is worthless. The art of cinema creates its own Mona Lisas. Generations that follow ours should have the same fulfilling experiences we've been able to have."

Since its beginnings as a museum, the central purpose of the Eastman House has been to collect, restore and display not only films and photographs, but also the machines that make them and other related items.

Much of the film collection's distinction can be traced to its founding curator, James Card. A passionate film-lover from childhood, the Cleveland native had amassed a personal collection of 800 movies when he came here to work for Eastman Kodak Co. in the mid-1940s.

The board formed to launch the Eastman House coveted Card's collection of mostly silent rarities. It came along with the man, who joined the museum staff and ultimately became director of the film department. "Lent to the Eastman House," he wrote in his 1994 memoir, *Seductive Cinema,* "my collection would become the nucleus of its own famous archive."

Card headed the film department for 29 years. In that time, the archive came to be recognized as a world-class institution, featuring what many scholars consider the world's premier silent-film collection. Among film archives, it's on equal footing with the greatest film museums in the world, including the Museum of Modern Art in New York City, the

Library of Congress in Washington, D.C., and the British Film Institute in London.

Other museums may have more silent films in total, but not as many that are important or rare. "In qualitative terms, the silent-film collection here is unsurpassed anywhere in the world," says current curator Cherchi Usai.

Not content to collect only early works, Card also worked with the Eastman Kodak Co. vice president in charge of motion pictures, Major General Edward Peck Curtis, to develop a conduit to Hollywood. "Ted" Curtis' friends included such movers and shakers as David O. Selznick and Jack Warner. To get a film delivered to Rochester, Curtis "only had to pick up the phone," Card wrote in his memoir. Eventually, such ties helped the Eastman House acquire extensive collections from Cecil B. DeMille and MGM Studios, along with many other Hollywood titles.

Card shared his passion with Rochester filmgoers. He conceived the elegant 550-seat Dryden Theatre, attached to the Eastman House, and began the Dryden Theatre Film Society, which regularly packed the theater to hear Card's enthusiastic film introductions. Many longtime Eastman House members still talk fondly of his lectures.

David Bordwell, a University of Wisconsin film professor and author of several nationally known books on cinema, grew up in Penn Yan, Yates County. He says he was inspired to his life's work by Card's movie programs. From his current perspective as a scholar, Bordwell sees the Eastman House as a "terrific source for research. People there may not be aware how famous it is. It's one of the world's major archives."

After Card's retirement in 1977, curator John Kuiper oversaw a volatile decade that witnessed dwindling funding and other problems for the museum. In the mid-1980s, there was talk of shipping all of the Eastman House collections to the Smithsonian Institution in Washington. Forceful community involvement and renewed efforts to find funding kept the treasures in Rochester.

Jan-Christopher Horak, who became senior film curator in 1987, took charge of the resurrection of the Eastman House film archive. "He got the department back on its feet with his emphasis on independent and avant-garde films and the American cinema of the European exiles," says Cherchi Usai, who took over from Horak. Horak also negotiated the most important acquisition – the Scorsese collection. Beyond the acclaimed filmmaker's own works, the collection features 3,000 titles, mostly American films of the 1940s, '50s and '60s. "That collection keeps growing constantly," Cherchi Usai reports. "Scorsese sends us a minimum of one new acquisition every week." (Since this was written, the collection has climbed to 8,000 titles.)

The archive continues to prosper under the Italian-born Cherchi Usai, who has been in charge of the film archive since 1994. (He would leave for a time, in the years to come, but would return in 2012.) Under his care, the collection has grown from about 17,000 titles to 23,000, of which a third are silent films and about 15,000 full-length features.

The Eastman House has intensified its restoration efforts, built the preservation and storage facility in Chili, created the world's first school of preservation techniques and developed fruitful relationships with key people in the film industry. They include filmmakers Spike Lee, Dennis Hopper, and the late producer L. Jeffrey Selznick (son of David O. Selznick), who was instrumental in funding the preservation school that bears his name.

Each curator over the half-century has brought a particular set of strengths and priorities.

"The Eastman House was fortunate to find Paolo (Cherchi Usai)," says Adrienne Mancia, a film program consultant at the Museum of Modern Art in New York City. "He's a historian and preservationist with good international links, and has broadened the archives. It's unusual to find an archivist like Paolo who tries to keep up with current cinema as well. Usually, they tend to look back on the silent era or the 30s as the 'Golden Age.' But Paolo is engaged with contemporary film culture."

Cherchi Usai's goals include strengthening film preservation, deepening relationships with the film industry, improving access to the archive and forging deeper ties to important film collectors. (He has since added a desire to further understand and find ways to archive as the cinema moves headlong into the digital age.) "Archives used to be hidden sanctuaries," he says. "That time is over. Access is fundamental. As part of that, we want to foster new audiences for films."

To that end, he and his staff have brought more pizzazz and variety to the nightly programming at the Dryden Theatre. Rare classics and serious imports now share the schedule with oddball cult films, a "bizarro" film series and occasional 3-D films.

For scholars and buffs, Cherchi Usai is overseeing an upgrading of the archive's computer cataloguing "to a more user-friendly system that'll hopefully allow people to access at least the titles of films that can be shown."

Cherchi Usai must also look at ways to keep the archive growing – and relevant. One avenue is cultivating film collectors the world over. "Without collectors, there would be no film museums," he says. "Jim Card, our founder, is an outstanding example of a collector who had the vision and guts to make the leap to a museum. We need collectors. They're like small, highly flexible scouting units for archives."

Like any curator, Cherchi Usai must play oracle. With storage space and funding limited, he must try to predict what will matter to later generations. "Sometimes I feel like a doctor looking at 10 gravely ill patients. And I have to tell them I only have enough medicine to save one of them."

Cherchi Usai must also anticipate "the earthquake to come, the time when the manufacture of film will end" and digital images rule. "Film is a phase in the much longer story of the moving image," he observes. "We're open to all the techniques. It's important that what we do now will be useful to viewers of 2100."

CHAPTER THREE

A REVIEW SAMPLER

This chapter features what I'll call a review sampler, a collection of reviews that represent the sort of film criticism I wrote over the years.

INTRODUCTION

THEY AREN'T NECESSARILY OF THE BEST MOVIES OR THE WORST MOVIES I EVER SAW. Remember, I typically reviewed three films or so per week, which equates to perhaps 150 films or more per year. That means from 1977 till I stopped regular reviewing upon my retirement in 2007, I wrote about roughly 4,600 films or more.

I've selected this small sampler just to give readers a taste. I've also picked a few classic films from the past that I had the opportunity to review because of DVD releases or important restorations. In many cases, these films represent the projects of some of the actors or directors represented in interviews or essays elsewhere in this book.

None of the reviews are especially long – length was seldom an available luxury in day-to-day print journalism, although my contemporaries who worked for certain magazines were fortunate to have it. You'll note that the later reviews are especially short, reflecting the more compact nature of print journalism, for better or ill, in the 21st century.

I'm often asked which print film critics and essayists influenced me (or were folks I have especially enjoyed reading over the years). That list would include, in order of my acquaintance with them, Judith Crist, Pauline Kael, Andrew Sarris, Roger Ebert, and Molly Haskell.

Yes, I realize Kael and Sarris were philosophical opposites in basic film theory, but both offered succinct, thoughtful, and entertaining reading. And yes, Ebert built his reputation on television, when he and the late Gene Siskel stuck their thumbs up or down. However, I've been much more a fan of Ebert as a writer, before, during and after his TV career.

Another critic I enjoy is Anthony Lane of *The New Yorker*, though he came along too late to be called an influence; I wasn't aware of him till after my retirement. But I find Lane's work thought-provoking and very amusing. He doesn't seem to like much, but nobody is better at slicing into a film. His put-down of the final Star Wars film remains the funniest single review I ever read. (As of this writing, you can find it at http://www.newyorker.com/

93

archive/2005/05/23/050523crci_cinema).

As for my own reviewing, I had a few basic concepts I tried to follow. First, I tried to give every film a fair shake, because I know the time and expense that goes into making one. That's not to say I won't skewer a turkey, because I will. But only after much thought.

Second, I think of myself as a shades-of-gray critic. In other words, few films are utterly without any redeeming value or are pure perfection. Nearly all fall in between. Not black, not white, but with shades of gray.

Third, I try not to give too much away. In terms of plot development, I'll take you up the hill, but I'll let you have the ride down for yourself. The unfairness of giving plots away was hammered into me at a very early age. I was giving a report in seventh grade on the then-showing *The Bridge on the River Kwai*. I began by saying (spoiler alert), "I suppose you know they blow up the bridge?" No, most of my fellow students, and my teacher, hadn't seen the film yet and didn't know about the climactic moment. Much complaining and uproar ensued.

I think of film reviewing as a basic form of self-analysis. I watch a film. I react to the film. I pay attention to how I react to a film. I think about what things or qualities triggered those reactions. I report my "findings" to the reader.

Finally, those who followed my reviews in the *Democrat & Chronicle* or elsewhere in the Gannett newspapers may recall a number rating of usually some number out of 10, assessing the value of the film. I have to be honest. I hate numbers or "stars" or any other device on a review that can be viewed as shorthand or tools for spoon-feeding readers. They're primarily an editor's device or preference, not a writer's.

They can also pose occasional problems, as happened the time a guy called to complain after he had piled his wife and children into a station wagon and taken them all to see David Lynch's *Blue Velvet*, a genius film filled with violence, sex, nudity, drugs, and all-around perversion. He was shocked as his family watched it.

He said, "You gave it a 10."

I said, "Yes, but did you read the review?"

"No," he said, "but you gave it a 10."

I said, "Well, if you'd read the actual review, you would have seen my several warnings about the nature of the film and its content. It's a great movie, but only for certain mature audiences."

That darn 10.

CITIZEN KANE

1941

WHEN I PUT THE BLU-RAY RELEASE OF THE 70TH ANNIVERSARY EDITION OF *Citizen Kane* into my DVD player, I only planned to give it a glance. I know the film intimately, have taught it in classes, and have probably seen it at least 20 times.

I planned to watch the first 10 minutes or so, simply to judge the Blu-ray quality for a possible review. The next thing I knew, two hours had passed and the end credits were scrolling. I couldn't take my eyes off it. I couldn't stop watching. I submit that that's one definition of an essential film.

Beyond the better-than-ever pristine quality of the Blu-ray, my umpteenth viewing reinforced my great admiration for this film and my agreement with most of the world's critics who have declared *Citizen Kane* the greatest film ever made. It's a ranking that has held firm in various polls for decades.

Why? Let me count the ways:

– The brilliant screenplay by Herman J. Mankiewicz and Welles explores the rise and fall of a powerful newspaper czar, based loosely on the life of William Randolph Hearst and played by Welles himself. The script employs flashback upon flashback, and it begins with a wonderful backgrounding device, a recreation of a *News of the World,* based on the way most people got visually presented news in the '40s, on a screen before the feature.

That newsreel provides the narrative "hook" that holds our attention. The plot is propelled by a newsreel reporter's search for the meaning of the newspaperman's deathbed word: "rosebud."

(One reason *Citizen Kane* would eventually engender potent anger in Hearst was that word, "rosebud." Apparently, Mankiewicz, who had been a guest at Hearst's San Simeon castle, had learned that "rosebud" was Hearst's pet word for the genitalia of his lover, Marion Davies.)

– The film includes memorable and often-poetic dialogue. Here, for example, is my favorite, a poetic statement from Kane's manager, Bernstein: "A fellow will remember a lot of things you wouldn't think he'd remember. You take me. One day, back in 1896, I was crossing over to Jersey on the ferry, and as we pulled out, there was another ferry pulling in, and on it there was a girl waiting to get off. A white dress she had on. She was carrying a white parasol. I only saw her for one second. She didn't see me at all, but I'll bet a month hasn't gone by since that I haven't thought of that girl."

– Gregg Toland's cinematography was brilliant. Toland was a genius cameraman who wanted to work with young newcomer Orson Welles because he knew Welles wouldn't be bound by any old-fashioned attitudes or techniques and would embrace new ideas. Thus, there's the famous "deep focus" in which visuals are simultaneously sharp at distance and close up, as well as the equally famous low angles that show ceilings and made Kane seem large and powerful.

– The use and manipulation of sound, which should have been expected from Welles, a radio genius of the '30s, was clever and realistic. One example: speeches in large halls echo, as they would in such circumstances.

– The editing by editor (and future director) Robert Wise and Welles, including the famous and concise account of the first marriage, was evocative; we observe the disintegration, portrayed in just a few moments strictly through behavior at the breakfast table.

– The performances by Welles and his "Mercury Theatre" actors, including Joseph Cotten, Everett Sloane and Dorothy Comingore, were stellar. The 24-year-old Welles is especially astonishing (as is his makeup) as he goes through decades of Kane's life.

Citizen Kane remains the ultimate cinematic masterpiece. Don't let all that intellectual prestige scare you, because *Citizen Kane* is also a fascinating and wonderfully entertaining movie. Even at 70 years old or more, it remains modern and relevant, and always will. It is, in fact, ageless.

OTHELLO

1952

A SUPERB, NEARLY FORGOTTEN FILM BY THE LATE ORSON WELLES HAS BEEN RESTORED to its proper place among his better works, thanks to the recent release of the reconstructed *Othello*.

One of the most thoughtful, artful and economically structured of all Shakespeare screen adaptations, Welles' *Othello* is also a great example of guerrilla filmmaking on the run. It was shot over four years, on two continents, as Welles and his company attempted to stay one step ahead of creditors.

Welles worked on the project between 1948 and 1952, in between independent acting jobs that he took for financing. (His legendary performance as Harry Lime in Carol Reed's *The Third Man* was one of those acting jobs.) *Othello* was made on locations throughout Europe and North Africa, with the principal settings in Morocco.

Given the hit-and-run nature of the project, *Othello* is a remarkably seamless and flowing work. Welles cut Shakespeare's play to the narrative minimum, creating a film that runs only 91 minutes; yet the story seems complete and utterly satisfying.

Welles plays The Moor as a brooding, moody fellow whose rise to violent jealousy takes a deeply inward route. Micheál Mac Liammóir, a talented, veteran Irish actor, plays the sharp-witted, envious Iago. (Mac Liammóir had given the teenage Welles his first professional acting job when the brash 16-year-old knocked on the door at Dublin's Gate Theatre in 1931.)

Desdemona, Othello's wife, was reportedly the most difficult role to cast, but the woman who won the role, Canadian actress Suzanne Cloutier, offers a regal beauty and a sympathetic presence.

Jealousy is, of course, the central theme of the play, as Iago torments Othello into thinking Desdemona has been unfaithful. By the story's end, the jealousy leaves few characters alive.

Typical of Welles' work, *Othello* is photographed in black-and-white, and the arches, domes, curved lines, and shadows and light of North Africa lend a distinctive, enveloping design to the film. At his best Welles was the most resourceful and inventive of the great filmmakers, and this was never truer than in this difficult production.

Othello's most famous sequence, for example, is the murder of Roderigo. When costumes weren't ready for the scene, Wells quickly improvised and the scene was redesigned to take place in a bathhouse. The actors are enveloped in towels and steam, and little else. The result is not only clever but also powerful; treachery and murder endanger individuals at their most vulnerable.

The restoration of *Othello* not only returns the film to public view, but also improves it. The evocative score has been completely re-recorded, much improving the fidelity, and the film has been struck from original nitrate negatives. The movie's weakest aspect – its audio-dialogue soundtrack – has also been improved.

Because of the fitful style of filmmaking, much of the original dialogue has been duped blind for the film, which means actors recorded dialogue without watching the film; thus, words do not always match mouth movements. The result originally was jarringly clumsy and generated the few negative comments the film received upon its initial release. Using modern audio technology, the original dialogue has been cleaned and equalized, and even processed electronically to better match the lip movement on the screen. Though still not perfect, it's a vast improvement.

If your understanding and respect for Orson Welles begin and end with *Citizen Kane*, you need to see more of this giant's films. The newly restored *Othello* is a great place to start.

REAR WINDOW

1954

WHEN IT WAS RELEASED IN 1954, *REAR WINDOW* PROMPTED A CRITIC TO COMPLAIN that James Stewart's character was nothing but a peeping Tom. Director Alfred Hitchcock responded: "Sure, he's a snooper, but aren't we all? I'll bet you that nine out of 10 people, if they see a woman across the courtyard undressing for bed, or even a man puttering around in his room, will stay and look."

That is the point of this masterpiece: We may not care to admit it, but we've always been a nation of peeping Toms. To prove it, Hitchcock uses this great film to make us voyeurs along with Stewart's housebound character. We share his guilt as a nosy neighbor. We share his triumph when he discovers a murder. And we share his terror as the killer approaches.

In 2000, *Rear Window* returned to theaters, looking better than ever in a print restored by archivists Robert A. Harris and James C. Katz. Over the last decade, the pair also restored the grandeur of *Lawrence of Arabia, Spartacus* and Hitchcock's *Vertigo.*

Compared to other projects, *Rear Window's* restoration is less of a spectacle: No fabled lost segments were discovered, no drastic errors were fixed, no splashy colors explode from the screen. Instead, Harris and Katz employed preservation techniques, along with Technicolor's much-admired dye transfer system, to spiff up the film so it looks more vibrantly realistic than before.

Small details are now vivid, from characters' blue eyes to the red glow on a cigar tip, from the details in a tavern across the street to the red-orange textures of bricks. The clarity allows you to see new things amid the familiar images. Also greatly improved are the film's darker scenes: The color black is richer, and various details previously hidden in the shadows are now evident.

But while the restoration is superb – and most welcome – the true blessing is that it returns *Rear Window* to the big screen. Although it would still be enjoyable in the DVD editions that followed this restoration, it's pretty special in the theater.

Wheelchair-bound photographer L.B. Jeffries (Stewart) uses his telephoto lens to watch various stories unfold among his neighbors in a half-dozen apartments outside his windows. Since they're all vignettes framed small within the context of the larger movie – similar to the picture-within-picture option on some of today's television sets – *Rear Window* benefits from a large screen more than most famous films.

The story's mystery arises when Jeffries discovers suspicious behavior in an apartment across the courtyard. He begins to think the tenant may have murdered his wife. Add to that one of Hitchcock's most delicious romances: The elegant Grace Kelly co-stars as Lisa Fremont, a Madison Avenue society woman who's deeply in love with Jeffries. He feels the same, but sees little hope for their affair. Delightfully, the mystery and the romance dovetail, as Lisa proves her mettle as an amateur sleuth.

Hitchcock made more than a half-dozen films that lesser directors would gladly claim as masterpieces. None surpass the suspense, romance, wit and wisdom of *Rear Window*. Since moviegoing itself is a voyeuristic habit, seeing a film that explores the idea is essential. And now that the windows are sparkling clean, the view is better than ever.

GONE WITH THE WIND

1939

GONE WITH THE WIND WASN'T HOLLYWOOD'S FIRST EPIC – *BIRTH OF A NATION*, *Intolerance* and the first *Ben-Hur* were among those that preceded it. We all know it wasn't the last epic. Or haven't you heard about *Titanic* and *Lord of the Rings*?

But *Gone With the Wind* remains Hollywood's most enduring epic, probably because it's also its most endearing epic.

The passionate saga of Scarlett O'Hara and Rhett Butler, played out against the flaming red backdrop of the Civil War, generates enough romance, historic drama and deep emotion to fuel a dozen great films. And now a spiffed-up, digitally polished 1998 reissue of the 1939 film is where it belongs: on the big screen, reclaiming its title as the longtime champion of the American movie palace.

Gone With the Wind may have come in fourth on last week's American Film Institute's Top 100 list, but it's usually No. 1 in popularity lists, and it remains the all-time box office hit, when receipts are adjusted for inflation. More importantly, *Gone With the Wind* remains the benchmark by which all other Hollywood epics are measured.

For example, many viewers and commentators called *Titanic* a *Gone With the Wind* for a new generation. It's an apt description:

– Both films were considered disasters in the making, as both went wildly over budget and months over schedule. *Gone With the Wind* was considered David O. Selznick's "folly." Titanic was considered "the ship that'll sink Fox." For the record, GWTW cost $4.3 million in 1939 dollars. Adjusted to $100 million in 1998 dollars, it was half as expensive as *Titanic*.

– Both were set against a historic event.

– Both featured a charismatic, fictional romance that captured the hearts of romantic viewers.

– Both are more than three hours long and feature elaborate visual effects and richly evocative theme music.

– Both cleaned up at their respective Oscar ceremonies. *Gone With the Wind* won eight out of 13 nominations; *Titanic* won 11 of 14.

– In both cases, the popular leading man was ignored. Clark Gable was nominated, but he was upset by Robert Donat (of *Goodbye, Mr. Chips*); Leonardo DiCaprio wasn't even nominated.

Ted Turner's New Line Cinema (*Gone With the Wind's* current owners) have put the film through a rare three-strip dye transfer process, which means it is in new, true Technicolor for the first time in generations. Indeed, the skies over burning Atlanta haven't been this vibrantly red since the original release in 1939; nor has Scarlett's stunning, makeshift "drapery dress" ever looked so beautifully green.

In addition, digital technology has been applied to "erase" scratches and blotches in the film. The film is being reissued in the original, appropriate screen shape. (Some editions in the '60s and '70s lopped off the top and bottom of the image, to stretch it artificially over a wide screen.) And the soundtrack, including Max Steiner's lush music, has been digitally remastered.

In sum, *Gone With the Wind* has never looked nor sounded as good as it does today – perhaps even on the day of its initial release. It's a good thing it's back on the big screen, where it belongs.

Working with three directors (Victor Fleming, George Cukor and Sam Wood), its hands-on producer David O. Selznick created a visually stunning work, with infinitely detailed sets, moody lighting, gorgeous matte paintings and lavish costumes.

Three of the four leads were superbly cast – Gable was never better or more perfect than as Rhett Butler; Vivien Leigh is the epitome of Scarlett O'Hara; Olivia de Havilland is sweet, but plausible as the saintly Melanie. Only Leslie Howard is a less-than-perfect choice as Ashley. As he himself argued at the time, he was too old, and the character is too darn wimpy to compete with Rhett.

Several of the supporting players also are memorable, particularly Oscar-winner Hattie McDaniel as Mammy, the true source of power in the O'Hara household, and Thomas Mitchell as Scarlett's robust father, driven to insanity by the war.

The exaggerated shiftlessness of Butterfly McQueen (as the dim-witted slave, Prissy) doesn't age as well; it's one of the aspects that have made racial attitudes in *Gone With the Wind* problematic for modern audiences.

The film does lack perfect balance. Most of its memorable moments occur in the first half: The crane shot over the hundreds of wounded in the Atlanta railway yard, the carefree romp of the barbecue at Twelve Oaks, Scarlett's outrageous behavior at the fundraising ball, the flight from Atlanta. The second half degenerates into a big-budget soap opera, although it's salvaged through the strength of the Gable and Leigh performances.

After Rhett leaves with his famous "don't-give-a-damn" speech, and Scarlett vows to find a way to get him back, we hope – we know – she will. As she says, "Tomorrow is another day."

Thanks to ongoing upgrades in digital technology, *Gone With the Wind* earns more tomorrows on the big screen. Don't let this classic pass you by.

PRIDE OF THE YANKEES

1942

In the summer of 2012, Rochester's triple-A baseball team, The Red Wings, made an agreement to share their beautiful stadium with another International League team, the Yankee farm team from Scranton Wilkes-Barre (because that team's stadium was being refurbished). To welcome "The Yankees" to Rochester, the Red Wing management asked me to write a piece, for the yearbook they sell in the stadium, about the most famous Yankee-related movie, The Pride of the Yankees. *Here's that piece.*

THE PRIDE OF THE YANKEES STARRED GARY COOPER AS THE FABLED YANKEE IRON MAN, Lou Gehrig. Despite the film's strong sentimental core, and the emphasis on romance, *The Pride of the Yankees* is an iconic baseball movie that routinely shows up on lists of all-time favorite sports films.

The life of Lou Gehrig *had* to be a movie. It was 1942, and we were at war, and America needed heroes. And looking back to July 4, 1939, we found one. That's when a dying man walked with great effort to a microphone at home plate, in a sold-out Yankee Stadium, and said, "Fans, for the past two weeks you have been reading about a bad break. Yet today I consider myself the luckiest man on the face of this earth."

These words came from a man in his mid-30s, crippled with amyotrophic lateral sclerosis, a disease that now carries his name. It killed Gehrig at 37, less than two years after he made the famous speech that one biographer has labeled "baseball's Gettysburg Address."

Though we elevate a lot of sports figures to heroic stature, Gehrig deserved that status. This was, by all accounts, an unpretentious, low-key, but strong and talented son of German immigrants who played with conviction and passion while maintaining a private life of high standards and decency. He stood in marked contrast to the rowdy shenanigans of fellow Yankees like Babe Ruth. Yet he also considered them brothers, on and off the field, and was their team captain from '35 to '39.

Gehrig was known as the Iron Horse because he never missed a game after he was first inserted into the Yankee lineup as the first baseman; eventually he racked up an unprecedented 2,130 straight games before he took himself out of the lineup on April 30, 1939. And in that period, Gehrig compiled a Hall of Fame stat sheet that included a .340 batting average, 493 home runs (including four in one June game in '32), and 2,721 hits. He was a seven-time All-Star and a six-time World Series champ.

It was a record that stood for nearly 60 years, until former Red Wing and Baltimore Oriole legend Cal Ripkin Jr. surpassed it by an incredible 502 games.

When producer Samuel Goldwyn was approached to make a film about Gehrig, he initially was skeptical. He knew that much of the decision-making about going to films was made by women, and didn't see the emotional appeal. Then someone showed him footage of Gehrig's Yankee Stadium speech and it left him in tears. He agreed to make the film, but he also steered writers Paul Gallico, Jo Swerling, and Herman J. Mankiewicz (who co-wrote *Citizen Kane*) to stress the sentimentality of the story and the romance between Gehrig and his wife, Eleanor. And that they did.

Gary Cooper was cast as Gehrig, and though it's hard to buy the 41-year-old as a college fraternity brother in the film's early scenes, he's eventually quite convincing.

The other problem with Cooper had to be solved by technical trickery: The actor was right-handed and could not master Gehrig's left-handed swing, so he was filmed swinging from the right side while wearing uniforms with reverse lettering. Editors then flipped the film negative. Cooper would even run to third base instead of first to complete the illusion.

Teresa Wright was cast as Gehrig's supportive wife (and, like Cooper, received an Oscar nomination). The great character actor Walter Brennan played a reporter and Gehrig's discoverer and supporter, marking the sixth of seven times Brennan and Cooper worked together.

A handful of Yankees played themselves, most notably Babe Ruth. Though Ruth had gained a lot of weight since leaving baseball six years earlier, he went into training and lost nearly 50 pounds to be more convincing in the film, out of respect for his old friend.

Though *The Pride of the Yankees* does sentimentalize much of the story, the basic facts are generally true. The filmmakers, however, did slightly alter the famous final speech, putting the most memorable line at the end (whereas Gehrig had placed it earlier in the speech).

As a lesson in moviemaking artistic license, here are the two famous speeches.

First, Gehrig's original:

"Fans, for the past two weeks you have been reading about the bad break I got. Yet today I consider myself the luckiest man on the face of this earth. I have been in ballparks for 17 years and have never received anything but kindness and encouragement from you fans.

"Look at these grand men. Which of you wouldn't consider it the highlight of his career just to associate with them for even one day? Sure, I'm lucky. Who wouldn't consider it an honor to have known Jacob Ruppert? Also, the builder of baseball's greatest empire, Ed

Barrow? To have spent six years with that wonderful little fellow, Miller Huggins? Then to have spent the next nine years with that outstanding leader, that smart student of psychology, the best manager in baseball today, Joe McCarthy? Sure, I'm lucky.

"When the New York Giants, a team you would give your right arm to beat, and vice versa, sends you a gift – that's something. When everybody down to the groundskeepers and those boys in white coats remember you with trophies — that's something. When you have a wonderful mother-in-law who takes sides with you in squabbles with her own daughter – that's something. When you have a father and a mother who work all their lives so you can have an education and build your body – it's a blessing. When you have a wife who has been a tower of strength and shown more courage than you dreamed existed – that's the finest I know.

"So I close in saying that I might have been given a bad break, but I've got an awful lot to live for."

Here's the movie version:

"I have been walking onto ball fields for 16 years, and I've never received anything but kindness and encouragement from you fans. I have had the great honor to have played with these great veteran ballplayers on my left – Murderers' Row, our championship team of 1927. I have had the further honor of living with and playing with these men on my right – the Bronx Bombers, the Yankees of today.

"I have been given fame and undeserved praise by the boys up there behind the wire in the press box, my friends, the sportswriters. I have worked under the two greatest managers of all time, Miller Huggins and Joe McCarthy.

"I have a mother and father who fought to give me health and a solid background in my youth. I have a wife, a companion for life, who has shown me more courage than I ever knew.

"People all say that I've had a bad break. But today ... today, I consider myself the luckiest man on the face of the earth."

JAWS

1975

IF SOMEONE SAYS "SUMMER MOVIE," I THINK OF ONLY ONE FILM: STEVEN SPIELBERG'S *Jaws*, from the summer of 1975. I remember, as if it were yesterday, driving to the Todd Mart Cinema to see the film – and I remember how it knocked me out.

It also knocked out the world, getting inside the viewer's psyche to the point that sharks have become the great, scary villains of the ocean, in our minds. We cannot put our toes in the ocean without hear John Williams' fabled da-dum da-dum music theme.

Just as important has been the long-lasting impact *Jaws* has had on the way films are targeted and marketed as blockbusters in the summer months. Spielberg established the template for summer films for decades to come; at the same time, he launched his own career into hyperspace.

All this comes to mind as I write this in the summer of 2012, because a stunning new Blu-ray restoration of the film is upon us, and the film has never looked as crisp and rich, or sounded so powerful and clear. The film is literally better than ever, with more bite than ever (if you'll excuse the expression).

There is so much to admire about *Jaws*, from the performances of Roy Scheider, Richard Dreyfuss, and especially Robert Shaw (as the cranky, eccentric Quint), to the Oscar-winning editing of Verna Fields and the iconic music of John Williams.

My favorite moment, technically speaking, occurs fairly early in the film, when Chief Brody (Scheider) is sitting on the beach and thinks he spots the shark among a large crowd of beach users. Spielberg shows the dizzying stress by dollying out and zooming in simultaneously. (This is known as the "vertigo effect," because it was used so effectively by Alfred Hitchcock in *Vertigo* in 1958.)

Fields not only set the standard for suspense editing with *Jaws*, but also had to work with film that was probably fragmented by the misbehaving mechanical shark and other challenges of filming on the open sea. Fields even contributed her backyard swimming pool at a key moment: there's a famous story that when the film was supposedly done and in post-production, Spielberg realized they needed one more "fright beat" at a certain point, so they added the head floating by the bite hole in the sunken boat. Since they were back in Los Angeles at this point, they shot it, believe it or not, in Fields' backyard pool.

A good backgrounder accompanies the film on the disc. It includes a discussion of the ins and outs of getting the script together. Mostly, it was about making it lean and singularly focused on man vs. shark. For example, a subplot involving a romance, of sorts, between the Dreyfuss character and Chief Brody's wife was quickly jettisoned (thank goodness).

Beyond the great script, there were also astonishing improvs, especially by the late Robert Shaw. They included, reportedly, the riveting story, told by Shaw, of the harrowing night in the ocean with sharks with the crew of the torpedoed *USS Indianapolis*.

Also, it still astonishes me that *Jaws* was rated PG. Yes, I know there was no PG-13 in 1975, but how such an emotionally disturbing film could escape an R, I'll never know. Near the end one character is literally bitten in half, for Pete's sake.

But, that said, *Jaws* was spectacular in 1975, and it's still spectacular today.

SAVING PRIVATE RYAN

1998

FROM ITS OPENING MOMENTS, WHEN BLOODY HELL ERUPTS ON OMAHA BEACH, Steven Spielberg's *Saving Private Ryan* is hard to watch. But it's important to see.

With its riveting combat drama played out against a D-Day backdrop, *Saving Private Ryan* is a masterpiece of World War II heroism. The film will hold your heart hostage for nearly three hours with its relentless, realistic carnage, its portraits of ordinary men displaying extraordinary courage, and its complex moral dilemmas.

In *Saving Private Ryan*, eight men barely survive D-Day, only to be asked to risk their lives to save another G.I. He's Private Ryan (Matt Damon), a paratrooper who must be found and sent home because his three brothers have all been killed elsewhere in the war, and the Army doesn't want his mother to lose a fourth child.

Tom Hanks stars as Capt. John Miller, the quietly competent leader of the squad given the Ryan duty. In a performance that ranks among the best by this two-time Oscar-winner, Hanks creates a new kind of war hero: a complex figure with fears and doubts, but a conviction to do his duty, if only so he can go home.

Spielberg guided Hanks and the capable supporting actors, including Edward Burns and Tom Sizemore, to performances that are totally free of machismo and bravado.

The humanity of the men is always evident, from the country-boy sharpshooter who says a prayer before each squeeze of the trigger, to the timid squad interpreter who cowers on a staircase, unable to lift his gun when a German soldier walks right by him.

Though *Saving Private Ryan* marks a return to the clear-cut good and evil of World War II films, Spielberg injects a new, terrifying realism – a tribute, perhaps, to the unblinking honesty of a filmmaker raised in the Vietnam era.

Filmgoers will be rocked by the horrors before them, especially in the 25-minute Omaha Beach invasion that opens the film. Young soldiers clutch crosses and Stars of David on chains around their necks while they vomit and shake in their landing craft. G.I.s drown in blood-red water, weighed down by their backpacks before they can even get to the beach. A dazed youth walks by, carrying his own detached arm. Another lies on his back, dying, crying for his mother.

The herky-jerky hand-held cameras of Oscar-winning cinematographer Janusz Kaminski bring the immediacy of news footage to the incredible carnage, as blood, body parts and dead fish despoil the surf of Normandy. But through such intensely violent scenes – and the actions of the men depicted so brilliantly in them – Spielberg brings credibility and immense weight to the drama that follows.

Filmgoers will understand better than ever the price many of our fathers and grandfathers paid to secure our freedom. In *Schindler's List*, Spielberg created the most powerful film ever about the tragic, horrific stupidity of hatred. In *Saving Private Ryan* – a film just as magnificent – he defines the true meaning of valor and sacrifice.

In the story of the need to save one man, Spielberg and screenwriter Robert Rodat have created a perfect metaphor for the effort to save all of us whose way of life would be preserved. The stunning, heartfelt realization of this great film is this: We are all Private Ryan.

THE TRUMAN SHOW

1998

IMAGINE THAT THE LIFE YOU LEAD IS BOGUS. UNBEKNOWNST TO YOU, YOUR SPOUSE, friends and co-workers are all actors. You're the unwitting star of your own TV show.

That's the premise of *The Truman Show*, the year's most entertaining film, and it's not as far-fetched as you may think. After all, we line up to tell our most intimate secrets on *The Jerry Springer Show*. Video cameras record us at traffic intersections and in stores while we shop. We stand on a curb at Rockefeller Plaza for three or four hours just to wave a sign at Al Roker and the *Today Show* viewing audience. Amateur videographers capture us when we're being arrested or when a twister levels our home.

A favorite mantra of the '60s was: "The medium is the message." But the '90s have brought an addendum: "The medium is the message – and we are the medium."

All that prying technology – and our willingness to embrace it – has a price: the loss of privacy, a cornerstone of our freedom. And quite frankly, all those cameras also alter our reality. As a character says in *The Truman Show*, "We accept what we're presented with as reality."

Who could have predicted that such a profound theme would be smack-dab in the middle of the latest Jim Carrey film? It's a drastically intelligent change of pace for the star of *Dumb and Dumber*.

Director Peter Weir, the astute Australian-born filmmaker, has reined in the manic antics of Carrey, as he did with Robin Williams in *Dead Poets Society*. Weir, who was also responsible for *Gallipoli* and *The Year of Living Dangerously*, guides Carrey to a powerfully restrained, amusing and touching performance.

Carrey plays Truman Burbank, a sweet-natured insurance salesman who lives and works in the sunny, impeccably clean beach community of Seahaven. He's happily married to Meryl, a cheery former cheerleader – and, we come to find out, an actress (played with spooky two-faced skill by Laura Linney).

Each sunny day (and every day is a sunny day), Truman goes to work, does his job, comes home for supper, has a few brews with a friend, and generally enjoys a simple, comfortable life. But a series of events soon suggests to Truman that all is not "normal." He begins to suspect he's the only person in his life who isn't pretending. And he tries to break free.

Overseeing the 24-hours-a-day, seven-days-a-week *Truman Show* from a faraway control room is Christof, a genius TV director, crazed artist and would-be father figure. He's played with subtle skill by Ed Harris. Christof clearly has delusions of divinity, and not just because he gets to begin each day by saying, "Cue the sun,"

The clever, highly original screenplay for *The Truman Show* is by Andrew Niccol, a New Zealander who also wrote (and directed) the recent *Gattaca*. The script, though, has been filtered through the remarkable artistry of Peter Weir. He frames the dark fable with bright, sunny, PG ambience and elevates the startling theme with stunning minimalist musical anthems by Burkhard Dallwitz, Phillip Glass and Frederic Chopin. Most important, Weir guides his diverse cast members to the most artful and effective performances of their lives.

The Truman Show is something special. Don't miss it.

MASTER AND COMMANDER: THE FAR SIDE OF THE WORLD

2003

WHEN YOUR CHARACTER IS CALLED MASTER AND COMMANDER, YOU'D BETTER BE A take-charge guy. That's Russell Crowe from stem to stern in Peter Weir's grand sea epic, *Master and Commander: The Far Side of the World*. In fact, when a friend saw how Crowe portrayed 19th-century British sea captain Jack Aubrey, he suggested the film ought to be shown at management seminars.

"Lucky Jack" is a courageous and wily warrior, a natural leader of men, a tolerably good fiddle-player and an amusingly bad punster. His men love him and will follow him across the seas to do battle against impossible odds for king and country. Mark down another impressive, larger-than-life achievement for the chameleonic Australian actor.

This eagerly awaited sea adventure, the first film made from the score of best-selling novels by Patrick O'Brian, is all anyone could ever have hoped for. Like O'Brian's thickly and precisely detailed books, Weir's film revels in fascinating period imagery and sometimes archaic, turn-of-the-19th-century dialogue, along with the robust cannon fire and bloody swordplay that are necessary for any tale of action before the mast.

The artful Weir has long been expert at putting exotic and unusual worlds on the screen – remember the Indonesia of *The Year of Living Dangerously*, the Amish country of *Witness* and the plastic artificiality of *The Truman Show*? Here he provides a view of the crowded and meticulously ordered life aboard a three-masted British frigate of the early 1800s.

Nearly 100 men share deck and sleeping quarters on a ship barely half the length of a football field. In a sense, *Master and Commander* is *Das Boot*, except 150 years earlier. In that classic World War II submarine film, men are crowded into a small, claustrophobic space and do battle despite being on a badly damaged ship. Their captain is nearly as charismatic and forceful as Aubrey.

Weir's movie bears a title nearly longer than the ship because it's based largely on two of O'Brian's 20 novels, *Master and Commander* and *The Far Side of the World*. Aubrey commands the *HMS Surprise* and is pursuing a larger, better-armed French frigate in the waters off South America and around the Galapagos Islands. It is 1805 and England is at war with Napoleon's France.

At Aubrey's side is friend, confidant, ship's doctor and (sometimes) ship's conscience Stephen Maturin (played with subtle grace by Paul Bettany, Crowe's imaginary college roommate in *A Beautiful Mind*). He offers the counterpoint of restraint.

But it's the two talented Australians, director Weir and star Crowe, who steer this $150 million enterprise to a rousing victory on the high seas.

L.A. CONFIDENTIAL

1997

SID HUDGENS, THE CONNIVING TABLOID EDITOR PLAYED BY DANNY DEVITO IN *L.A. Confidential*, always ends his juicy reports with a tag line: "Off the record, on the QT and very hush-hush."

In the same spirit – just between you and me, of course – I hear that thanks to this first-rate new film, easily the most engrossing, exciting Los Angeles crime drama since *Chinatown*, the 1997 Oscar race is off and running. (Indeed, the film would be a major player at that year's Oscars, but would be undone by a giant luxury liner called *Titanic*.)

Director and co-writer Curtis Hanson has masterfully adapted James Ellroy's deliciously dark, demented novel of the same name, trimming its convoluted plot and refining its epic scope, but preserving the hard-boiled Ellroy style. For a director who made his name with lean, B-movie chamber pieces like *The Hand That Rocks the Cradle* and *Bad Influence*, *L.A. Confidential* is a leap ahead, elevating Hudgens to the top rank of American filmmakers.

L.A. Confidential oozes period style, recreating the marvelous landmarks, fashions and music of the City of Angels circa 1950.

The film details the exploits of three very different and highly competitive police officers as they become entangled in several plot strands: the investigation of a mass murder at a diner, a change in the town's gangland hierarchy, Hollywood corruption involving drugs and hookers, and bribery and betrayal among fellow cops.

Bud White (Russell Crowe) is a gruff, hard-nosed detective who isn't afraid to take the law into his own hands; he's also got a peculiar weakness for helping damsels in distress.

Ed Exley (Guy Pearce) is an up-and-comer whose self-righteous veneer of integrity fails to mask his ambition.

Jack Vincennes (Kevin Spacey), a veteran detective who's infatuated with fancy suits and fine women, loves rubbing shoulders with Hollywood types. He especially enjoys his role as technical advisor on a TV cop show (humorously modeled on *Dragnet*). Jack also makes a good living on the side, providing tips to tabloid editor Hudgens about high-profile busts. (Blending fact and fiction, Jack is supposedly the cop who famously busted actor Robert Mitchum for marijuana.)

The three officers have little in common and don't much like each other. But they're thrown together in a case whose murky complexity would do Raymond Chandler proud. Along the way, they cross swords with LAPD Capt. Dudley Smith (James Cromwell), the district attorney (Ron Rifkin), a high-class pimp and would-be producer (David Strathairn), and call girl Lynn Bracken (Kim Basinger), whose main claim to fame is her resemblance to actress Veronica Lake. Illusion being the name of the game in L.A., then and now, they all have things to hide. Gleefully helping to peel back the layers is tabloid slimeball Hudgens, who narrates the tale.

The script, by Hanson and co-writer Brian Helgeland, marvelously maintains the balance among the various plots, and Hanson organizes it all with wit, intrigue and clarity. Speaking strictly on the record and not at all hush-hush: don't miss *L.A. Confidential*.

MIGHTY APHRODITE

1995

WOODY ALLEN ALWAYS SAYS HIS AUDIENCE TAKES HIS FILM ROLES TOO LITERALLY, THAT we're too quick to confuse him with his screen persona. He even made a whole movie about it called *Stardust Memories,* way back in 1980.

But Allen doesn't make it easy to avoid thinking his characters are like him. In film after recent film, he's played middle-aged guys hung up on younger women. And in *Husbands and Wives,* his screen marriage fell apart in tandem with the collapse of his real-life relationship with Mia Farrow.

Now, in *Mighty Aphrodite,* Allen plays a guy who tells his wife he opposes her plan to adopt a baby. How can a viewer not think of Farrow's famous and ever-increasing brood of adopted children? Methinks the Woodman is winking as he nudges me in the ribs with his elbow.

But whether the references are the result of coincidence or coyness, there is a positive side: Woody Allen continues to make funny movies. And that's all that should really matter to filmgoers.

There's an irony here: During the most difficult time in Allen's personal life, he's made three of his most unpretentious, angst-free and flat-out funny movies of recent years. *Manhattan Murder Mystery, Bullets Over Broadway* and the new *Mighty Aphrodite* have marked a return to the spirited wackiness of his films before he turned "serious" with comedies like *Annie Hall* and dramas like *Interiors.*

Though *Mighty Aphrodite* falls short of the inspired backstage lunacy of *Bullets Over Broadway,* it easily equals or even surpasses *Manhattan Murder Mystery* in laughs per minute.

In *Mighty Aphrodite,* Allen plays Lenny, a New York City sports writer. His wife, the chic Amanda (Helena Bonham Carter), is so busy operating an upscale art gallery that she won't take time for pregnancy. She wants to adopt. Lenny opposes the idea but eventually succumbs.

The result is the arrival of an unusually bright little boy, Max, who brings the couple considerable joy. But Max also makes Lenny curious: who could have brought such an intelligent, handsome young man into the world? His birth mother must have been somebody special. Without telling Amanda, Lenny decides to find Max's mother.

He gets an address, but when he knocks on the door, a sexy, tightly dressed woman answers and says, "Are you my 3 o'clock?"

No, she's not a psychologist (at least, not one with a diploma). She's a delightfully dim-witted hooker and occasional porno actress who goes by a variety of names, including Judy. She's a jovial, oddly innocent and unabashedly enthusiastic purveyor of sex – the sort of role once earmarked for Judy Holliday. Here she's played with gusto by Mira Sorvino in a career-launching performance.

Since this hooker is also the mother of his adopted child, Lenny makes it his duty to redeem Judy, or whatever her name is. He begins a crusade to educate and improve her, and to get her away from the sex trade.

First, she needs a regular boyfriend, so Lenny recruits Kevin, an up-and-coming boxer and a decent guy who's also dumber than a fence post. This and other plans go awry, of course, as does Lenny's own love life, especially when his wife has an affair.

This material is rife with humorous potential, in the urbane *Manhattan* mode familiar to Allen fans. (Still, the profanity and sex jokes are a new element; *Mighty Aphrodite* is Allen's naughtiest movie to date, though it's never exploitive.)

A marvelous one-joke gag provides additional laughs – and sustains itself throughout the film: Allen employs a Greek chorus to comment on Lenny's behavior. While many filmmakers have used the chorus device in modern guise, Allen goes to the source. The actions of these 1990s New Yorkers come under the scornful gaze of a real Greek chorus, commenting from the Parthenon. Garbed in ancient robes (and led by Oscar winners F. Murray Abraham and Olympia Dukakis), the chorus shifts hilariously between the thees and thous of antiquated conversation and the deses and dems of modern-day New Yorkers. They're part Sophocles, part Borscht Belt. They even perform a Cole Porter production number, which we might consider a warm-up to the musical Allen reportedly has next on his filmmaking schedule.

About the only thing the chorus doesn't comment on is how much the fictional Lenny and the real Woody have in common. If they did, they'd probably say: "Who ya kiddin', Woody? Of course, you're a lot like Lenny. But it's OK, schnook. We had a lotta laughs."

PULP FICTION

1994

MIA, THE GANGSTER'S MOLL, LIES IMMOBILE ON THE APARTMENT FLOOR, THE VICTIM of a drug overdose. Vincent Vega, one of the gangster's hit men, has been assigned to baby-sit the girl. And now she's dying.

Frantically, he's brought Mia to a friend's apartment. together, they're trying to figure out how to use adrenaline to revive her. The friend fills a hypodermic needle, but says it has to be driven hard into the chest. As Vincent takes aim with a needle big enough to drug a horse, the hyperactivity in the room freezes, and the tension is palpable. And then – WHOMP! – Vincent rams the needle home.

It's a classic Quentin Tarantino moment in *Pulp Fiction*, the latest work from the young renegade writer-director who's become the *enfant terrible* of Hollywood. Like the ear-cutting scene in his first film, *Reservoir Dogs*, it's the outrageous moment when black humor and fear collide, setting off intense sparks.

The scene also is a rich metaphor for Tarantino's contribution to the films of the '90s. In *Pulp Fiction*, he delivers another distinctive shot of adrenaline to the world of the movies. Like Mia the moll, the audience sits bolt upright, jolted to life.

In *Reservoir Dogs*, in his screenplay for *True Romance* and in his story for *Natural Born Killers*, Tarantino brought together graphic violence, a love of gangster lore and a peculiarly poetic brand of foul-mouthed dialogue. But his previous work is only a prelude to the accomplished *Pulp Fiction*, which won the top prize at this year's Cannes Film Festival. It's the most original movie of the year. For viewers able to handle its thrills, it's also the most entertaining.

But it offers more than sensation. Sometimes lost in the visual excitement and violence is a basic fact: the director is also a first-rate storyteller. The new film offers a trio of tales, cleverly interwoven into a whole that's even greater than its parts. Anthology films seldom work. One of the tales usually dominates the proceedings, throwing the film out of balance. *Pulp Fiction*, though, is seamless – yet another accomplishment.

Along the way, Tarantino jump-starts the sputtering careers of John Travolta and Bruce Willis. Travolta, in particular, bites into the meatiest role of his life as Vincent Vega.

In the first story, Vega is ordered to be company for his boss's girlfriend, Mia. Since she's sexy and fun (and played by Uma Thurman), that would seem a choice assignment. However, the last guy to do the job was blown away by the jealous boss, simply because he dared to give Mia a foot massage.

Imagine Vincent's concern when Mia overdoses.

In the third story, Vincent and his Bible-quoting partner, Jules (a fabulous, fire-breathing Samuel L. Jackson), have a problem. They've blown a guy's head off in their car, and it's a mess. They've driven to a safe house and must await the arrival of the mob's cleanup specialist (a natty Harvey Keitel).

The second story stars Bruce Willis as Butch, a battle-scarred, tank-town boxer, hired by the mob to take a fall. Spurred by memories of his father, he wins the fight and puts his life at risk. In one of the many ways the stories interlock, Vincent Vega is dispatched to kill him.

Tarantino isn't content with simply connecting three stories. He also fools inventively with the time frame. Characters who die in the second story are still alive in the third. Yet I not only followed the narrative logic, I admired it.

As an added bonus, Tarantino frames the three stories with an interlocking prologue and epilogue that on their own would make an engrossing little film. Tim Roth and Amanda Plummer play "Pumpkin" and "Honey Bunny," extravagantly funny young lovers whose romance peaks whenever they rob convenience stores or diners.

Though Tarantino sets his stories in the seedier corners of modern Los Angeles, his inspiration clearly is the melodramatic crime fiction of 1940s pulp magazines.

The production design of *Pulp Fiction* matches the extremes of the stories. The film's ultimate set piece is a Hollywood restaurant with a '50s motif that outrocks the Hard Rock Cafe. Reportedly there have been offers to franchise it as a real restaurant, complete with its Buddy Holly busboys and Marilyn Monroe waitresses.

Quentin Tarantino in the restaurant business? Hey, who knows? Maybe that industry also needs a shot of adrenaline.

JACKIE BROWN

1997

IN HIS WONDERFULLY ENTERTAINING *JACKIE BROWN*, FILMMAKER QUENTIN TARANTINO sidesteps any notion that he'll be saddled with a career of *Pulp Fiction* retreads.

Casting aside that earlier film's off-the-wall energy, quick cuts and loony narrative style, Tarantino wisely uses his new crime caper to explore slower rhythms, more leisurely scenes – and significantly more meaningful character development.

Tarantino shows his developing maturity as a filmmaker as well as his appreciation of the quirky style of Elmore Leonard, the author of *Rum Punch*, upon which *Jackie Brown* is based. The Leonard-Tarantino match is a marriage made in movie heaven; *Jackie Brown* is an effervescent crime tale in which the filmmaker's trademark dialogue, camera work and musical choices all blend marvelously with the author's well-defined characters and goofball plotting.

If that's not enough, Tarantino also uses his distinctive eye for nearly forgotten talent to cast his story. (Remember, this is the guy who saved John Travolta from movies with talking babies.)

Tarantino correctly saw the central characters of *Jackie Brown* as middle-aged unde-achievers who could finally get something right in life, and cleverly cast two overlooked veteran actors who know firsthand how their characters feel. Pam Grier and Rochester native Robert Forster make memorable acting comebacks, delivering delightful, contrasting performances that approach perfection. They hold our attention and sympathy throughout the film – and even manage to outshine such talented co-stars as Robert De Niro and Samuel L. Jackson.

As the strong, resourceful title character, trying to outsmart cops and criminals alike, Grier takes the independent spirit and warrior-like edge she brought to her '70s blaxploitation flicks and adapts them to a more grounded and appealing tale of the '90s.

But if she's the heart of *Jackie Brown*, Forster's decent, diligent and devoted Max Cherry is its soul. The least flashy of the film's main characters, Max eventually emerges as its conscience.

Jackie is a Los Angeles-based stewardess for a budget airline with flights to Mexico. Two cops (Michael Keaton and Michael Bowen) bust her for carrying currency across the border for L.A. gun dealer Ordell Robbie (Samuel L. Jackson). Jackie is just one of several women Ordell employs to run his errands.

On the advice of Max, her smart, sweet-natured bail bondsman, Jackie offers to help the cops catch Ordell. But meanwhile she sets up a con game of her own.

Ordell is a formidable ally – he's as street-smart as they come, and he has absolutely no scruples about killing to conduct business. Ordell also has a partner named Louis who is even more dangerous, mostly because he's as dense as he is deadly. (Louis is played, in a slow-building gem of a performance, by De Niro.)

Rather than telling Leonard's tale slam-bang, writer-director Tarantino eases into the relationships, fully exploring each character and how they fit into the puzzle.

He ultimately shifts gears – quite winningly – to romance, hinting at sparks between Jackie and Max. When Max first gazes longingly at Jackie, he shows a restrained but remarkably moving reaction; it may be Forster's best moment yet as an actor. (Indeed, Forster got an Oscar nomination.)

To help flavor the saga, Tarantino dips into his record collection to rediscover black soul classics of the '70s, including songs from earlier Grier blaxploitation films, such as *Coffy* and *Foxy Brown*.

His language, though, is as salty and irreverent as always. He's already upset some viewers with the heavy use of the N-word that peppers Samuel L. Jackson's dialogue, though the distasteful word seems at home in the mouth of a distasteful man like Ordell.

Ultimately, *Jackie Brown* won't make the same sort of splash as *Pulp Fiction*. But if viewers are willing to watch Tarantino's new film on its own terms, they'll be richly rewarded.

APOCALYPSE NOW REDUX

2001

I AM AMONG MANY CRITICS WHOSE ADMIRATION FOR FRANCIS FORD COPPOLA'S 1979 Vietnam epic, *Apocalypse Now,* came with an asterisk: If I called the film a "masterpiece," I modified it with "flawed."

It's time to drop the asterisk and erase "flawed." Why? Because *Apocalypse Now* has evolved. It's not the same film. And because we've evolved, too. We're not the same audience.

Apocalypse Now Redux is a magnificent new edition of the Coppola film. Restructured in subtle but important ways – and with 49 minutes of previously unseen footage – this landmark film is not to be missed.

It is clearer now that Coppola created a profound metaphor for the entire Vietnam experience, but audiences in 1979 were too close to step back and take in this broader view. And with the addition of a fabled but previously unseen French plantation sequence, the presence of the French in the bloody history of Vietnam is reaffirmed, and the overview of the conflict is complete.

But that's only one of several major additions to *Apocalypse Now,* which adapts Joseph Conrad's novel *Heart of Darkness* to the Vietnam era. As in the novel, a man takes a long, difficult journey up a jungle river to destroy a demented, dangerous man.

The journey is taken by a military special op named Capt. Willard (Martin Sheen), on instructions to terminate Col. Kurtz (Marlon Brando) "with extreme prejudice." Kurtz was once a great officer but has left the military behind, gone native and set up a kingdom of jungle warriors. As we observe Willard's trip upriver, we go on a journey through the Vietnam experience, with all its horrors, paradoxes, humor and idiocy.

In addition to the plantation scene, Coppola and his Oscar-winning editor and sound designer, Walter Murch, now weave in:

– A few more scenes with Robert Duvall's fabulous Col. Kilgore character, the surf-riding officer who loves "the smell of napalm in the morning."

– Another scene involving the Playboy bunnies, who had been shown entertaining the troops. Now, their sexual favors are bartered for a helicopter's gasoline – a stunning example of human exploitation in a war of exploitation.

– The only sequence that shows Brando in daylight, as his character reads to Willard war reports from *Time* magazine, showing the hypocrisy of the conflict.

The movie's end, which stirred much confusion in 1979, is largely unchanged. But now it makes more sense in the broad metaphoric sweep of the film.

In going back to the dailies and rebuilding *Apocalypse Now*, Coppola and Murch said their goal was to make the film they had always intended. Coppola says he rushed to wrap up the original because of the looming 1979 Cannes Film Festival.

Coppola has written: "We were terrified the film was too long, too strange and didn't resolve itself in a kind of classic big battle … so we shaped the film that we thought would work for the mainstream audience of its day. More than 20 years later, I (saw) the picture. … What struck me was that the original – which had been seen as so demanding and adventurous when it first came out – now seemed relatively tame, as though the audience had caught up with it."

Clearly, we're further removed from the conflicted emotions of the Vietnam War, and have seen far more at the movies – more violence, more technique. Coppola was inspired to tackle a new version that adhered more to original themes "related to the morality in war."

Indeed, audiences hungry for reality in 1979 were sometimes dumbfounded by the film's operatic melodrama and its penchant for metaphor. The film's violent, ritualistic ending was especially strange and unsettling.

In the new version, the journey upriver can be more easily seen as a trip back in time: First, we encounter the '70s, with American soldiers led by the surf-loving Kilgore. Next, we travel through the dark hell of Vietnam, crossing the DMZ into Cambodia, after stopping at a border camp where drugged-out, '60s-style soldiers have no clue "who's in charge." Farther upriver, out of the fog comes a squad of Frenchmen guarding a plantation, where a French family lives as if unaffected by time. We're now back in the '50s, when France was a strong player in Southeast Asia. Finally, we reach the river's beginning – Kurtz's compound – where painted natives carry spears and bloody heads decorate the shore. We've returned to the primal.

Coppola has said *Apocalypse Now* was designed "to let audiences feel what Vietnam was like: the immediacy, the insanity, the exhilaration, the horror, the sensuousness and the moral dilemma of America's most surreal and nightmarish war." With *Apocalypse Now Redux*, it can be said: mission accomplished.

CAPOTE

2005

AMBITION CAN BE DANGEROUS STUFF, AND PERHAPS MORE SO WHEN IT'S CLOAKED IN artistry. Writer Truman Capote made that painful discovery in the early 1960s when he pursued the book that would ultimately make him a literary legend.

Philip Seymour Hoffman brilliantly portrays the eccentric and troubled writer in *Capote*, a film that examines those key five years of the author's life.

Inspired by an article in the *New York Times* on murder in Kansas, Capote travels to the farmlands to research what he hopes will be an article for *The New Yorker*. Once two men are arrested for the crime, Capote sees the makings of a book, in which he hopes to use the techniques of fiction on a nonfiction subject. He says it will be a nonfiction novel, and he ultimately titles it *In Cold Blood.* "Sometimes, when I think how good it could be," Capote writes a friend, "I can hardly breathe."

But Capote discovers his book won't come cheap. First, he struggles with acceptance in the American farm belt, where his high-pitched voice and flamboyant manner are unlike anything ever seen on a Holcomb, Kan., street corner. In fact, to cushion his eccentricities, Capote enlists his old friend, writer Harper Lee (Catherine Keener), to accompany him. She often paves the way for her extreme friend as they meet with various authorities, including chief investigator Alvin Dewey (Chris Cooper).

Much more seriously, Capote finds himself in a quandary when he meets accused killer Perry Smith. The young man comes from a troubled upbringing with which Capote identifies. He also finds himself drawn to the darkly handsome man. It may even be that Capote falls in love with him. At any rate, he vows to do whatever he can to help Smith (Clifton Collins Jr.) and his partner, Dick Hickock (Mark Pellegrino) get proper legal representation.

But here's the rub: Capote will have a potent finale for his book only if the killers are executed.

Director Bennett Miller and writer Dan Futterman have evocatively adapted aspects of Gerald Clarke's *Capote: A Biography*. They've also faithfully incorporated the known information and suggested imagery from Capote's famous book and from Richard Brooks' great 1967 film version. In other words, *Capote* serves as an eloquent and equally artful companion piece to Brooks' *In Cold Blood*.

The heart of *Capote*, though, is to be found in Hoffman's astonishing performance. After the initial shock of hearing Capote's familiar squeak of a voice, and seeing his no-nonsense walk and his flamboyant mannerisms, we realize Hoffman is going far deeper, giving us a portrait of uncommon subtlety and emotional depth. Through this remarkable work, we understand the ultimate tragedy of the artist emotionally shattered by his ambitions for his art.

THE QUIET AMERICAN

2002

THE QUIET AMERICAN, GRAHAM GREENE'S CLASSIC NOVEL OF ROMANTIC INTRIGUE IN the decaying French Indochina of the 1950s, has been artfully adapted into one of the best films of 2002.

Though only now going into broad release, the film had a preliminary Oscar-qualifying run in a few big cities. It resulted in a best actor nomination for its star, Michael Caine.

At the film's center is Caine's absolutely perfect performance as Thomas Fowler, the story's narrator, a cynical, world-weary British correspondent who is content to hide out in Saigon with his young Vietnamese mistress.

Partly an evocative thriller and partly a moody metaphor for the earliest U.S. incursions into Vietnam, *The Quiet American* explores a volatile romantic triangle that's about to be overtaken by broader, more serious issues.

As the film opens, Fowler meets the title character, a brash, seemingly naive young American named Alden Pyle (Brendan Fraser). Pyle is in Vietnam purportedly to provide medical aid. But that might be a cover story.

Fowler is more immediately concerned with the friendship that develops between Pyle and Phuong (Hai Yen Do), the older man's lovely young lover. The self-righteous Pyle makes it his mission to save Phuong from a doomed life in Vietnam. He wants to lure her away from Fowler, marry her and take her home to Boston.

So, while Fowler, Pyle and Phuong remain friendly and respectful on the surface, tension runs deep. Like America's involvement in general, the situation can't end well.

Caine virtually disappears within Fowler and gives viewers a complex, morally ambivalent and utterly fascinating character. This will be remembered as one among a handful of his greatest performances.

Fraser is ideally cast as the fresh-faced, idealistic American, while newcomer Hai Yen Do makes Phuong a young woman of innocence, beauty and mystery.

The Quiet American is the first major Western production to be shot in Vietnam, and 1950s Saigon and its environs have been meticulously re-created. The highly esteemed cinematographer Christopher Doyle provides robust visuals of the steamy green jungles, the primordial countryside, and the shadowy, slightly seedy colonial structures, streets and squares of Saigon.

The script, by Christopher Hampton and Robert Schenkkan, is remarkably loyal to Greene's text. Director Phillip Noyce engineers an ideal pace and mood along with the first-rate performances.

It may seem remarkable that Noyce could release two superb films in one season (the other being *Rabbit-Proof Fence*). However, *The Quiet American* had been completed a year earlier. Miramax delayed its release in the complex political atmosphere that followed September 11, 2001 because the film could be viewed as anti-American.

Once seen, that all seems silly because the story is of another time. Besides, the cautions it raises about Vietnam have been justified in our 20/20 hindsight.

THE CIDER HOUSE RULES

1999

MICHAEL CAINE IS REMARKABLE IN THIS LYRICAL ADAPTATION OF A JOHN IRVING NOVEL.

It's the 1940s and the only reason to get off the train at St. Cloud, Maine, is children. Either you want to adopt one or leave one behind – or perhaps not give birth to one.

The St. Cloud of author John Irving's imagination in *The Cider House Rules* is the location of an orphanage sitting high on a hill. There, a kindly, conscientious physician named Larch cares for the children, whom he calls "princes of Maine, kings of New England."

He also quietly performs illegal (at that time) but relatively safe abortions.

In this lyrical film from director Lasse Hallström, Dr. Larch (Michael Caine) has refused to play favorites with the orphans over the years – with one exception. Not having been chosen for adoption by any of the couples who visit the home, Homer Wells (Tobey Maguire) has grown into a young man at the orphanage. So Larch has become Homer's mentor and virtually his father. Larch has taught Homer medical skills; the youngster can deliver babies and help with other operations, even though he's never even gone to high school.

Then Homer comes of age and dreams of a world outside St. Cloud – of seeing the ocean, going down the highway, meeting other people. He also finds himself opposed to Larch's abortions.

So Homer moves on – just to another part of the state, where he works at an apple farm. There he learns the proper way to pick the fruit off the tree, and so much more, from the migrants with whom he bunks. He also develops a complicated but passionate relationship with the lovely Candy Kendall (Charlize Theron) while her boyfriend fights in the war in Europe.

Through tragic circumstances, Homer learns that certain rules apply and others don't, whether they're hung on the wall of the cider house where he and the migrants bunk, where the apples are processed, or are deeper moral laws that govern our lives.

As Irving intended with his 1985 best-selling novel, *The Cider House Rules* powerfully states a pro-choice position on abortion. That may be a problem for some viewers, even though the issue is artfully examined and not clumsily hammered home.

Hallström's superb screen adaptation (with a script by Irving) also offers an engrossing, poignant coming-of-age saga, as well as a portrait of a compassionate physician and several touching stories of orphans.

As he ably demonstrated in *My Life as a Dog* and *What's Eating Gilbert Grape?*, Hallström is a skilled observer and manipulator of children. They are present in some of the best moments here: eager youngsters preparing themselves for an adoption inspection by spitting down their hair or practicing their smiles, or gathering boisterously to watch a weekly screening of *King Kong*.

The Cider House Rules has been beautifully filmed, taking full advantage of the red and golden colors of a New England orchard in autumn, the crisp snow of winter, the welcome sun of spring.

The range of performances is equally impressive, especially Maguire's as the quietly determined and passionate Homer Wells and Delroy Lindo's as the chief migrant picker, who is both wise and cursed. Theron seems a bit upscale to play the daughter of a lobster fisherman, but she eventually wins us over with her sincerity and grace.

Best of all is the remarkable Caine. He tackles an accent that's not his own for the first time in decades and sounds convincingly like a New Englander. More important, he fully generates the decency and conviction of Dr. Larch, one of the most fascinating characters he's brought to the screen in his long, storied career.

TITANIC

1997

BY NOW YOU'RE PROBABLY SICK OF HEARING THAT JAMES CAMERON'S $200 MILLION *Titanic* is the most expensive movie ever made. Who cares, as long as the money is on the screen?

There's never been a film of more stunning visual splendor, starting with the magical way the underwater ruin of 1997 turns seamlessly into the floating luxury liner of 1912. The amazing sights continue for more than three hours, until the great ship breaks horrifically in half and sinks into the deep. The effects are so astonishing, and the experience so realistic, that *Titanic's* very real flaws can be forgiven. But they need to be noted, for the film endures rough dramatic seas before reaching its breathtaking finale.

Writer-director Cameron has chosen to blend a romantic fiction with the maritime history – though it's hard to imagine why anyone would think such stirring drama needed embellishment. Cameron's fiction is a Romeo-and-Juliet variation in which a steerage-class dreamer (Leonardo DiCaprio) romances a wealthy, first-class young woman (Kate Winslet), despite the protestations of her obnoxious fiance (Billy Zane) and her snobbish mother (Frances Fisher).

All are caricatures, thanks to Cameron's simplistic approach to class prejudice. On his ship, the folks in steerage have robust fun and idealistic ambitions; first class is populated by overdressed, unfeeling elitists. Despite the superficial writing, the spirited DiCaprio is still charming – he's the best and maybe the only thing on the ship that doesn't need a boost from digital effects.

Otherwise, the ship and the attention to history are what make *Titanic* worth seeing. The meticulously recreated ship, the grandest of ocean liners, gets top billing throughout the epic film, from the fine china and grand stairway in first class to the rows of roaring furnaces below the engine room.

In the moments when the romantic plot works – usually when Zane isn't around – it does help draw you into the personal lives of the Titanic passengers. And just when Cameron's soap opera threatens to go overboard, you're moved by the real-life stories of crewmen and other passengers.

They include the famously "unsinkable" Molly Brown (Kathy Bates); the stern, reserved captain (Bernard Hill) walking gamely into the ship's wheelhouse to await his fate; and the ship's famous lounge orchestra, playing music to soothe passengers even as water laps at their ankles.

Of these cameos, the most affecting involves master shipbuilder Thomas Andrews, brilliantly played by Victor Garber. You last see him standing alone with a brandy near the first-class fireplace. On his face is the awareness that his greatest achievement has turned into the new century's most famous disaster.

In such quiet, haunting moments – and in the horrifying spectacle that triggers them – Cameron's *Titanic* achieves its most telling effects.

THE QUEEN

2006

STEPHEN FREARS' *THE QUEEN* TAKES US ON AN INTRIGUING, INSIGHTFUL JOURNEY INTO that odd British institution: the modern monarchy. We become flies on the wall during a key moment in history that nearly triggers a magisterial crisis. Through it, we see the royals as a family and as human beings, trapped in a gilded cage of bloodlines and tradition.

And the complexity, intelligence and veiled emotions of Elizabeth II are evident in the Oscar-worthy performance of Helen Mirren.

Tony Blair (Michael Sheen) has been prime minister for only a few weeks, and has only just been formally introduced to Elizabeth II at Windsor Castle. Then a tragedy shakes the monarchy: Princess Diana is killed in a car crash in a Paris tunnel.

The days following Diana's death force the monarchy into a rare bit of self-examination. For several days, the royals issue no statement and refuse to fly the flag at half-staff. They escape to Balmoral Castle in Scotland, where Prince Philip (James Cromwell) takes the boys hunting.

Blair, who has a limited view of the monarchy, gradually understands that he must convince the royals to take an active part in the nation's mourning. He must make Elizabeth understand a disagreeable fact: The public loved Lady Di more than they love their queen.

Frears, who's tended toward edgier, more rebellious fare through his career, brings a remarkably even hand to *The Queen*. He lifts the story out of the realm of political debate and puts a human face on the monarchy. Like Blair, we come to understand that Elizabeth II had no choice in her birthright.

Mirren strongly conveys an Elizabeth who is firm, clearly in charge – at least of her household – and is still trying to adapt to a world that long ago left most kings and queens behind it. In one especially affecting moment, she's alone in the Balmoral countryside, and she comes upon a beautiful stag that has long been the target of the hunters in her family.

She and the deer stare at each other for a long time, but when she hears the approaching hunters, she shoos the animal away.

It's a fabulous metaphor for a queen who is trying to save a way of life from those who would destroy it.

THE PAINTED VEIL

2006

JOHN CURRAN'S *THE PAINTED VEIL* STARS EDWARD NORTON AND NAOMI WATTS IN A richly evocative adaptation of W. Somerset Maugham's novel about romantic desperation and the hope for redemption, as a troubled couple is challenged by life and death in the exotic China of the 1920s.

For filmgoers who long for the days when adventurous filmmakers such as David Lean placed fascinating, flawed characters in sweeping, historic settings, *The Painted Veil* is a most welcome motion picture. And no, I don't suggest that *The Painted Veil* is old-fashioned. Instead, I'd say it's classic.

Kitty (Watts) is a spoiled upper-class Brit who marries Walter (Norton), a middle-class physician, for the wrong reason (she wants to escape a domineering mother). They move to Shanghai, where Kitty is seduced by a British bureaucrat (Liev Schreiber). Walter discovers the affair and comes up with his own diabolical punishment for his wife: When he's called away to a remote village to help combat a dangerous cholera epidemic, he insists that Kitty join him.

Of course, Kitty is initially angry, bitter and bored, but she eventually warms to the idea of being helpful. Perhaps she can assist nuns who care for orphans? The sisters are led by a warmly perceptive mother superior, played with subtle restraint by a nearly unrecognizable Diana Rigg (far removed from her Emma Peel *Avengers* days).

Walter, meanwhile, runs a clinic and instructs villagers in healthier habits, all under the watchful eye of nationalist soldiers and a neighborhood warlord. In the '20s, China was starting to move away from the fractious warlords, forging a national identity, though a civil war lay ahead between the forces of Chiang Kai-shek and Mao Zedong. Although this historic perspective is not central to the story, the elements add unsettling turmoil to the couple's struggles.

Walter and Kitty also befriend a fellow Brit, a deputy commissioner played well with colonial decadence and rumpled charm by Toby Jones (who played Truman Capote in *Infamous*).

Curran and screenwriter Ron Nyswaner keep untangled the threads of the literate story, and Curran underscores the richly emotional elements by taking full advantage of the breathtaking Chinese locales.

RAISE THE RED LANTERN

1992

THE TALENTED ZHANG YIMOU, THE FIRST CHINESE FILMMAKER TO DEVELOP AN audience in the West, through his stunning *Red Sorghum* and *Ju Dou*, returns with his latest, the Oscar-nominated *Raise the Red Lantern.*

Once again, Zhang tells a folk tale that is rich in meaning and allegory and profound in its simplicity. It can be absorbed at face value, as an eye-opening portrait of an aspect of life in feudal China, or be viewed as a fascinating political allegory about the corruption and injustice of totalitarianism.

Gong Li, Zhang's frequent muse and the star of *Red Sorghum* and *Ju Dou,* here plays Songlian, a young woman in 1920s China who agrees to become the fourth wife of a polygamous wealthy nobleman named Chen.

Chen installs each of his four wives in duplicate stone houses, joined by a central courtyard. He designates his choice for companionship each night through a ceremony in which bright red paper lanterns are hung at the house of the "chosen one." The "lucky" wife is also given a ritual foot massage, the dinner of her choice, and all sorts of attention.

Instead of rebelling against the injustice of being chosen or not chosen, the women all clamor, scheme, and compete to be No. 1. They willingly demean or try to destroy the competition. In other words, they play into the nobleman's hands, viewing the nightly selection as a great prize that makes their lives worth living. The self-centered plotting of each of the women leads to no good – and tragedy is the ultimate result.

The symbolism is clear. When the subjects of totalitarianism try to live within the system, they're playing by rules they can't control. Ultimately, they become victims.

As played by the beautiful and imaginative Gong Li, Songlian is certainly not always sympathetic, and evoking such emotional complexity in the midst of a simple tale is part of Zhang's considerable gift as a filmmaker. Songlian is a prideful, self-centered and ambitious woman who's not above spiteful behavior and who eventually learns a painful lesson.

In *Raise the Red Lantern,* director Zhang demonstrates increasing maturity as a world-class filmmaker. His narrative is lean and to the point, and he keeps his focus firmly on the clash among the four women by avoiding any temptation to make the nobleman a flesh-and-blood character. He is important to the women, but not to us. We don't even see his face throughout the film.

Zhang also is an impressive visual artist. In the three of his films that have reached the United States thus far, his use of the color palette is the most evocative and lyrical in movies since Federico Fellini first turned to color with *Juliet of the Spirits.*

Note here, for example, the importance of red imagery – in the extensive use of the lanterns, and the reddish glow they cast over the characters. It is the color of passion and of pain – and it underscores both elements in this remarkable motion picture.

VOLVER

2006

IT'S ONE THING TO LOAD UP A MOVIE PLOT WITH A MOTHER'S LOVE, A FATHER'S DEATH, the abuse of a child, a murder, great cooking, a struggle with cancer, family secrets, a touching performance of a flamenco ballad, the appearance of a benevolent ghost – in fact, everything but the kitchen sink.

It's quite another to make it all work without a bit of strain. And it's even more impressive if it works with rich humanity, unbridled satisfaction and even joy.

That's the considerable accomplishment of filmmaker Pedro Almodóvar in *Volver*, the Spanish master's latest and greatest film. The film, whose title translates to "The Return," is a guaranteed player at the upcoming Oscars. (In the end, shockingly, it failed to earn a best foreign language film nomination, though its star, Penélope Cruz, was nominated as best actress.)

By returning to her native Spain to perform brilliantly in *Volver*, Cruz vaults into the top ranks of international actors. She's Raimunda, the robust, caring mother at the center of the multi-layered story. Both the character and the performance convey the delightful earthiness and inherent wisdom of the women portrayed by Sophia Loren in her great Italian films for Vittorio De Sica, including *Marriage Italian Style* and *Yesterday, Today and Tomorrow*.

Although no director has ever been as fascinated by and supportive of women as Almodóvar, in *Volver* he outdoes himself. Though the plot is fictitious, the characters are designed as a memory and tribute to the women in Almodóvar's childhood.

Besides Raimunda, the women of *Volver* include her teenage daughter (Yohana Cobo), her funny and not especially bright sister (Lola Dueñas), a loving, longtime neighbor who is as close as a sister (Blanca Portillo), and the mysterious, deceased mother (Carmen Maura), who makes a ghostly return to her family. All the performances are memorable –

and shared a rare best actress ensemble prize at May's Cannes Film Festival.

Nonetheless, two stand out: the aforementioned Cruz, who plumbs new emotional depths with maturity and heart, and the much-admired Maura (the star of *Women on the Verge of a Nervous Breakdown*). An early Almodóvar muse, Maura returns to the master after an 18-year estrangement.

The films of very few modern directors can be described simply with the filmmaker's name (like the Hitchcock films of yesteryear). But *Volver* can be. It's an Almodóvar film. And that makes it one of the best.

THE BILLS GAME

1993

The last two reviews in this cross-section of my film reviews are personal and a little off-the-wall. The first was inspired by a historic NFL game that's beloved in upstate New York by fans (like me) of the Buffalo Bills. It is not a movie review, of course, but an attempt to write about an event in the style of a movie review. It's followed by a review of a film that is worthwhile for me, strictly because of the memories it generates.

I saw an estimated 200 movies in 1992. None provided as much drama, as many thrills, or the emotional rush of being in the drizzle-drenched crowd at one football game in 1993: Buffalo 41, Houston 38.

Movies have made me feel as if I'm floating on air – no mean feat at my weight. Movies have brought me to loud applause or moved me to tears. But no movie ever caused me to jump up and down like a jumping jack or to hug other people and grab strangers joyously. The event that did that for me was seeing the encounter that will forever be known to upstate New York as The Game.

The Game offered more action than *Under Siege* or *Trespass*, more heart than *Lorenzo's Oil* or *Scent of a Woman*, greater confrontations than *A Few Good Men,* a bigger surprise than *The Crying Game*, and a more stunning miracle than *Leap of Faith*. And in classic Hollywood fashion, the great rush of excitement came after the viewer was taken to the absolute deaths of despair. When the Oilers ran back that second-half interception to go out 35 to 3, a football game could not get any worse for a Bills fan.

If you think of the game as a classic Western, a handful of settlers would be running out of ammo while 12,000 Sioux surrounded their wagon train. If it were a vampire flick, the stake would have missed Dracula's heart as the sun sets. If it were a gangster movie, the mob would have you lined up against a garage wall on St. Valentine's Day.

And in each case, the good guys would still win. The Bills roared back like John Wayne leading the cavalry to the wagon train, like Dr. Van Helsing armed with a steam drill, like Elliot Ness and the Untouchables blasting their way into a Chicago garage. But, you argue, movies have heroes and villains. Well, how about these:

– Houston cornerback Chris Dishman, prancing and dancing like a peacock with each Oiler score, taunting Buffalo fans and players along the sidelines. He was the Oiler you loved to hate.

– Houston quarterback Warren Moon, a class act and a dangerous opponent, doing everything right in the first half, playing like he was affected by some strange phase of the moon. He's the villain for whom you feel empathy.

As for heroes, Rich Stadium was full of them:

– Bills quarterback Frank Reich, usually a second-stringer, as quietly strong, courageous, and resourceful as Gary Cooper in *High Noon*.

– Bills kicker Steve Christie, who placed every kick-off, onside kick and field goal with the precision of Indiana Jones with a bullwhip or Robin Hood with an arrow.

– The fans. Despite the stories about fair-weather fans who left early, I'm here to tell you that the vast majority of the 75,000 people at Rich Stadium – at least 65,000 to 70,000 – stayed throughout the drizzle and the wind and the cold. The steadfast fans not only were rewarded with a game that they'll recount to their grandchildren, but in addition their screaming, stomping and whistling had the Oilers befuddled, and Moon seeing stars.

So, I'll admit it, the game turned this movie critic into a raving loon, eagerly dispensing a solid 10 on the event. I'm just glad it was a real football game and not a movie. If somebody tried to turn Sunday's event into a screenplay and put it on the screen, I wouldn't believe it for a minute.

THE PERFECT GAME

2009

THE PERFECT GAME IS NOT A PERFECT MOVIE, BUT IT'S A FUN, FEEL-GOOD EFFORT, a real uplifter in the tradition of *Rudy*, and I'm glad I finally caught up with it. It's a tale of Little League baseball, based on a real-life incident of 44 years ago. I was out of town when the film played for only a week in a theater here last year, and have been eager for an opportunity to see it on DVD. I had a special reason...

The film tells the story of a ragtag team of shoeless Mexican kids who cross the border with their coach (Clifton Collins, Jr.) and parish priest (Cheech Marin) on a mission to test their mettle against more polished and better-outfitted American Little League teams. To everyone's surprise, the Monterrey, Mexico, kids keep on winning, until they find themselves in Williamsport, PA, where they're to play as the first international entry in the Little League World Series. And again, to everyone's surprise, they win when a kid named Angel Macias pitches like an angel, throwing a perfect game.

Here's the fun part: *The Perfect Game* wasn't informing me; it was reminding me, because I was there. I was a 12-year-old boy on Aug. 23, 1957, and I rode my Raleigh bike from my home in South Williamsport across the Susquehanna River to Memorial Park in Williamsport for the big game. And I'll never get over it, as the Monterrey kids, behind Angel's pitching wizardry, defeated La Mesa, CA, 4-0.

I remember biking home after the game, running into our house and announcing to my parents, with the naiveté of a 12-year-old, "Those kids could beat the Yankees!"

But the story gets better. Years later, I discovered that elsewhere in that crowd of 5,000 people had been a 10-year-old girl named Bonnie, with her grandfather, also enjoying the game. I met that girl 12 years later, and married her less than a year after that. Ultimately, in more ways than one, it was a perfect game. And it was fun to see it recreated.

CHAPTER FOUR

MY MOST MEMORABLE ENCOUNTERS

A joy of my life has been the opportunity to meet famous actors and filmmakers who've had a part in creating films that have meant the most to me over my lifetime.

I remain astonished that I spent time with Lillian Gish (arguably, the first movie star), Louise Brooks (another rare silent movie legend), Jimmy Stewart, (a key figure in Hollywood's Golden Age), two of my favorite directors, David Lean and Woody Allen, Sophia Loren (the first great love – lust? – of my adolescent movie-going life), and Ray Charles (the artist who has meant more to me than any other performer).

These are my most memorable encounters over my career...

LILLIAN GISH

TO THIS DAY, I'M STILL ASTONISHED THAT I MET AND HAD CONVERSATIONS WITH A woman who was present at nearly the beginning of cinema, and was one of the stars of the seminal *Birth of a Nation.*

Meeting Lillian Gish underscores for me the relatively short life of motion pictures, compared to other major art forms. The birth of film is usually dated at 1895, when people gathered in a Parisian salon to watch the short films of the Lumière brothers, projected onto a sheet. A mere 15 years later, Lillian Gish was working with D.W. Griffith.

Gish came to Rochester's Eastman House in 1986 for a special screening of her 1920 Griffith silent classic, *Way Down East*, with full orchestra accompaniment. I'll never forget Gish, then 92, jumping out of her seat at the film's conclusion to run up and congratulate the orchestra conductor. This spunky, bright woman would live on for seven more years, dying at 99.

For her appearance in Rochester, Gish and I talked twice, on the phone before she arrived, and then, when she was at the Eastman House. I'll never forget meeting a contemporary of Griffith, Chaplin, Pickford, John Barrymore, and so many others. That's why meeting her was among the most memorable encounters of my career.

The actress on the phone was happy to have a chance to mention her new film, due to open within a few weeks.

"It's called *Sweet Liberty*, and stars Alan Alda, who also directed it," the actress said. "He's such a marvelous man, just like he was on *M*A*S*H*. If you want to know why I did the film, just look at his face. Of course I would work with him!"

This is hardly a debuting starlet enthusiastically promoting her new movie. No, the actress played Alda's mother in *Sweet Liberty*, and it was far from her first movie. In fact, *Sweet Liberty* marked her 77th year in films, for the actress is 92-year-old Lillian Gish, and the actress is the embodiment of the motion picture industry in one tidy, frail-looking woman.

Alan Alda's movie was the most recent on the list of her credits that included *Birth of a Nation, Intolerance, Orphans of the Storm,* and *Broken Blossoms* for D.W. Griffith, *The Scarlet Letter* and *The Wind* for Victor Seastrom, *Duel in the Sun* for King Vidor, *The Unforgiven* for John Huston, and *The Wedding* for Robert Altman. And she wasn't done yet; a year after we talked, Gish finished her career with a wonderful performance in Lindsay Anderson's *The Whales of August.*

The actress came to Rochester to be honored at ceremonies at the George Eastman House. A reconstructed print of her 1920 classic, *Way Down East,* was shown, accompanied by the Eastman-Dryden orchestra.

Way Down East is the D.W. Griffith melodrama that almost brought Gish's career to a premature close. In the film's famous, exciting conclusion, Gish's character collapses on ice floes that are breaking up on a river. To film that scene, Gish did not use a double. The sequence was staged on the ice at White River Junction, Vt., in zero-degree temperatures. Gish says she was on a slab of ice at least 20 times a day for three weeks.

"For the scene in which my character faints on the ice floe, I thought of a piece of business and suggested it to Mr. Griffith, who thought it was a fine idea. I was always having bright ideas and suffering for them," Gish said. "I suggested that my hand and my hair trail in the water as I lay on the floe, as I drifted toward the falls. Mr. Griffith was delighted with the effect. After a while, my hair froze, and I felt as if my hand was in a flame. To this day, it aches if I'm out in the cold for very long."

Gish said she felt she had to do the stunts herself to make the character real. "We were all so shocked when Mr. Griffith bought *Way Down East* to use it for a film," she said. "It was an old-fashioned melodrama from the previous century, and we never thought it would be successful. If it was going to work, I had to make that silly woman real. So that's why we did the scene. Besides, we didn't have stand-ins in those days."

By the time she did *Way Down East*, Gish and her sister, Dorothy, were veteran stars in the Griffith stable. They met Griffith at his New York studios in 1909 when the child stage actresses came to visit a fellow child actress, Gladys Smith. (They didn't know Smith's name had already been changed to Mary Pickford.) They were introduced to Griffith, who immediately used both sisters and their mother in a crowd scene, as members of an applauding audience. It was the beginning of careers that would eventually earn Dorothy Gish a reputation as a pert, funny film comedienne, and Lillian Gish the label of being the Eleanora Duse of the silent screen and the most successful serious actress in early movies.

From the beginning, Griffith capitalized on Lillian Gish's delicate beauty, often placing her in perilous situations. Eventually, in such films as *Way Down East*, and in her tragic portrayal of an abused child in *Broken Blossoms*, Gish demonstrated remarkable strength of character behind the gentle facade.

Gish left Griffith in the early 1920s to join the growing list of stars at MGM. For that studio, she made a superb series of films – *The White Sister*, *The Scarlet Letter* and *The Wind* – that unfortunately have not been shown as frequently as the Griffith classics. Her film career trailed off in the 1930s, thanks, she argued, to MGM boss Louis B. Mayer. "He told me I was lucky to have an audience, because audiences usually leave you if you have unhappy endings in your films," she remembered. "I have had one unhappy ending after another in my films. But Mayer added that I was on a pedestal in my real life and the fans resented it. 'You've never had a scandal in your real life, and that fact will ruin you,' he said. Mayer added, 'Let me arrange a scandal for you.' I thought about it for a while, but decided it would be too much to have to act in private life as well as in the films. So I said no."

Mayer handed *Anna Karenina,* then in preproduction for Gish, to "that Swedish girl" (Greta Garbo) and let Gish go. Gish headed back to the theater, where she had worked as a child. Before long, her career regained its momentum, but in a different medium. She starred on stage as Ophelia opposite John Gielgud's Hamlet, and appeared opposite Burgess Meredith in *The Star Wagon,* and in touring productions of *Life with Father.*

Gish returned to Hollywood in 1946 as part of the prestigious cast assembled by David O. Selznick for *Duel in the Sun.* Later she played the indomitable Rachel in Charles Laughton's cult classic, *The Night of the Hunter*, and the mother in Huston's *The Unforgiven.*

Gish also starred in television productions, including *Arsenic and Old Lace* (which had originally been written for the Gish sisters years earlier, but they could not work out their schedules when it first came to the stage). She also was the first to play the lead in the TV version of Horton Foote's *A Trip to Bountiful*, for which Geraldine Page won an Oscar when it was remade as a film.

Among her last performances were one as the mother who dies in a hilarious scene in Robert Altman's *The Wedding,* and a cameo in the PBS four-part production of *The Adventures of Huckleberry Finn.*

Gish had the longest lasting career in the history of the movies, making movies from 1912 to 1987. Speaking at age 92, Gish said she had no plans to retire – ever. "What would I do? I keep getting lots of scripts, and I do what I can," she said. Indeed, she would soon begin production on *The Whales of August.*

Asked if she has any particular philosophy about acting, she replied, "You must never let them see you 'act.' Don't act a part – be it."

In a letter written after the release of *Way Down East* in 1920, John Barrymore told D.W. Griffith that Gish's performance was "the most superlatively exquisite and poignantly enchanting thing I have ever seen in my life." He went on to say that he had seen Duse and Sarah Bernhardt and thought Gish matched them "for sheer technical brilliance and great emotional projection, done with almost uncanny simplicity and sincerity."

Although she had done superb work in sound films, Lillian Gish still believed the silent films were the industry's high point. She noted, "Silent film was a universal language. They changed the world. Their power is evident because now the whole world looks like America. These films could be understood everywhere. Do you realize when my book – *The Movies, Mr. Griffith and Me* – was published in 1969, there were enough people in Burma who knew who I was that an edition was printed in the Burmese language?"

ESSENTIAL LILLIAN GISH

The Birth of a Nation
Broken Blossoms
Way Down East
Orphans of the Storm
The Scarlet Letter
The Wind
The Night of the Hunter
The Unforgiven
The Whales of August

JAMES STEWART

James Stewart, one of Hollywood's most beloved actors, talked with me in March 1982, in connection with his appearance at Rochester's George Eastman House to receive the museum's prestigious George Eastman Award. He was then 73. Stewart died in Beverly Hills, CA, in 1997 at 89, but left behind a shelf full of enduring films, including Rear Window, Vertigo, Mr. Smith Goes to Washington, *and* It's a Wonderful Life.

During his two days in Rochester, he put people so amiably at ease that when my wife met him in a reception line after the award ceremony, she immediately threw her arms around him and gave the bemused actor a kiss. "I couldn't help myself," Bonnie told me afterward.

THE EASY-GOING, FRIENDLY, HONEST AND DECENT FILM STYLE OF JAMES STEWART – mixed with an attractive dose of vulnerability and hesitancy – wasn't as natural as it may have seemed.

"It's sort of a trick," said the enduring and talented star. "It's working at the craft so you're competent enough to make it appear 'natural.' Being yourself on camera doesn't really work that way. Filmmaking is a very technical craft."

His efforts over more than four decades and nearly 80 films have been rewarded with five Academy Award nominations, a best actor Oscar, two New York Film Critic best actor awards, and the consistent and strong affection of the movie-going public.

In Rochester, Stewart received his Eastman Award from an old friend, retired Air Force Gen. Edward Peck Curtis, who had been Eastman Kodak's representative in Hollywood after his military career was over. "I've been in Rochester several times," Stewart said, "because of my association with Gen. Curtis, which goes back to my military days." Stewart served in World War II and participated in 20 missions, including bombing raids on Bremen, Frankfurt and Berlin. He was much decorated and was promoted to colonel before his discharge in 1945.

His noted film career has ranged from a quartet of suspense films for Alfred Hitchcock, including *Rear Window* and *Vertigo*, and Westerns for John Ford and Anthony Mann, to light comedies like *Harvey* and heartwarming stories for Frank Capra like *It's a Wonderful Life* and *Mr. Smith Goes to Washington,* as well as George Cukor's *The Philadelphia Story,* for which Stewart won the Oscar. (Most observers believe Academy voters were trying to make up for failing to give Stewart the honor a year earlier for *Mr. Smith Goes to Washington.*)

Stewart said, "*It's a Wonderful Life* is my sentimental favorite. It was the first picture for me and Frank Capra after we got out of the service. It's a true type of film, in that it wasn't from a play or a book or something, but a simply stated idea. It's an honest film with lots of heart."

He said he's also been enthusiastic "about all the Alfred Hitchcock films I've done. I always thought *Rear Window* was an interesting film, and I really liked doing *The Man Who Knew Too Much.*"

Stewart agreed with many critics who suggest his most expert performance was his portrayal of the country lawyer in Otto Preminger's *Anatomy of a Murder.* "It was a beautifully directed character. It also was a tremendous asset to be filming the picture in northern Michigan, where the story actually takes place."

Stewart said everyone working on *Anatomy* was tired all the time because "Duke Ellington came on location to compose the music for the picture. He would work in the hotel dining room at night and after working all day we would hang around all night and listen to the music."

He said he never finds himself wishing he could redo any of his film characters. "That's sort of like doing remakes. When it's up there on the screen, that's it. Of course, I always feel I could've done better."

Stewart admitted, unlike some actors, that he watched his old movies when he had the opportunity. "Yes, I watch them," he said. "I find it interesting. For example, some films are much more effective on television than others, say the Westerns, for example.

"The one that's played the most on TV is *It's a Wonderful Life*," he observed, adding, "The BBC shows it in England every Christmas Eve. It also was very popular on radio on the old Lux Theater. I remember that Lionel Barrymore, Donna Reed, and I used to get together every New Year's Eve for four or five years to do it on the radio."

Stewart was fortunate to have worked for several Hollywood's greatest directors. They also were fortunate, because he was often the focus of some of their best films. Stewart talked to me about his appreciation for some of those directors:

– Alfred Hitchcock: "An original, in a class all by himself. For one thing, he's got a different attitude about it. He gets completely involved in the picture-making process, even to his sense of being part of the public relations of the picture. Most directors stay in the background, but Hitchcock's made himself a well-known public character. He's by far the best-known director ever."

– Frank Capra: "Again, an original. He had his own sort of niche, also in a class by himself. He had the tremendous capability to put heart and sentiment on the screen without it feeling wishy-washy."

– John Ford: "Here again, we have an original. He's the best example of a director who uses the medium to its fullest extent. He believed that if you cannot tell a story on film, visually, you are not using the medium properly. I remember him constantly tearing out pages and pages of script dialogue."

– Anthony Mann: "He was an excellent director who unfortunately died young. He was developing more and more every day. He had just gotten started. We got together on a picture and hit it off. I went on to do eight pictures with him, including *The Man from Laramie* and *The Glenn Miller Story*. He was a very good action man. It is a special talent to make action effective on screen without getting overly violent."

– Otto Preminger: "Another original. Yet he had a different slant. *Anatomy of a Murder* is a good example of Preminger at his best. He takes actual happenings and films them where they occurred and puts them on the screen. We got along wonderfully. I have great respect for him."

– George Cukor: "If you look at his credits, it's a very impressive career. He is noted for being expert [at] directing women. He also uses the medium correctly. He's not as angry at the spoken word as Ford was. But he uses it sparingly. He also gets freshness out of material that's not really new. *The Philadelphia Story,* for example, had been a long-running play."

Did Jimmy Stewart ever have any interest himself in directing?

"I suppose every actor wants to direct at some point, but I never really considered it seriously. I did direct a couple GE theater programs on TV, and a show about the Strategic Air Command. It isn't something you can just do. It's a tremendously difficult and technical job."

Stewart said then that he had no plans to retire. "I don't think retiring is much in an actor's makeup."

He had recently completed his 77th film, *The Magic of Lassie*, which would end up being his last feature film.

He and his wife were also active in wildlife conservation, scouting and other interests. Stewart married Gloria McLean in 1949 and the couple had gone on to become one of the most popular and durable in Hollywood. Asked how they had been able to maintain such a strong marriage in a town not famous for such marriages, he replied, "If I knew the answer to that, I think I could set up shop."

Although he's been in the public eye for 43 years and had been active in many social and philanthropic causes, Stewart developed a mild reputation as a shy, introverted guy. But, he said, "That shyness thing is overrated. I've always felt that in the picture business, your private life is not always your own."

"I've never felt shy in my relationship with the audience."

ESSENTIAL JAMES STEWART

Mr. Smith Goes to Washington
The Shop Around the Corner
The Philadelphia Story
It's a Wonderful Life
Winchester '73
Harvey
Rear Window
The Man Who Knew Too Much
The Spirit of St. Louis
The Man from Laramie
Vertigo
Anatomy of a Murder
The Man Who Shot Liberty Valance

DAVID LEAN

MASTER FILMMAKER DAVID LEAN SAID THERE ALWAYS CAME A TIME WHEN HE HAD TO "kiss a film goodbye." But, only a year before his death in 1991, Lean enjoyed a rekindled affair.

His classic 1962 film, *Lawrence of Arabia*, was restored to its original brilliance, had a triumphal reissue in major cities, and has become a treasure on DVD and Blu-ray. And it continues to climb higher on lists of the greatest films ever made.

Lean couldn't have been happier. That's what he expressed to me during an hour-long interview in a Manhattan hotel in the winter of 1990.

"I think *Lawrence* was the most exciting period of my whole professional life," he said. "A wonderful experience, and it was terrific to shoot in all those places that most people never get to see." Lean's enthusiasm for the restoration – and his joy at the resurgence of interest in the great 27-year-old film – was obvious and infectious.

Though nearly 82, Lean was outgoing, amiable, passionate, and keenly intelligent. Moderately tall, with an impressive shock of white hair, he emphatically underscored key words as he talked.

And, just so you don't assume this is simply a great artist looking back over a career that included *The Bridge Over the River Kwai, Great Expectations, A Passage to India,* and *Doctor Zhivago,* know that Lean at this point had enthusiastically embarked on preproduction for a new film, an epic version of Joseph Conrad's *Nostromo*, which he hoped to begin filming that spring.

It was not to be. Thus, this notoriously slow and meticulous filmmaker finished a brilliant career of more than 40 years with only 16 features to his credits.

The primary topic on this day in New York, of course, was *Lawrence of Arabia*, Lean's Oscar-winning epic with Peter O'Toole as T.E. Lawrence, the eccentric British adventurer who attempted to unite the feuding Bedouin tribes of Arabia during World War I. I was meeting with Lean because the film had just been restored to its original 220 minutes, an effort that took two years for archivist Robert Harris and required complex technology.

Lean himself was called back into the fray because some 20 minutes of the soundtrack were missing – and he had to direct surviving original stars O'Toole, Omar Sharif, Alec Guinness, and others in re-recording moments of dialogue.

"I'm in complete control of a film when I'm doing it – particularly when I'm cutting. I go to a lot of trouble when I'm putting it together," he said. "And then, in the dubbing, when you put in the final sound effects, and the music, and the wind noise, and the rustle of leaves, it suddenly becomes a very real thing, and from that moment on, it takes off and is on its own, and has nothing to do with me at all.

"In this case, though, I went out to Los Angeles for about a month for the finishing touches of the reissue. As I went back into it again, it became mine again. But when we put it on the screen for the Columbia people who'd never seen it, it was off on its own again.

"I remember going to see the premiere when it first came out in Washington in 1962. After, at a dinner party, I was talking to this lady who was very interested in the film and asking all sorts of questions. After a little, she looked at me and said, 'Excuse me, were you there?' and I said, 'I sure was.'

"But even now, as I look at it on the screen, it fools me. The movies are an extraordinary medium. They are very compelling, aren't they?"

Lean said he was "absolutely astounded" when he first heard *Lawrence of Arabia* had been restored, simply because he didn't think it was possible. "Films disintegrate," he explained, "and I'm used to my films disintegrating. I remember, I asked for a 16 mm print of *Great Expectations* once, and I was told, 'We can't get it on a printer.' It shrunk, and the sound was lost.

"In England, at least, it's partly because of the damp weather, but it's also because of the distributor's attitude. If it doesn't make money anymore, it's not worth anything, so they chuck out film reels from the vaults. Now suddenly video's come along, and they're all rushing into the vaults to see what remains."

(Since Lean and I talked, the higher qualities of DVDs and Blu-rays have made it even more important for disc-makers to uncover, polish up and release quality prints. Criterion, for example, eventually put out a beautiful copy of Lean's *Great Expectations*.)

The possibility of video release also prompted the *Lawrence* reissue; a brief theatrical run was an added bonus. If *ever* a film was designed for the big screen, it's *Lawrence*.

The irony of smaller-screen technologies triggering re-issues of his wide-screen epics wasn't lost on Lean, for he was the master of screen visuals. Think of the long shots of tribesmen on camels in *Lawrence*, or the train in the moonlight, scurrying across the countryside in *A Passage to India*, or the deep, cold snows on the steppes of Russia in *Doctor Zhivago*.

Also, after we talked, Lean's films became battle cries in the fight to get the television industry to accept the widescreen letterbox format. The scene most often used to make the argument has Lawrence and his Arab guide on either side of a desert well as Sherif Ali (Omar Sharif) approaches from a great distance away. It's impossible to see all three key characters on the conventional TV screen. Fortunately, the letterbox wars were won: not only are films now routinely letterboxed, but modern flat-screen TVs also employ, naturally, the widescreen dimensions.

Lean said going back to *Lawrence of Arabia* after more than a quarter of a century also allowed him to fine-tune a few key sequences – and to correct one of the most incredible post-production errors in film history.

"When we looked at this restoration for the first time in the studio a few months ago, I said, 'Wait a minute!' I consider myself a deft hand at lefts and rights, and I noticed the camels were going left to right in the first reel, and then right to left in the second reel," Lean said. "We checked and we found that on a change of reel, Peter (O'Toole's) wristwatch jumps from the right wrist to the left wrist. It turns out they'd flopped an entire reel. They flopped the whole damn thing."

The error apparently had been made in the creation of a 35 mm version in 1966. Thus, every theatrical, video or TV print since 1966 included 10 minutes of film with the images reversed.

Lean said he tinkered with a few other aspects of the film as well, including some moments of re-recorded dialogue with Peter O'Toole. After he did it, Lean reported, he told O'Toole, "'You know, Peter, I think you did that better than you did originally.' And he said, 'Well, you know, I've learned a little since then.'"

And then the day came when Lean had to once more let go of *Lawrence*. "I've got a reputation for not letting go of something, but it's absolutely untrue. I will go on and on and on, but then I'll say, that's it.

"And it's the same with takes with an actor. There are some actors who you've rehearsed a bit, and at take two, you assume they'll never get any better. But with other actors, you tickle their talent, and they get better and better, until you say 'print' with take 10."

Lawrence of Arabia obviously reinforced David Lean's already-substantial reputation in 1962. (*The Bridge on the River Kwai* had won seven Oscars, including Best Picture in 1957.)

However, *Lawrence* turned unknown actor Peter O'Toole into an international star. He didn't win the best actor Oscar, but only because he was up against Gregory Peck's iconic portrayal of Atticus Finch. O'Toole's Lawrence remains, in my opinion, the greatest performance that didn't receive an Academy Award.

Ironically, O'Toole wasn't the first choice for the role, or even the second choice. The role was offered to Marlon Brando, but he declined. Next up was Albert Finney, who came very close to doing it.

"We did a four-day test of Finney," Lean said, "He eventually turned it down, and I think it was because of contract terms. I'd guess they wanted to put him under some sort of slave contract. Absolute guess." (It's not a bad guess. Egyptian actor Omar Sharif was "discovered" for *Lawrence*, but had to sign a long-term contract that called for him to receive only a piddling $15,000 a picture for several years.)

When Finney declined, Lean said, "It was panic time. I spent my time in the movie theaters in London. I saw every movie around. I was watching something called *The Day They*

Robbed the Bank of England, and I suddenly saw this chap playing a silly-ass Englishman, sitting on a bank of a river, fishing. And I thought, *That's a good face, and he can certainly act. And,* I thought, *he certainly looks like Lawrence.* The only trouble: he was six-foot-two, and Lawrence was five-foot-five. To cut a long story short, that was it." O'Toole's face and talent beat out height issues.

Lawrence of Arabia also reunited Lean with the character actor who could probably be considered his lucky charm, the great Alec Guinness. Alfred Hitchcock had Jimmy Stewart, John Ford had John Wayne, Martin Scorsese has Robert De Niro. And Lean had Guinness, who had key roles in *Great Expectations, Oliver Twist, The Bridge on the River Kwai* (for which he won the Oscar), *Doctor Zhivago,* and *A Passage to India.* And, in *Lawrence,* he played Arab Prince Feisal.

Lean and Guinness famously fought often. "Alec's agent called it a great big love-hate relationship, and I suppose that's true," Lean said. "But when it goes well, and we see eye-to-eye, we have a good time."

Lean remembered having to trick Guinness during production of *Great Expectations,* their first film together. The actor was fine in rehearsal, "but as soon as he thought we were filming, he'd seize up. He was so shy and nervous. So, when he thought we were rehearsing, I went through an elaborate charade and had the cameras running."

In his autobiography, *Blessings in Disguise,* Guinness wrote that despite their frequent arguing, "I owe David my film career. David is a man of genius cocooned with outrageous charm. Any skill in front of the camera that is still left me is entirely due to his early guidance."

As we talked about his various films, from *Great Expectations* and *Brief Encounter* to *Lawrence* and *Doctor Zhivago,* Lean denied there are any common threads running through them. "You guys (film critics) are always looking for common threads," he said. "I simply have an affection for great love stories and for adventure."

However, a *stylistic* thread is undeniable – Lean was one of the great masters of visual storytelling and visual splendor. Think of the famous moment when Lawrence blows out a match and the film cuts instantly to the burning, sun-drenched desert of Arabia. Many people consider it the greatest single cut in the history of film.

Asked where he acquired such visual acumen, Lean said it was strange. "I was brought up a Quaker, and as a boy I couldn't go to the cinema. It was considered a wicked place. Then we had a woman who worked for us – Mrs. Achetin. She loved movies. I'd go down to the kitchen and talk to her when I was 9 or 10. And she'd tell me what the movies were like. She'd imitate Charlie Chaplin and run around the kitchen, and I'd roar with laughter.

"And then I finally went to the movies. They were magic to me. I saw people – met people, as it were – and saw places I thought I'd never see in real life. It was the opposite of drab suburbia.

"Once I went to the Tivola, and I saw a couple of Rex Ingram's films. He did the first *Four Horsemen of the Apocalypse,*" Lean said. "I realized for the first time that somebody was sitting behind the camera, selecting what it shot.

"I never dreamt of becoming a director, but I got a job in a silent film studio. It was difficult to believe that I had such a privilege. I remember once touching a camera that had photographed such-and-such a picture, and I remember thinking it was a sort of honor to touch it."

After a pause, Lean remembered another influential moment from his youth.

"When I was 10 or 12, an uncle gave me a box Brownie camera. I was a complete dud at school, and it was extraordinary in those days to give such a young boy a camera. I took pictures, and discovered I had a talent for it.

"I can't explain it," Lean said. "Composition is a question of balance. It's like everything else in art. It's the same with writing and music. It's all balance. And I found I had a talent for it."

THE ESSENTIAL DAVID LEAN

Brief Encounter
Great Expectations
Oliver Twist
Hobson's Choice
Summertime
The Bridge on the River Kwai
Lawrence of Arabia
Doctor Zhivago
Ryan's Daughter
A Passage to India

WOODY ALLEN

I began reviewing films as a graduate student at Syracuse University in 1968-1970. I'd hardly call it a job, really. I contributed reviews a few times a month to a suburban advertising tabloid. The pay was pretty basic: the cost of admission to the movie. (Hey, when you're a grad student every little bit helps.) After I met my fellow grad student, and future bride, Bonnie, I insisted they double my salary so she could join me.

An added benefit was the chance one day to attend a luncheon being held by a publicity outfit promoting Take the Money and Run, *a new film by an up-and-coming comedy filmmaker named Woody Allen. Charles Joffe, one of the film's producers, attended.*

And that was my introduction to the world of Woody Allen, a world I've very much enjoyed traveling through over the years. From the silly/brilliant comedies like Bananas *to the more mature work of* Annie Hall *and* Match Point, *Allen has remained for me a major figure in world cinema, one of the great filmmakers. He won an Oscar as recently as 2012 for his screenplay for* Midnight in Paris, *his most popular film in decades.*

I've made sure to see everything he ever made, I read his New Yorker *pieces, I traveled to Manhattan to see one of his Off-Broadway plays (*The Floating Light Bulb*), and Bonnie and I made the pilgrimage to Michael's Pub to catch Allen playing traditional clarinet jazz during one of his famous, sacrosanct Monday night gigs.*

Then, in the fall of 1994, I got the rare opportunity spend a day with Allen on the set of the film that would eventually become Mighty Aphrodite, *and to conduct a no-holds-barred hour-long interview.*

Over my career, I always hated "on-the-set" stories, because as a journalist you're looked down upon by some actors, who expect you to wait in their trailers and often admonish you not to get in their sight line when they're performing. Ugh. I can remember being told that once by grade B action star Dolph Lundgren, and I thought, "Right, what are you doin', Hamlet?"

However, Woody and his actors had no such compunction. I was able to stand next to Woody as he stood next to the camera, directing a scene at the betting windows of Belmont Park Racetrack. Then I was invited to share lunch with Woody and his cast and crew, who ate together on Styrofoam plates on picnic tables. Then we had the interview.

I've also included my choices for "Essential Woody," as well as my version of Woody's famous "what makes life worth living" speech.

IN ONE OF THE BEST-KNOWN EXCERPTS FROM THE WORKS OF WOODY ALLEN, a character answers the question "Why is life worth living?" as follows: "There are certain things I guess that make it worthwhile... Groucho Marx, to name one thing... Willie Mays, the second movement of the Jupiter Symphony and Louis Armstrong's recording of 'Potatohead Blues,' Swedish movies... those incredible apples and pears by Cezanne, the crabs at Sam Wo's..."

That was 15 years ago, in Allen's screenplay for *Manhattan*.

"But I was wrong," Allen says now.

"It's interesting. I got a letter from a lady after that was in the film saying to me that I didn't mention my child, because Meryl Streep and I had a child in that picture. At that time, I had not had children in my (real) life," he says. So "I was mentioning Chinese restaurants and music and everything. Then, when I had children, I realized how correct she was, and how shallow, well, not shallow, but misguided, I had been. Of course, the children would now be the thing I mention. Once you have children, they become the top priority."

By talking personally about a line from his movie, Allen might seem to be mixing up his own life and the lives of his characters. Allen says he has no trouble separating the two, but many of his fans have had a hard time making the distinction.

Perhaps that's why they were especially shocked by Allen's tabloid-style troubles that were publicized shortly before this interview: the explosive breakup of the Farrow-Allen relationship, triggered by the revelation that he had secretly been dating Farrow's 21-year-old adopted daughter, Soon-Yi Previn.

Farrow responded with accusations, eventually judged unfounded, that Allen had molested his and Farrow's adopted daughter, Dylan. Allen, in turn, sued for custody of his children, and lost.

But despite all the turmoil, the court appearances, the nasty name-calling and battles among tag-team lawyers, Woody Allen didn't break stride as one of America's most dependable and distinctive filmmakers. One can argue endlessly about the wisdom or stupidity of his private behavior, but Allen's persistence as an artist can't be denied. During these domestic wars, Allen completed three other films (*Husbands and Wives, Shadows and Fog, Manhattan Murder Mystery*) in addition to a one-act play to be staged in New York City, and a TV film of his play *Don't Drink the Water*. And opening the week we talked was *Bullets Over Broadway*, a film comedy about an idealistic young playwright who becomes entangled with gangsters, molls and a high-strung veteran actress while trying to mount a new play.

The film was the chief topic on a sunny, crisp autumn day. We sat in a glassed-in executive box overlooking Belmont Park, a Long Island racetrack. The 58-year-old Allen had set aside an hour for an interview, part of an obvious effort to make himself more accessible to the media. He'd also been available recently for round-table interviews, occasional magazine pieces, radio sound bites and even a session of meet-the-public computer access.

This interview, though, took place at a movie location for his next film (eventually titled *Mighty Aphrodite*). Nearby, his crew set up a scene for the romantic comedy, in which Allen plays a sportswriter. I mentioned that Allen had managed a lot of work during what must be an especially stressful time in his life.

"But that's because there's no correlation between that situation and my life," he said calmly. "When things were going on it was a matter for lawyers. They'd handle it and I'd go work. People are always surprised that there could be stress in my private life and not in my professional life. But they're two separate things.

"I never lost a step because I never took it seriously. I thought it would all be over in three weeks. I worked at my normal rate because I was not as involved in that as the public and the press. That was their fun and amusement.

"I'm not a workaholic," Allen added, "but I normally am a daily worker. I take plenty of time off to practice my clarinet, to watch basketball games, go for walks. But I do work at a steady pace, which is how people get things done."

Allen sat with his legs crossed. He was wearing the khaki pants, tweed sport coat, open-collar shirt and loafers that are so identified with his image. Moments earlier, he was in character, a sportswriter taking a bimbo girlfriend to place a bet at the racetrack window. The scene was complicated by the choreographed meanderings of about 50 extras, playing bettors. Allen and his crew patiently worked through it and wrapped the scene after eight or nine takes.

Now, as he talked, he shifted gears to *Bullets Over Broadway*.

The film is set in the Broadway of the 1920s, the time of Damon Runyon and assorted Times Square guys and dolls, and the central character is the young playwright played by John Cusack. Clearly, the role would have been perfect for the Woody Allen of an earlier time.

"Age was the only factor when I decided not to play it. I had thought of making the part a college professor who tried his hand in the theater. But it wasn't worth it to force it, because it requires a young, idealistic person, especially for his scenes with the older actress, so Cusack seemed perfect."

Allen said he had the idea for a story about what makes an artist and decided to place it in the old Broadway setting. Runyon was an influence, but only in the most general sense. "I have the same regard for the Broadway area of that time that he did," he reports, "and I feasted on his stuff when I was growing up."

The irony in *Bullets Over Broadway* is that the true artist in the story is its least likely candidate, a mobster's henchman played by Chazz Palminteri.

"That's the theme of the film," Allen explained. "Some people have all the outer trappings of an artist. You're constantly running into people who live in the Village who talk constantly about art and eat the cheese and bread, and have all the debates. In the end, it doesn't matter. When it comes time to do the art, though, it could be anybody who does it, somebody who you least expect to be an artist."

Allen acknowledged that he has no idea how *Bullets Over Broadway* will be received, but he said he was sure of one thing: "There will be people who see this film and will make the wrong connections."

Since he and Farrow broke up, he said, people have been searching for signs, some sort of Rosetta Stone of scandal, amid the dialogue and wisecracks in his films. Allen, though, denies any such intent, even in *Husbands and Wives*, the 1992 film that seemed to many observers like a blueprint for the breakup.

"I know," he says, "and it was totally unrelated and compartmentalized. It was conceived years ago. It had no relation whatsoever to my situation."

But people have been doing that, he said, shrugging, ever since *Take the Money and Run* in 1969. "People thought when *Annie Hall* came out that I grew up in a house under a roller coaster, and that the film showed how Diane Keaton and I met, and how we parted. It's astonishing to me."

Allen said he believes that his recent problems may finally counter such confusion. At a personally troubling time, Allen made three of his most lighthearted and angst-free films – *Manhattan Murder Mystery, Bullets Over Broadway* and the TV production of *Don't Drink the Water.*

"I hope one of the positive by-products of all the awfulness is that there is a more authentic perception of me," Allen says. "Someone like Charlie Chaplin was not the character offstage that he was onscreen. But the difference was perceptible to people because he put on a mustache and a hat and all that. I don't do that. I dress like this when I come to work, and I look like this on the screen. So it's hard for people to make the differentiation.

"I'm very different than the characters I play on the screen, but it's tough for people to understand that. It's possible because there's been so much publicity over the last couple years that they will now have a more authentic way to perceive me. But it's hard to know."

Allen said he's never understood the confusion, because he feels his life has always been an open book. "For some reason, it became fashionable to write in the press that I was reclusive. But I did television shows, I hosted *The Tonight Show* several times, I spoke publicly about my psychoanalysis. I walk the streets in New York. I do my own shopping. I go to Madison Square Garden.

"But people think I sit home, reading Kierkegaard secretly. None of this is so. It's true,

I'm a private person in that I don't like to run down the street signing autographs. I am shy about that. But I've never been closed about anything in my life," he says. "I've gotten a lot of mileage out of it, actually."

And, as promised, here's my version of "why is life worth living."

Near the end of Woody Allen's great 1979 movie *Manhattan*, Allen's character ruminates on the things that make life worth living. The quotation has gone on to be one of the most popular excerpts from his many works.

Before I tackle my version of the quote, here is the original:

"Well, all right, why is life worth living? That's a very good question. Well, there are certain things I guess that make it worthwhile. Uh, like what? Okay. Um, for me ... oh, I would say... what, Groucho Marx, to name one thing... and Willie Mays, and... the second movement of the *Jupiter Symphony*, and... Louie Armstrong's recording of 'Potatohead Blues'... Swedish movies, naturally... *Sentimental Education* by Flaubert... Marlon Brando, Frank Sinatra... those incredible apples and pears by Cezanne... the crabs at Sam Wo's... Tracy's face... "

With the caveat that my wife, children, and grandchildren are truly the key elements that make life worth living, and sticking as close to Woody's formula as possible, here are my choices:

"Well, all right, why is life worth living? That's a very good question. Well, there are certain things I guess that make it worthwhile. Uh, like what? Okay. Um, for me...oh, I would say...what, Ray Charles, to name one thing... and Ernest Hemingway, and... John Coltrane's *A Love Supreme*... and Chuck Berry's recording of 'Johnny B. Goode'... Edward Hopper's paintings, naturally... *Treasure Island* by Stevenson... Humphrey Bogart, Marlon Brando... those incredible Sophia Loren movies by De Sica...the turtle soup at Commander's Palace... Bonnie's face..."

An explanation: My favorite city in which to eat is New Orleans, and Commander's Palace is my favorite Big Easy eatery. Also, I stuck to the Allen formula, but my list would be a little longer, so I could also include the movies of John Ford and Preston Sturges, Steve Cropper's guitar solos, the performances by Duke Ellington's amazing orchestra, and Muhammad Ali's dancing and jabbing in the ring. Oh, and Woody Allen, and, like Woody, Groucho Marx.

ESSENTIAL WOODY ALLEN

The Films: The flat-out funny early comedies, *Take the Money and Run, Bananas, Sleeper,* and *Love and Death;* the prestige breakthroughs, *Annie Hall, Manhattan,* and *Hannah and Her Sisters;* the show-biz tribute trilogy, *The Purple Rose of Cairo, Broadway Danny Rose,* and my all-time favorite Allen picture, *Radio Days;* the oddball technology wonder, *Zelig,* and the later gems, *Match Point* and the Oscar-winning *Midnight in Paris.*
Stand-up Comedy: Much of Woody's early stand-up comedy is still available on record-

ings and mp3s at iTunes and amazon.com, etc. The one essential routine to hear is called "The Moose." (It's also on YouTube in an archive TV version.) It's hysterical.

Short Stories: Woody has written several funny short stories over the decades, especially for the *New Yorker*. All but the most recent volume (*Mere Anarchy*) are collected in *The Insanity Defense*. However, even better is to get the *The Woody Allen Collection*, the audio version of all the things in *The Insanity Defense* and *Mere Anarchy*, with this key added incentive: They are read by Allen himself, which greatly adds to the pleasure. The greatest of the short stories? Probably "The Kugelmass Episode," about a CCNY professor who magically gets to have an affair with Emma Bovary. Its concept is emulated, to a degree, in Allen's film *Midnight in Paris*.

LOUISE BROOKS

It's because I live in Rochester, the home of the George Eastman House, that I've had the chance to meet so many filmmakers and stars of the Golden Age. The Eastman House is one of the world's most important archives for film, film restoration and film artifacts. Through the Eastman House, I've spent time with Lillian Gish, Meryl Streep, Spike Lee, Gregory Peck, Jimmy Stewart, Kim Novak, Lauren Bacall, and Audrey Hepburn. But no relationship was more meaningful to me, or more lasting than that with silent film legend Louise Brooks, and it continued for the last several years of her life, when she lived as a recluse in a small apartment at 7 N. Goodman St., off East Avenue on Rochester's east side.

I wrote about Louise many times, but this piece is my favorite. I wrote it in 2006 to introduce a superb book that features a rich collection of Brooks photos from the George Eastman House collection. They were originally published by Rizzoli New York in Louise Brooks: Lulu Forever, *by Peter Cowie, and are reproduced here with the permission of Rizzoli International Publications, Inc.*

CAN A MOVIE ACTOR BECOME AN ICON WITHOUT HAVING ONE POPULAR MAINSTREAM motion picture to her credit? Louise Brooks did it.

Certainly, she has worthy films to her name and a few breathtaking performances. But all save one are silent films, and three are from Europe. Her few highlights are *Pandora's Box* and *Diary of a Lost Girl*, from Germany's G.W. Pabst; *Prix de Beauté*, a Franco-German silent-sound hybrid; and two American silents – William Wellman's *Beggars of Life* and Howard Hawks' *A Girl in Every Port*.

Brooks came *this* close to having one mainstream hit, when she nearly co-starred with James Cagney in *The Public Enemy*, in a role that, instead, made a star out of Jean Harlow.

But it never happened. Instead, Brooks ended her film career as a co-star in two B-movie Westerns, one with Buck Jones and the other with a pre-stardom John Wayne. She left films and moved on to a dark period in Manhattan, hanging around an Eastside bar, working briefly as a department store clerk and existing largely as a "kept woman."

Brooks might have remained a movie curio, an asterisk in histories of European silent cinema history, were it not for the passionate curiosity of film curator James Card, the first man to head up the film archive at the George Eastman House in Rochester, NY. The motion picture collection at George Eastman House, one of the major film archives in the United States, was begun in 1949 by Card (1915-2000). It is housed in the expansive East Avenue mansion of the late George Eastman, founder of Eastman Kodak Co., along with a world-class museum of photography.

Thanks to Card's vision and unrelenting enthusiasm from '49 to '77, and that of curators who have followed him, The Eastman House film archive continued to grow as a leading force in the field with holdings now of more than 25,000 titles and a collection of stills, posters and papers totaling more than three million artifacts. The Eastman House also is one of America's five great centers of film restoration. Card's devotion was especially strong for the silent era of filmmaking (1895-1928), the Golden Age of Hollywood (the 1920s-1940s), and silent German cinema (which eventually led to the rediscovery of Brooks).

Card regularly championed film history by honoring its pioneers through the creation of the George Eastman Award, which has brought luminaries from Lillian Gish to Audrey Hepburn to the museum. Card also opened the museum's doors to the public through one of the longest running and uninterrupted film screening programs in the United States at the museum's Dryden Theatre.

It was at Dryden screenings that Card began to introduce the public to Brooks' films, and that was where I first saw *Pandora's Box* and *Prix de Beauté*. Though the famous Kenneth Tynan profile of Louise Brooks in *The New Yorker* is generally credited with the launching of the latter-day Brooks cult, Card proudly states in his memoir, *Seductive Cinema*, "It was in 1951, twenty-eight years before the Tynan article, that we began screening Louise Brooks films." And, in 1953, Card brought to Eastman House, and restored, Brooks' three great European films.

Card's passion was infectious. "William Everson told me once that his idea of hell would be to have a great collection of films, but no projector," he said. "My idea of hell is having a great collection of films *and* a projector, but no one to *show* them to."

But Card's greatest find was Louise Brooks herself. Visiting an old friend (and former Rochesterian) John Springer, a veteran Manhattan film publicist, Card mentioned how much he'd love to discover the whereabouts of Louise Brooks. Imagine his shock when Springer said she was a neighbor on the lower East Side. They met, and Card eventually persuaded Brooks to come to Rochester, where she could indulge her recently discovered passion for writing essays about filmmaking by using the resources and films of the Eastman House collection.

She moved to Rochester in 1956 and never left, except for a few brief forays to events in

Paris and Manhattan, where she was honored with special screenings of her films. And she began writing her series of perceptive, witty and insightful articles about fellow stars, film-makers, and making movies in Hollywood and in Europe.

Thus, Brooks became both one of the most important researchers at the Eastman House and one of its greatest objects of research. Kenneth Tynan eventually made his way to Rochester and wrote his much-praised 1978 *New Yorker* article, and Brooks' iconic stature was firmly established.

Upon her death in 1985, Card described her to me as "an extremely realistic and de-manding perfectionist. She was an enormously powerful individual, as a dancer, thinker and searcher for the absolute essence of things.

"I think she'd like to be remembered for her writing rather than her films, but I think she will have the same enduring stature as Humphrey Bogart has," Card continued. "Her performances were really timeless. Her acting was so steady."

John Springer said then, "Card convinced Louise that the great film scholars considered her one of the industry's great fabulous individual women. He really let her realize that she was more than just an old has-been."

And now, more than 20 years after her death, her legend and beauty endure.

Indeed, the Brooks mystique derives as much from her stunning appearance and sense of style as from any of her naturalistic film portrayals. Surely far more people have been engaged by the Brooks depicted in many photographs than by the actress seen in her rare film appearances.

For myself, as I write this, I glance up to see Louise looking back at me from the Edward Steichen portrait on my wall, and I'm reminded of the time I spent with this star-tling woman.

On a shelf of her one-bedroom apartment on Rochester's Goodman Street, Louise Brooks kept a tattered two-volume edition of Marcel Proust's *Remembrance of Things Past.* Every single page of that epic work featured intense ink-pen notations and underlines. The flyleaves were crammed with notes. There was no white space in the book at all. Louise had not simply read Proust – she had devoured him, poring four times through the giant series of novels.

Of all the items in her tiny apartment, that book may say the most about the intensity and the searing intelligence of Louise Brooks. I think I'll remember that book more than anything else about the apartment I frequently visited.

I got to know Louise Brooks in the late 1970s, while researching an article about John Wayne. Brooks had finished her career in 1938 in *Overland Stage Raiders*, a matinee Western that was among Wayne's early films (one year before he achieved stardom in *Stagecoach*). Louise had written about Wayne as the introduction to a book about the actor. When I phoned, she told me she'd be happy to talk about the man she labeled "Duke by Divine Right."

I had often heard from my fellow reporters at the *Democrat & Chronicle* that a once-fa-mous silent screen actress now made her home in Rochester, but this was before the Louise

Brooks revival that brought her into the spotlight.

I talked with Brooks several times after the Wayne conversation, and eventually began visiting her regularly. I lived only six blocks away. As her arthritis and emphysema took greater hold in the last years, the visits also often included little errands. She was difficult as the end approached, for she wanted to remain sharp of mind, but was having trouble doing it. At this last stage, she was still a legend with remarkable stories to tell, but was also increasingly an elderly, infirm woman who simply needed help.

But even in her seventies, Louise Brooks remained a strangely charismatic and sensual woman. Her famous black helmet hairdo had been replaced by a long mane of salt-and-pepper hair, and her weight had dwindled to 80 pounds. Yet her eyes dazzled visitors, and until only the last year or so, her conversation was as crisp, free-spirited and rebellious as ever.

Louise maintained interest in a variety of topics, from the arts to politics. I remember conversations in which we assessed things as diverse as John Travolta's abilities as a dancer and Geraldine Ferraro's nomination for the vice presidency. In both cases, Louise was impressed.

Mostly, though, she *loved* to talk about sex, which she considered one of the most powerful and defining aspects of life. She speculated endlessly about the sex appeal and/or sexual preferences of any number of folks.

Visitors to Rochester often made a pilgrimage to Goodman Street, and they were often former stars themselves, brought to the city for honors at the Eastman House. I was there when Sylvia Sidney came, but her loud, raspy voice and boisterous manner made Louise nervous, and she bad-mouthed Sidney as soon as she'd left. More to her liking was Luise Rainer, whom I escorted to see Brooks. Louise quickly identified with another intellectual, a fellow rebel who couldn't get out of Hollywood quickly enough.

Louise stayed in her unadorned single bed in a tiny bedroom off her austere living room. Visitors would often find the apartment dark, but she'd turn on a light whenever she heard the door open. (Close friends knew her apartment was unlocked in those last years – she'd rather risk burglary or worse than have to get up to answer the door. Friends simply walked in.)

Walking across the living room toward her bedroom, I was always struck with sadness by the sight of her typewriter sitting unused in a corner. The onslaught of emphysema and arthritis eventually made it impossible for her to write, and she refused any offers to tape-record her thoughts or to take dictation. Louise viewed writing as a hands-on art. She wanted to manipulate words and sentences the way a sculptor manipulates clay. If she couldn't do that, she would no longer write.

As she became increasingly convinced that emphysema was making her senile, Louise would write down nearly everything anybody said to her, no matter how insignificant the information. To Louise, the mind was everything, and she fought hard to keep hers alert.

When she talked about her career, one message kept reappearing. "I never wanted to be an actress. I wanted to be a dancer."

But in her last years, she wanted more than anything to be a writer. It could have been the most appropriate vocation for a woman who lived in what Card called "intense isolation."

Despite the resurgence of her fame, Louise never became a happy individual. She seemed particularly struck by the irony that a career as a highly regarded writer came at a time when she was too ill to continue to pursue it. "Now William Shawn wants me to write for *The New Yorker*, and I can't do it," she'd say.

Anyone who met Louise Brooks during her final years in Rochester went away impressed by her caustic wit and incredibly perceptive mind. But for those who'd seen her riveting portrayal in *Pandora's Box* or read her stunning memoir, *Lulu in Hollywood*, there was always a sadness for what might have been – if she'd been properly appreciated and challenged by the filmmakers of her day, if she hadn't so ferociously burned every bridge she ever crossed, and if she'd discovered and unleashed her undeniable skills as a writer at a time when she was better able to fulfill them.

Louise was often the victim of her own impulsive whims. But she deserved better from a life she always approached with unadorned honesty and highly original talent.

ESSENTIAL LOUISE BROOKS

A relatively surprising number of rare Brooks films are available on DVD.
The must-sees are:
G.W. Pabst's *Pandora's Box* and *Diary of a Lost Girl*
Augusto Genina's *Prix de Beauté*
William Wellman's *Beggars of Life* (on *The Actors: Rare Films of Louise Brooks Vol. 3*)

SOPHIA LOREN

HOW'S THIS FOR A FAN STORY?

In my freshman year in 1963 at St. Bonaventure University, my roommate was a nut for Barbra Streisand (who was just emerging out of Greenwich Village bistros as a star, thanks to her first three brilliant albums). He put up what seemed like 100 photos of Streisand on his side of the room. Yes, I admired Streisand's early albums, but I didn't want to look at her constantly.

So, not to be outdone, I began to haunt used-magazine outlets and movie memorabilia shops, and assembled more than 100 photos of Sophia Loren for *my* side of the room. And, I must say, it was the far more popular side of the room when friends visited.

I can't explain my affection for Loren. Actually, I don't imagine I have to. After all, she's long been a world-class beauty. (I remember an interesting magazine article at the time that argued that Sophia's features were all wrong – too big a mouth, eyes too close together, etc. – *but* when she put it all together, perfection!)

Honestly, I also loved Loren as an actress, more so as I became exposed to her superb Italian films. If you saw only Loren's American films, you don't know half the story. Her greatest work, by far, was for Italian filmmaker Vittorio De Sica, and those are the films with which I fell in love and for which she'll long be remembered.

The three masterpieces are *Two Women* (1960), for which she won the first Oscar for an actor performing in a foreign language; *Yesterday, Today, and Tomorrow* (1963), in which she played three great comedic roles (and danced a legendary striptease for her frequent co-star, Marcello Mastroianni); and *Marriage Italian Style* (1964), which also co-starred Mastroianni.

I met Loren (twice), when she came to Rochester as part of two U.S. tours in the mid-'80s, promoting her line of perfume at McCurdy's department store. Each time, I was led into her hotel suite, and she stood there, in graceful elegance, and offered a warm hand. We had brief conversations both times – much to my delight, as you can imagine. And she laughed out loud at my college story.

I only regret that she declined to do any extensive interviews on her visits to Rochester (this was during a dispute with the law in Italy on tax evasion charges, and she was avoiding prying interviews). I would have loved to talk to her at length; her story of rising from poverty and beginning as a crowd extra in *Quo Vadis* is compelling stuff.

Still, we did meet – twice – and had informal conversations. She was gracious and charming. So, yes, there were encounters. And they were memorable.

ESSENTIAL SOPHIA LOREN
Boy on a Dolphin
Desire Under the Elms
Houseboat
It Started in Naples
Two Women
El Cid
Yesterday, Today and Tomorrow
Marriage Italian Style
Arabesque
Sunflower
A Special Day

RAY CHARLES

Of all the artists, actors, directors, and musicians who caught my eye and ear over the decades, none moved me as deeply as Ray Charles. And, among the many blessings of my life, there's the fact that I got to spend some times with Ray, beyond the half-hour interview a journalist might normally enjoy.

I told the story of my special relationship with Ray Charles in a column I wrote a few days after his death, and it follows in this chapter. But first, here's the piece I wrote on the day Ray died.

Ironically, I first heard about it while working at the Rochester International Jazz Festival, interviewing saxophonist David "Fathead" Newman, Ray Charles' primary sax and flute soloist over the years. I went back to the office and wrote the following, before returning to introduce Fathead to a nightclub audience.

Four months after the musician's death, the film biopic Ray *opened to unanimous raves and earned Jamie Fox an Oscar. Ray approved Fox's casting, and he organized the film score before he died.*

MUSIC LOST A BIG PART OF ITS SOUL ON THURSDAY, JUNE 10, 2004. RAY CHARLES, the blind singer and pianist often introduced as "The Genius," died at his Beverly Hills home of acute liver disease, a spokesman said. Family and friends surrounded him. He was 73.

Through a half-century of performing, Charles broke down all the musical barriers – bringing gospel into the blues, playing jazz like a master, crooning top-selling country hits, and leading powerhouse bands, large and small. His many hits included "I Got a Woman," "What I'd Say," "Georgia on My Mind," "Hit the Road, Jack," "Unchain My Heart," and "I Can't Stop Loving You."

"He was very gifted, with so much natural ability," said David "Fathead" Newman, Charles' long-time saxophonist and lifelong friend. Newman, 71, learned of Charles' death during a sound check at the Montage Grille, where he was preparing to play for the Rochester International Jazz Festival. Newman immediately excused himself to go back on-stage to play alone for five minutes. Then he said, "I owe Ray my career. He'll be missed."

Newman, who went on as planned at 6 p.m., said he'd be thinking of Charles while he was on stage. I was honored to introduce Fathead, and will always remember the gasp that greeted us when I told the packed house, "Some of you may not yet know, but we lost Ray Charles today."

Charles was blind at age 7 and orphaned at 15. Yet he rose out of Georgia poverty to become an icon of American music, as readily identifiable by his trademark sunglasses as by his voice.

Though he originally patterned himself after honey-voiced early idols Nat King Cole and Charles Brown, Charles found success when he unleashed his distinctive, rough-hewn baritone. The boxed set of his early Atlantic recordings is not hyperbolic in being called *The Birth of Soul.*

Charles' sound then became a major influence on a generation of other singers, including Van Morrison, Joe Cocker, Bill Medley of the Righteous Brothers, and many more.

"Soul is when you can take a song and make it part of you," Charles once said. "It's a part that's so true, so real, people think it must have happened to you. I'm not satisfied unless I can make them feel what I feel."

"My favorite song is the song that I'm in the mood for at that particular time," he told me in a 1972 interview. "If you've got the blues, you put on something that makes you want to cry more. It's strange but true. Well, I'm the same way."

After forging a substantial R&B and jazz career on Atlantic in the 1950s and early '60s, Charles jumped to ABC-Paramount and explored ballads, big band music and more. His *Modern Sounds in Country and Western Music* was a top-selling album that opened the doors to country to many artists and listeners. His top-selling Grammy winner, "I Can't Stop Loving You," came from that disc. It secured one of 12 Grammys that Charles won, with most honors coming between 1960 and '66, which was the pinnacle of his recording career.

Eventually, Charles toured in his own plane, opened a Los Angeles recording studio and founded his own label, called Tangerine. He performed music and acted in several films, including *The Blues Brothers, Ballad in Blue,* and *Swingin' Along,* and sang the memorable title songs for *The Cincinnati Kid* and *In the Heat of the Night.*

He was equally at home on albums with jazz vibraharpist Milt Jackson and country singer Willie Nelson.

"He left a wonderful legacy of recordings," said saxophonist John Nugent, the producer of the Rochester International Jazz Festival.

Charles was born Ray Charles Robinson in Albany, GA, in 1930. (He later ditched the "Robinson" to avoid confusion with boxing great "Sugar" Ray Robinson.) His father was a handyman and his mother stacked boards in a sawmill. The family moved to Gainesville, FL, when Charles was still a baby.

At 5, Charles witnessed his brother's drowning in a laundry tub. Two years later, he lost his eyesight. Though glaucoma has been suspected, nothing was ever checked.

He tinkered with a neighbor's piano as a child, and later studied music at the Florida School for the Deaf and Blind in St. Augustine. He also learned to play the trumpet, saxophone and clarinet, and to read music in Braille.

Orphaned and finished with schooling at 15, Charles decided to go to the farthest point on a map that he could from Florida. It was Seattle, where he played in local clubs in a group called The Maxim Trio, with Nat Cole as the influence. He also met the teenage Quincy Jones, who became a lifelong friend and musical associate.

Charles played piano with blues and country bands and recorded a few tasty but obscure tracks for the Swingtime label before Atlantic Records bought his contract in 1952. Two years later, Atlantic released the single "I Got a Woman," which created a stir for being the first rhythm and blues record to incorporate gospel chords and vocal inflections. Charles had an even bigger hit with the boogie-based "What I'd Say" in 1959.

Though the music always soared, Charles struggled with a heroin addiction for 20 years. But after an arrest in Boston in 1965, he went cold turkey, by himself, without the aid of a rehab center or hospital.

Charles toured extensively throughout his career, typically playing an hour set, sitting at the piano in front of his orchestra. He'd sway so broadly at the keyboard, he sometimes seemed on the verge of losing his balance. And his legs would kick and stomp with the music. At his final bow each night, following the curtain-dropping "What I'd Say," Charles would mime the action of giving the audience a big hug.

I saw Ray Charles in concert many times, in Rochester, in Pittsburgh, at St. Bonaventure University and in Niagara Falls. My last opportunity came on Oct. 28, 2002, when Ray performed after being presented with the Lifetime Inspiration Award by the Rochester-based Lifetime Assistance Foundation. He told the appreciative audience, "You sure know how to make an old man happy."

Here's the column I wrote a few days after Ray's death. This is where I get personal.

Whatever Ray sang was the truth.

Growing up white in a small Pennsylvania town in the 1950s and early '60s, I had almost no contact with African Americans, and no inroads into the so-called Black Experience.

And then I heard Ray Charles.

Someone once called Ray's voice the voice of man. All I know was, I'd never heard anything as rough-and-tumble spirited, as rock-bottom emotional, as painful and as exuberant. The scream he unleashed before the last verse of "Tell the Truth" was more primal, more wrenching, more free, than anything I'd ever heard. Tell the truth, indeed.

It was time to put aside my teenage musical obsession and get into music of incredible emotional richness. Ray Charles opened the door, and I walked in to hear Sam Cooke, Otis Redding, the Temptations, Sam & Dave.

At my all-white high school, my buddy Mike Byers and I would constantly share our obsession with the latest Ray Charles record. And, forgive me Ray, I even sang "Hit the Road, Jack" at a school assembly.

But Ray the pianist also released fabulous, blues-infused jazz albums. His "Sweet Sixteen Bars" remain for me the sweetest 16 bars in all of music. So that led me to Charlie Parker and Duke Ellington and John Coltrane.

But Ray wasn't done with me. He was also my entree into the arts, contributions, strengths and stories of black America. Ray's music had that profound an effect.

So fast-forward a few years to 1967, my senior year at St. Bonaventure University in Olean, NY. A student came to ask a favor. He knew from my campus radio show that I loved Ray Charles. "He's performing here soon. Would you like to pick him up at the airport and escort him?" Are you kidding?

I didn't have a car, but that was a minor point. I called Mike Byers in Pennsylvania and told him if he could drive his car up to Olean, we'd be Ray's drivers. We were a bit concerned because Mike's college car was an old junker, but we joked, with the irreverence of college kids, "He's blind – he'll never know."

So the day came – along with a rare May snowstorm. We got Ray at the Bradford, PA, airport. He flew in with one of the backup-singing Raelettes. Both climbed into the back seat and we drove them to St. Bonaventure. We stayed with Ray all day.

When Ray shook my hand, he recognized I was a big guy, and he put his hand on my head to see just how big.

During his show that night, Ray thrilled me when he paused after a song to introduce the next, saying "The young man who picked me up at the airport told me this was his favorite song, so I'm going to play 'Georgia on My Mind' for him."

Several years later, I went to interview Ray Charles for the *Rochester Times-Union* before a concert at the Niagara Falls Convention Center. As I entered his dressing room, I mentioned that snowy day in Olean in 1967. Ray extended his hand high above his head, approximating my height.

Surprisingly, Ray Charles had remembered me. Not surprisingly, I'll never forget him.

CHAPTER FIVE

THE FINAL CURTAIN

In this chapter, fittingly called "The Final Curtain," I present some samples of appraisals I wrote when a major star or director died. I developed a bit of a reputation around the office for doing these pieces. I think it may be because I was inspired emotionally when we lost someone whose work meant something to me over my years as a moviegoer. And it was an honor to try to put into words what many filmgoers were feeling.

I've also attached to each appraisal a short list of the essential work by the late artist. Let's start with a glorious dancer ...

FRED ASTAIRE

FRED ASTAIRE DANCED ON THE CEILING IN *ROYAL WEDDING* AND IN MIDAIR IN *THE Belle of New York*. Though delightful, neither stunt was necessary. Filmgoers knew Fred Astaire had been dancing on air from the start. He only touched ground to show his humanity.

The death of Astaire on June 22, 1987, took away one of Hollywood's greatest icons, a supreme talent who changed the face of the movie musical forever. It was Astaire who so eloquently demonstrated how dance could express emotion and tell a story. Though others had danced on screen before him, none before Astaire had found the key to blending the dance and the narrative into seamless entertainment.

Starting with Ginger Rogers and continuing with Vera Ellen, Cyd Charisse, Eleanor Powell and Rita Hayworth, Astaire was famous for his ability to work with a partner. Though he created many memorable solo moments, the lasting Astaire image is of an elegantly attired couple, gracefully swirling around a lavishly appointed set.

Astaire's most important partner, though, was his audience. In his most important films – his early Ginger Rogers movies – Astaire grabbed America by the hand and showed it how to dance its way through the Great Depression. When America sought escape from its woes, it turned to the ultrafashionable, ultraromantic world of Fred Astaire.

It has come to be a part of Hollywood mythology that Astaire's screen test met with this assessment: "Can't sing. Can't act. Balding. Can dance a little." Though the story is now considered apocryphal, it survives because it might have seemed at first glance to be true.

In reality, Astaire was a surprisingly good singer beloved by songwriters for the straightforward and honest interpretation he gave their lyrics. The greatest composers, from Irving Berlin to Cole Porter, fought to contribute songs to an Astaire film. They knew the tunes were in good hands.

Astaire was also a superb actor – not only in the much-lauded character parts he played in his last years, but also in the way he created and embellished one of the most lasting images in screen history.

But, of course, it is as Hollywood's greatest dancer that Fred Astaire will be remembered and most frequently enjoyed. From the start, with his first leading performance in *The Gay Divorcee* in 1934, Astaire took charge of the way dance would be presented in his films, and the purpose it would have in the narrative.

In previous musicals, songs and dance were done in between the plot. "OK, let's stop the story and have a song" was the prevailing attitude. To accommodate this attitude, many early productions were so-called "backstage musicals" that took place in the world of the stage shows, so the musical numbers could be part of the show that the characters were putting on. They didn't have to make sense as plot points.

Astaire, on the other hand, worked hard to fully incorporate his numbers into the plot. Every Astaire number – and there were hundreds – advanced the story and character development.

Think of Astaire and Rogers trying to be at odds with each other in the song "Isn't This a Lovely Day (To Be Caught in the Rain)" from *Top Hat*. Though the dialogue indicates a dismissive attitude between them, their honest emotions of love surface in the way they can't help dancing together.

Or think of Astaire gently lulling Rogers to sleep with a soft-shoe on sand in the same film.

Or how about the shocking sequence in *The Sky's the Limit* when Astaire shows anger and anguish by trashing a bar with his feet? He proved that rage or sorrow could be expressed as clearly in dance as love and joy.

Astaire also showed Hollywood the proper way to photograph dance – by showing all of the dancers' bodies in the shot. He knew it was the dance and not the camera that would carry the day, and that it is the entire body that dances, not just the feet. Tricky partial shots are almost never seen in an Astaire film. (This is a lesson many directors still have not learned; even today, filmmakers often try to get fancy during dance numbers and obscure the scene with cleverness.)

Then there is the issue of pure dance. Though he chose to work in a popular medium and not in the world of fine arts ballet, Fred Astaire is considered by most great dancers and dance critics to have been the finest dancer who ever lived. We are a people who hunger for superlatives; we want to call Fred Astaire "the greatest dancer," and he probably was. But cases can certainly be made for Gene Kelly – and for the great ballet dancers such as

Nureyev and Baryshnikov.

Ultimately, such superlatives aren't important. What is important is that Fred Astaire created sublime art that was also wonderful entertainment, and he did it for the masses, on films and home videos that will be enjoyed for generations to come.

That is the great consolation. Fred Astaire died in Hollywood in 1987, but he'll dance in my living room tonight.

ESSENTIAL FRED ASTAIRE

Top Hat (1935)
Swing Time (1936)
The Gay Divorcee (1934)
Silk Stockings (1957)
Holiday Inn (1942)
The Sky's the Limit (1943)
The Broadway Melody of 1940 (1940) (if only for the "Begin the Beguine" number with Astaire and Eleanor Powell, often cited as the greatest tap exhibition in film)
On the Beach (1959) (best non-dancing role)

GENE KELLY

"GOTTA DANCE! GOTTA DANCE! GOTTA DANCE!" WHEN GENE KELLY SINGS THAT FAMOUS refrain in *Singin' in the Rain*, we believe it. That is a key to his greatness: Kelly, who died Feb. 2, 1996, conveyed such a joyful passion for dance that we are convinced he had no choice. He needed to dance the way you and I need to breathe.

Maybe that's why he didn't care that he was getting soaked as he tapped and splashed and swirled his way through a downpour in the single greatest moment in the history of the movie musical, his performance of the title song from that same *Singin' in the Rain*.

In those moments, Kelly not only expressed the love for what he did, but also displayed immense skill and artistry. With Kelly as their shining light, the MGM movie musicals of the 1940s and '50s became the most glorious of all. *An American in Paris, The Pirate, Invitation to the Dance, On the Town, Summer Stock* and *Singin' in the Rain* – they're all Kelly films, and they're the cream of the crop.

The American Film Institute counts *Singin' in the Rain* among the 10 greatest films ever made, and it was included in the first 25 films designated as national treasures by the Library of Congress.

It remains Kelly's most accessible and popular film, but dance fans may love *An American in Paris* even more. Created in 1951, a year before *Singin' in the Rain, An American in Paris* offers an artful blend of Gershwin music, romantic ballet, the graceful athleticism of Kelly, and the sophisticated charm of his young discovery, Parisian Leslie Caron.

The film was typical of Kelly, for he was a man on a mission. He was determined to win over the masses through the joy of dance – in any form. That's why, at the height of his fame in 1956, Kelly fought and won a battle with his studio to create an all-ballet, no-dialogue film titled *Invitation to the Dance*.

Dance could ask for no better salesman.

Born Eugene Curren Kelly in Pittsburgh on Aug. 23, 1912, he was coerced by his actress mother into taking dance lessons from early childhood. Kelly was more interested in sports. "Actually, I wanted to be a hockey player," he once told me. But eventually he discovered he had a talent for dance, as well as a love for teaching it to others.

Kelly's talents took him from a revue in Pittsburgh to the Broadway stage in 1938. After success in musicals such as Cole Porter's *Leave It to Me* and Rodgers and Hart's *Pal Joey*, he was signed to a Hollywood contract. He made his film debut in 1942 with Judy Garland in *For Me and My Gal*.

Though he also appeared, sometimes quite successfully, in nonmusical roles and directed several nonmusical films (including the 1970 Western *The Cheyenne Social Club*), Kelly obviously will be best remembered for his dancing.

His talent was so distinctive and memorable that it led to one of the longest-running, never-settled debates among movie buffs: Who was Hollywood's greatest dancer, Fred Astaire or Gene Kelly? Kelly once addressed the issue himself in a *Los Angeles Times* interview.

"People would compare us, but we didn't dance alike at all," he said. "Fred danced in tails – everybody wore them before I came out here – but I took off my coat, rolled up my sleeves and danced in sweatshirts and jeans and khakis." But that was only the outward sign of the differences between the two. Astaire, the great symbol of 1930s musicals, was a master of ballroom and tap styles, a stylish romancer on the dance floor and the epitome of black-tie elegance.

Kelly came along a decade later and brought elements from both ends of the dance spectrum. On one hand, he was trained in ballet and incorporated that form into several of his movies. On the other, he was a casual, working-class kind of guy, the man next door.

Kelly stressed this image by often dressing down in his films. But there was a practical basis for the white socks he often wore: He thought they helped viewers follow his feet.

He also brought a certain athletic masculinity to dance, which probably made it easier for some boys to survive dance lessons in the 1950s.

While Astaire shone best in duets with women (particularly Ginger Rogers) or in solo numbers, Kelly often danced "with the boys." He also loved to work in odd couplings (including one memorable sequence with cartoon characters Tom and Jerry in 1945's *Anchors Aweigh*).

In *Can't Help Singin'*, a definitive history of the American musical on stage and screen, critic Gerald Mast writes that Kelly, "more than any other MGM performer, rose to the big time by becoming big-time in his heart." Mast also addresses the Astaire-Kelly debate, explaining,

"While Astaire seeks a private place, a personal stage where he and one other can dance, Kelly takes dancing with him into the everyday world."

That's true: Splashin' in the rain, Gene Kelly took dance out of the ballrooms and into our lives. Now, thanks to DVDs and downloads, and as I said about the late Fred Astaire, we will continue to welcome Gene Kelly into our living rooms. To watch Kelly move while he sings, "Gotta dance," I just gotta push "Play" on my DVD player.

ESSENTIAL GENE KELLY
The Cross of Lorraine (1943) (non-dancing)
Singin' in the Rain (1952)
An American in Paris (1951)
On the Town (1949)
Brigadoon (1954)
Anchors Aweigh (1945)
The Pirate (1948)
Summer Stock (1950)
Inherit the Wind (1960) (non-dancing)

MARLON BRANDO

I often say I've had two favorite actors: one pre-Brando, the other post-Brando. The pre-Brando actor is Humphrey Bogart. The post-Brando actor is, well, Marlon Brando. He was the great demarcation line for a seismic shift in acting styles. What follows is my appraisal of Brando upon his death on July 1, 2004. Then there's a more personal and specific discussion of his brilliance as an actor.

MARLON BRANDO – THE MOST ORIGINAL, INFLUENTIAL AND CHARISMATIC ACTOR OF his age – died Thursday, July 1, 2004 of lung failure at UCLA Medical Center in Los Angeles. The star of such cinema classics as *On the Waterfront* and *The Godfather* was 80.

When Brando burst upon the Hollywood scene in the early '50s in *The Men* and *A Streetcar Named Desire*, he revolutionized the concept of acting, bringing the moody, visceral Method style to the fore. Though early critics complained that he seemed to be mumbling, audiences found an explosive reality unlike anything they had seen before.

Brando's performances paved the way for modern screen actors, from such contemporaries as James Dean and Montgomery Clift to such later stars as Robert De Niro, Al Pacino, Meryl Streep, and Johnny Depp. "He influenced more young actors of my generation than any actor," longtime friend and *Godfather* co-star James Caan told The Associated Press. "Anyone who denies this never understood what it was all about."

Francis Ford Coppola, who directed *The Godfather*, told reporters, "Marlon would hate the idea of people chiming in to give their comments about his death. All I'll say is that it makes me sad he's gone."

Difficult and self-possessed, Brando was never bland on screen. Even his most infamous failures, for example as the flamboyant title character in *The Island of Dr. Moreau* or the gunslinger in drag in *The Missouri Breaks*, were the results of extremely daring choices. One of the many ideas that worked was having Don Corleone, his character in *The Godfather*, play with an orange slice in his mouth just before the character's death.

Brando never settled for the conventional, onscreen or in life. Both realms were peppered with eccentricities and behavior that became Brando lore:

– As a young actor in Hollywood, he often infuriated studio suits by wearing blue jeans to functions and by sitting in a haze in the corner, banging on bongos.

– After falling hard for Tahitian culture and women during the filming of 1962's *Mutiny on the Bounty*, he bought a Pacific island, which later became a financial burden.

– He seemed to have little control over his weight, often eating half-gallons of pistachio ice cream in one sitting. When he showed up for his key role in *Apocalypse Now*, director Coppola had to hide as much of the actor's ballooning weight in dark shadows as he could, since he was portraying a supposedly robust soldier.

– Brando, who became a passionate advocate of Native American rights and visited Wounded Knee during an Indian rights demonstration, sent an actress who claimed to be an Indian named Sacheen Littlefeather onto the stage to accept his 1972 Oscar for *The Godfather*.

– He often refused to learn the lines of a script, preferring the placement of cue cards around the set or the use of a hearing aid into which an assistant would say the lines just before Brando was to act them. Though some viewed his approach as lazy, Brando argued that he was simply keeping the dialogue as spontaneous as possible, enhancing the reality.

– Despite his legendary status, Brando's reputation for trouble had limited his opportunities by the early '70s. But Brando so desired the role of Don Corleone that he was willing to make a screen test with Coppola. He stuffed Kleenex in his cheeks to achieve the Don's thick-jowled look, and he spoke in a deep, harsh whisper that became much imitated.

– Isolated in a home atop Los Angeles' Mulholland Drive next door to Jack Nicholson, Brando often connected with the outside world incognito, using fake voices to converse with fellow ham radio operators.

His later years were marred by family tragedy. His son, Christian Brando, shot and killed the lover of his half-sister, Cheyenne. Christian was jailed after a celebrity trial that included Marlon's painful testimony. Five years later, Cheyenne committed suicide. Legal fees reportedly drained the actor's fortune.

Yet, through it all, Brando remained a two-time Academy Award winner who was routinely labeled the greatest actor of his generation. His last screen performance was in 2001's *The Score*, with Robert De Niro and Edward Norton, two of the many actors who reflect his influence. Typically, in *The Score* Brando chose an unorthodox approach for his character, playing him gay when the script indicated no such characteristic.

Other memorable performances included the biker in *The Wild One;* a controversial Method approach to Shakespeare as Marc Antony in *Julius Caesar;* Emiliano Zapata in *Viva Zapata!;* Paul, the enigmatic and lustful loner in *Last Tango in Paris;* and Carmine Sabatini, a witty take-off on his own Don Corleone character, in *The Freshman*.

An Omaha, NE, native, Marlon "Bud" Brando developed a difficult reputation early, getting kicked out of private schools and a military academy. Influenced by an artistic mother but pushed by a stern father, Brando eventually gravitated to New York and into an acting career.

He studied Constantin Stanislavsky's techniques at the New School before enrolling at the Actors Studio to work with Lee Strasberg and Stella Adler. Brando applied his Method training to summer stock and eventually landed a Broadway role in 1944 in *I Remember Mama*. But nothing prepared audiences for his volatile, landmark portrayal of the brutish Stanley Kowalski in Tennessee Williams' *A Streetcar Named Desire in* 1947. The play remains a legend and Brando's cries of "Stella!" echo through the collective Broadway memory.

He made the leap to film with a supporting role as a paraplegic in the post-war drama *The Men* in 1950, and then re-created his Kowalski role on film for director Elia Kazan in 1951. Kazan and Brando reteamed for *On the Waterfront* in 1954, and the actor won his first best actor Oscar.

Brando made fewer than 40 films, a relatively small legacy for an 80-year-old actor of such protean talent. A contrary fellow if ever there was one, Brando followed his own eccentric muse, which clearly limited his output. But his relative lack of productivity could never overshadow the immense scope of his unique vision and his one-of-a-kind talent.

Marlon Brando was the actor as artistic rebel, and he changed the face of American film and theater. Throughout his career, you could almost hear him aping Johnny, his biker character in 1953's *The Wild One*. Johnny is asked, "What are you rebelling against?" He replies, "Whaddya got?"

Brando's Method

An anguished man stands in a yard, his torn T-shirt soaked with rain. He looks to a second-floor apartment, grabs the sides of his head and bellows, "Stella!" It was Marlon Brando in *A Streetcar Named Desire*, first on a New York stage and then on the world's movie screens. And he was launching a revolution.

It was a cry from an emotional depth that audiences had not yet been exposed to, a level of feeling that was both disturbing and exciting.

It was the cry that shook the acting profession, challenging actors to plumb untapped personal emotions, giving birth to the type of acting that is now universally accepted as the norm on stage and screen.

It was Method acting, a style evolved from the teachings of Russian director Constantin Stanislavsky. He believed actors must psychologically identify with their characters and that this identification is at least as important as mastery of vocal projection or body movement. It was no longer enough to observe human behavior and copy it. Now you had to look inward. It wasn't enough to do something. Now you had to understand what motivated the action.

Method acting was first popularized in the United States by the Group Theatre and later by Lee Strasberg at the Actors Studio, both in Manhattan. Marlon Brando became the style's first great proponent.

Though Brando's work in *A Streetcar Named Desire* set the stage, Method acting really captured the public's imagination with the actor's Oscar-winning portrayal of Terry Malloy, the former boxer turned informant in 1954's *On the Waterfront*.

Acting is about choices, and Brando's choices in *On the Waterfront* are sublime. Consider the moment in the park when co-star Eva Marie Saint drops her delicate glove. Kazan kept the cameras moving. Most actors would simply pick up the glove and hand it to Saint. Brando picks it up and playfully slips his hand into it. It's a tight fit, a quiet but potent way to demonstrate his character's size and brute strength in the face of the gentle girl at his side.

Later in *Waterfront*, Brando and his co-star, Rod Steiger (as his brother), enact what many consider the greatest scene in all of film. They're in the back seat of a taxi, where the windows are covered, strangely, with blinds (to hide the fact that the low-budget scene was being shot in a garage, with stagehands shaking the car to simulate movement).

The scene ends famously with Malloy's famous, impassioned regrets about what could have been: "You don't understand. I coulda had class. I coulda been a contender. I coulda been somebody, instead of a bum, which is what I am, let's face it."

Brando says the line with a deeply pained reality, creating a belief in the character that fuels the entire, Oscar-winning film. Whenever Brando's imagination melded perfectly with a character – as it did in *On the Waterfront* – we believed everything he said.

ESSENTIAL MARLON BRANDO

A Streetcar Named Desire (1951)

Viva Zapata! (1952)

Julius Caesar (1953)

The Wild One (1953)

On the Waterfront (1954)

The Fugitive Kind (1959)

One-Eyed Jacks (1961)

Mutiny on the Bounty (1962)

The Chase (1966)

Reflections in a Golden Eye (1967)

The Godfather (1972)

Last Tango in Paris (1972)

Missouri Breaks (1976)

Apocalypse Now Redux (2001)

The Freshman (1990)

KATHARINE HEPBURN

KATHARINE HEPBURN'S HIGH STANDARDS WERE HER HALLMARK.

For about 70 years, until her death on June 29, 2003, Katharine Hepburn was the glorious aristocrat of motion pictures. The all-time Oscar champ, with 12 best actress nominations and four statuettes, Hepburn had a prodigious acting talent that was equally on the nose in screwball comedies and in Eugene O'Neill dramas. And she had the strength of character to go toe-to-toe with some of the most robust actors of her time, from Cary Grant and Humphrey Bogart to Peter O'Toole and John Wayne. At a time when women frequently were window dressing in films, Hepburn always put herself on an equal footing – at least – with her male co-stars.

Most famously, she teamed with Spencer Tracy in nine movies, creating a memorable team that was to the movies what Alfred Lunt and Lynn Fontaine were to the stage. Tracy and Hepburn were the reigning royalty of the cinema, a perfect blend of contrasting elements. He was rugged, substantial and weighty; she was smooth, graceful and light as a sprite. Though each was a superb actor, as a team member, each made the other better. Garson Kanin, the playwright (and Rochester native) who helped bring them together, once wrote of the coupling that "rich and vibrant though it was in the beginning, the ripening years brought it to a rare perfection."

It wasn't public knowledge at the time, but Hepburn and Tracy also engaged in a passionate love affair that lasted from their meeting in *Woman of the Year* in 1942 until Tracy's death, just after the completion of *Guess Who's Coming to Dinner* in 1967.

Born 96 years ago in Hartford, CT, Katharine Houghton Hepburn had blue-blood New England roots, impossibly high cheekbones and even higher artistic standards. She always credited her physician father and her highly opinionated, suffragist mother for her lifelong intellectual curiosity and determined independence.

Many years after her mother's death, Hepburn summed up her mother's message by writing in her 1991 memoir, *Me*, "Don't give in. Fight for your future. Independence is the only solution. Women are as good as men. Onward!" It was probably no coincidence that she so often played accomplished women – a lawyer, a newspaper reporter, a pro golfer.

Her belief in sexual equality extended to her wardrobe; she was one of the first women in Hollywood to regularly appear in slacks. (Her influence was so strong that she received an award from a fashion organization for helping to put women in pants.)

Starting with her memorable role as a middle-aged spinster in 1951's *The African Queen* and continuing into the 1990s, Hepburn blazed another trail: She maintained her status as a leading lady despite the onrush of age. Three of her record four Oscars came after she was 60. Actresses then and now have acted into their 60s and 70s, but usually in supporting roles (Judi Dench, for example). But Hepburn always was a lead performer and never saw her age as something to hide. Obviously, Meryl Streep has followed Hepburn's lead.

Though Hepburn's voice initially was considered too thin and reedy for an actor, eventually it became one of the most recognizable instruments on the planet. She spoke with superb articulation and with a specific if indeterminate accent that suggested elegance and intelligence. As David Thomson writes in *The New Biographical Dictionary of Film*, "Her very voice rose above the mainstream, like a lace hem being lifted above mud."

Hepburn was a star almost from the start. In only her second year in Hollywood, 1933, Hepburn won an Oscar for *Morning Glory* in addition to filming her all-time personal favorite film, *Little Women*. But the mid-'30s went up and down for Hepburn. A few misguided film roles, forced on her by studio bosses, led a group of exhibitors to place an ad in the Hollywood trades declaring Hepburn "box office poison."

The exhibitors knocked Hepburn's perceived lack of sex appeal. And undeniably, Hepburn never sent out conventional sexual vibes, compared with the eternally mysterious Greta Garbo of the '30s or the voluptuous Marilyn Monroe or Sophia Loren of the '50s and '60s. But Hepburn had an austere beauty, a witty intelligence, impressive integrity and self-confidence – elements the public always embraced more than the exhibitors might have expected. Hepburn took the "poison" rap as a challenge and bounced back with three smart movies – a trio of the greatest screwball comedies ever made: *Bringing Up Baby, Holiday* and *The Philadelphia Story*. There was no looking back.

Late in her career she occasionally recharged her batteries on the stage. In 1970, she starred in *Coco*, a Broadway musical on the life and times of Coco Chanel. The show brought Hepburn to Rochester in February 1971, where I saw her during the five-night run. The show was splashy and entertaining, but certainly not remarkable. Like everyone else, I was there to see Hepburn – and she did not disappoint.

I still remember her entrance as she walked with bounce and determination down a long, curved stairway at center stage. Her performance was more memorable than the show; even her singing was uniquely affecting, if not of typical Broadway quality.

By the mid-'90s, Hepburn's career had slowed to an occasional made-for-TV film or a small movie cameo. In later years, her appearances were marked by an unmistakable shaking of her head and extremities, reportedly caused by "essential tremor" and not the Parkinson's disease many believed she had.

Hepburn kept her longtime brownstone in Manhattan and was frequently spotted around town on a bicycle. But in her last years, she lived increasingly in her beloved Connecticut home along the Connecticut River, where she died, the last surviving legend of Hollywood's Golden Age – and one of the reasons it had such a glow.

THE ESSENTIAL KATHARINE HEPBURN

(With Cary Grant): *Bringing Up Baby* (1938), *Holiday* (1938), and *The Philadelphia Story* (1940).

(With Spencer Tracy): *Woman of the Year* (1942), *State of the Union* (1949), *Adam's Rib* (1949), *Pat and Mike* (1952), *Desk Set* (1957), and *Guess Who's Coming to Dinner* (1967).

These classics: *Little Women* (1933), *The African Queen* (1951), *Summertime* (1955), *A Long Day's Journey into Night* (1962), *The Lion in Winter* (1968), and *On Golden Pond* (1981).

ELIA KAZAN

ARTHUR MILLER, TENNESSEE WILLIAMS, MARLON BRANDO, JAMES DEAN, WARREN Beatty and even Andy Griffith. These artists came to dominate the theater and films of mid-20th century America – in large part because of the vision of Elia Kazan.

The 94-year-old Kazan, arguably the most original and influential filmmaker and theater director of the 1950s, died Sept. 28, 2003, at his Manhattan home. He presented audiences with a shockingly new way to look at the world. His blending of a gritty and combative realism with a surprising, poetic lyricism was unlike anything that had been seen before on a movie screen or a stage.

Miller's *Death of a Salesman* and Williams' *A Streetcar Named Desire* were both directed on Broadway by Kazan. But the director's passionate, uncompromising film work was even more influential, including the screen adaptation of *Streetcar*, *A Face in the Crowd* (with Griffith's breakthrough performance), and the landmark dockworkers drama *On the Waterfront*, which won eight Oscars.

His earlier films were replete with a social fire that first struck in left-wing organizations and theater groups of his youth. *Gentlemen's Agreement*, for example, examined anti-Semitism in America, while *Pinky* portrayed a black woman trying to pass for white in a racist society.

As a filmmaker, Kazan tussled frequently with studios and censors because he insisted on presenting a daring, mature approach to human relations, behavior, language and sexuality. But Kazan's work with actors may be his greatest legacy. As a co-founder of the Actors Studio and a proponent of the Method approach to acting, Kazan used his films to launch the careers of several performers who espoused the motivation-centered, immersion acting style. They included James Dean, Karl Malden, Kim Hunter, Warren Beatty and especially Marlon Brando.

It's unlikely that any actor before or since has electrified and divided audiences as much as Brando did in both the stage and film versions of *A Streetcar Named Desire,* and even more as dockworker Terry Malloy in *On the Waterfront.* Though Brando's acting under Kazan was dismissed by traditionalists as mumbling, others appreciated it for its affecting realism. Method has become the dominant film acting style in the decades since Brando's "I coulda been a contender" speech in *Waterfront.*

Despite Kazan's obvious importance, his life has long been shadowed by his behavior in the Red-baiting days of the House Un-American Activities Committee. Kazan did name names before the committee in 1952 and has been ostracized by many in the arts community in the decades since.

But this great artist's talent and influence are undeniable. Regardless of his personal flaws, it is appropriate to consider the words Arthur Miller put in the mouth of Willy Loman's widow in *Death of a Salesman:* "Attention must finally be paid to such a man."

ESSENTIAL ELIA KAZAN

Gentleman's Agreement (1947)
Panic in the Streets (1950)
A Streetcar Named Desire (1951)
Viva Zapata! (1952)
On the Waterfront (1954)
East of Eden (1955)
Baby Doll (1956)
A Face in the Crowd (1957)
Splendor in the Grass (1961)
America, America (1963)

JACK LEMMON

IN THE GREATEST EXIT LINE IN MOVIE HISTORY, IN *SOME LIKE IT HOT*, JOE E. BROWN tells Jack Lemmon, "Nobody's perfect." He could have added, "But you're mighty close."

Lemmon, who died June 27, 2001 at 76, earned two Oscars and six other nominations.

He was equally skilled in two arenas: at home amid laughs in *The Odd Couple* and *Grumpy Old Men,* and in searing drama in *The Days of Wine and Roses* and *Glengarry Glen Ross.* Often, Lemmon's sensitivity and range balanced comedy and drama in such projects as *The Apartment.*

It's no wonder Lemmon was the favorite actor of legendary director Billy Wilder, who starred him in seven films. Lemmon's drag-dressing, tango-dancing Daphne in Wilder's *Some Like It Hot* – which many consider the greatest comedy Hollywood ever produced – was just one of at least a dozen especially memorable characters brought to life by the talented actor in 53 years of work.

The Boston-born son of the owner of a doughnut factory, Lemmon followed his prep school and Harvard classes with a stint in the Navy and work in radio and the theater.

He first grabbed attention in 1955 as the hapless Ensign Pulver in *Mister Roberts*, making us laugh when he jammed the ship's washing machine with soap suds and then triggering our tears as he reacted to the tragic death of Henry Fonda's character. The role earned the relative newcomer his first Oscar nomination. With Pulver, Lemmon established the template for many of his comedic roles: an eager, well-intentioned klutz with a streak of decency, frequently swimming upstream against a fickle fate. It was a character that would show up, with subtle differences, as the fastidious Felix in *The Odd Couple*, as the belittled office worker with the key to The *Apartment,* as the beleaguered *Out-of-Towner,* and as one of the *Grumpy Old Men.*

Lemmon's pairing with Walter Matthau – an equally great (but different) comedic actor – as Felix and Oscar created the ultimate yin and yang of comedy film characters. Until Matthau's death last July 1, their chemistry remained perfect both on screen in a dozen films and off screen in their friendship.

"Matthau didn't do anything wrong. Lemmon didn't do anything wrong," Wilder, who directed the pair in three films, says in the book *Conversations With Wilder*. "I would like to make pictures with them all my life."

Lemmon, though, also was a superb dramatic actor, a point he proved repeatedly, starting with his wrenching, Oscar-nominated portrait of an alcoholic in *The Days of Wine and Roses* in 1962. He reinforced his interest in serious themes with his Oscar-winning portrayal of desperate Harry Stoner in 1973's *Save the Tiger*. Lemmon plays a scheming, bankrupt factory owner who stoops to arson. The role, which he did for union scale, demonstrates a seldom-discussed aspect of Lemmon's greatness: his willingness to explore dark, edgy parts and disturbing subjects.

Other aggressive film roles included the nuclear-plant whistle-blower in *The China Syndrome*, the father seeking his kidnapped son in the Third World in *Missing*, and the jaded parish priest in *Mass Appeal*.

He also starred in a well-received 1985 Broadway revival of Eugene O'Neill's *A Long Day's Journey Into Night*. One of his sons was played by the up-and-coming Kevin Spacey, who has considered Lemmon a mentor ever since.

While some of his contemporaries drifted into semi-retirement or easy paydays, Lemmon still sought out edgier projects, including Oliver Stone's *JFK*, Robert Altman's *Short Cuts*, David Mamet's *Glengarry Glen Ross*, and Kenneth Branagh's *Hamlet*. Late in life, Lemmon also contributed first-rate work to the television revivals of *12 Angry Men* and *Inherit the Wind*.

His last major role was his 1999 TV portrayal of Morrie Schwartz in *Tuesdays With Morrie*. The terminally ill Morrie taught one of his former students the importance of living life to the fullest.

That's what Jack Lemmon did for all of us, in an impressive and affecting half-century of performances.

ESSENTIAL JACK LEMON

Mister Roberts (1955)	*The Out of Towners* (1970)
Some Like It Hot (1959)	*Save the Tiger* (1973)
The Apartment (1960)	*The China Syndrome* (1979)
Days of Wine and Roses (1962)	*Buddy, Buddy* (1981)
Irma la Douce (1963)	*Missing* (1982)
The Fortune Cookie (1966)	*Glengarry Glen Ross* (1992)
The Odd Couple (1968)	*Grumpy Old Men* (1993)

STANLEY KUBRICK

GREAT FILMMAKERS ARE RARE ARTISTS WHO TEACH US NEW WAYS TO SEE. STANLEY Kubrick, who died March 7, 1999, at 70, was a great filmmaker.

And so many of the visions he brought us remain firmly in the mind's eye: a bone thrown by a caveman turning into a spaceship in *2001: A Space Odyssey;* a demented Malcolm MacDowell in *A Clockwork Orange* beating a woman to death with a giant phallic statue to the tune of "Singin' in the Rain"; Jack Nicholson's nightmarish encounters with the dark spirits of the Overlook Hotel in *The Shining;* and the utterly debased and dehumanized soldier, sitting in a latrine in *Full Metal Jacket* with a gun barrel in his mouth.

Who will ever forget All-American cowboy Slim Pickens in *Dr. Strangelove,* riding a hydrogen bomb to oblivion as if it's a bucking bronco? He slaps the sides of the bomb with his Stetson and yippee-ki-yays like there was no tomorrow. And, guess what: There wasn't.

In such films, Kubrick confronted his audiences with an audacious daring and unique visions, the likes of which hadn't been seen in Hollywood since Orson Welles.

Like Welles, Kubrick fled to Europe, preferring to live and work in England. But unlike Welles, Kubrick managed to keep working through the studio system and still preserve his eccentric artistry. Perhaps because at least some of his films had been major successes, his meticulous, infamously slow work process and odd ideas were tolerated.

Famous for insisting on innumerable takes and retakes, and for reworking films in post-production, Kubrick adhered to only one schedule: his own. He made only 13 features in nearly a half-century of work. His films were rare events. But they *were* events.

The last example – *Eyes Wide Shut,* with Tom Cruise and Nicole Kidman – was notorious for its long delays and reshoots. A sexual thriller, *Eyes Wide Shut* was shot in great secrecy on sound stages in England over 15 months. Like many Kubrick films, it puzzled some viewers, frustrated others, and thrilled still others.

Like a great trapeze artist, Kubrick took chance after chance with risky material and never used a net. And though an obvious master of innovative technique, he explored ideas that were even more challenging, typically revolving around mankind's quest for meaning in an increasingly complex and oppressive world.

Kubrick's most famous film – *2001* – was typical. The director instinctively understood that to convey a warning on the threat of technology in modern society, he would have to make a film that was, itself, a technological landmark.

Whether his source material was a 17th-century novel like *Barry Lyndon* or a modern pop horror novel like *The Shining,* Kubrick put his personal stamp on every film he made over his nearly half-century of work. No filmmaker, for example, more consistently cast aside sentiment and warmth to concentrate fully on intellectual issues and philosophical concerns.

Though dark humor was found in all his films, Kubrick rarely turned fully to comedy. The one exception, of course, was *Dr. Strangelove,* when he proved that audiences will even laugh – uproariously – at the portrayal of the nuclear obliteration of humankind.

A Kubrick film usually offered an inward journey both for the central character and for the filmgoer. The ending of *2001* is justifiably famous (or infamous) for the mind-altering stream-of-consciousness "trip" in the final reel. But, really, every Kubrick film from the early '60s onward took the filmgoer's mind for a ride.

Kubrick was notably a recluse, and he rarely granted interviews. But he once explained his filmmaking philosophy in a *Playboy* interview. He said his goal was to create "a visual experience (that) directly penetrates the subconscious with an emotional and philosophical content … just as music does."

"Kubrick strikes me as a giant," Orson Welles once said. Fellow director Sidney Lumet put it another way: "Each month Stanley Kubrick isn't making films is a loss to everybody."

Now that he's gone, we'll realize that more than ever.

ESSENTIAL STANLEY KUBRICK

The Killing (1956)
Paths of Glory (1957)
Spartacus (1960)
Lolita (1962)
Dr. Strangelove (1964)
2001: A Space Odyssey (1968)
A Clockwork Orange (1971)
Barry Lyndon (1975)
The Shining (1980)
Full Metal Jacket (1987)
Eyes Wide Shut (1999)

INGMAR BERGMAN

IN MY YOUTH, GROWING UP IN A SMALL PENNSYLVANIA TOWN, I HAD NO EXPOSURE TO any films beyond those in the Hollywood spectrum. The only time I saw a foreign film before college was during a visit to my older brother, when he was in college in Pittsburgh, and he made me swear not to tell our parents that he was going to sneak me into *And God Created Woman*, the then-scandalous French film with a naked Brigitte Bardot. (By today's standards, it'd probably earn a PG-13.)

Flash forward to St. Bonaventure University, where a professor was trying to get a film club going during my freshman year in 1964. He invited students to a basement classroom for a screening. (Since only four or five showed up, it was the one and only meeting of the group.)

The professor showed a scratchy 16 mm print of Ingmar Bergman's *The Virgin Spring*, and I was dumbfounded. This brilliant medieval tale of rape and a father's horrific revenge opened my eyes to a new level of emotional, philosophical and even downright metaphysical cinema. It was the point when my love of the movies took on a world view, which is something I've never lost, and also something I sometimes fear is missing from the film interests of many younger viewers today.

Bergman's death (on July 30, 2007) brought those memories rushing back, along with so many images. Film employs a visual language, and the memories are visual and not necessarily of dialogue. With Bergman, I remember:

The specter of death leading his victims across the horizon in *The Seventh Seal*; the feuding couple in bed, realizing their relationship is ending, in *Scenes from a Marriage*; the old man seeing the ghosts of his youth in *Wild Strawberries*; the boy exploring with wide-eyed wonder the gift of a magic lantern (a precursor of a movie projector) in the luscious *Fanny and Alexander*; the two faces molding into one personality in *Persona*; and so many more.

In the wrenching *Cries and Whispers*, each scene fades to blood red, instead of the standard black, because, Bergman said, "I've always imagined red as the color of the soul."

Bergman also famously pioneered the use of the extreme close-up, attempting to find the human soul or psyche within his characters. His partner in this effort was the great cinematographer Sven Nykvist.

Bergman was also well-served (and vice versa) by a stable of superb actors, including Max von Sydow, Liv Ullmann and Bibi Andersson, who've also done American films, and others, like Gunnar Björnstrand, Ingrid Thulin, Harriet Andersson and Erland Josephson, with international reputations built almost exclusively through the Swede's films.

In the wake of his death, at least three different writers have called Bergman the Shakespeare of film, and it's so true. Like Shakespeare, he was comfortable in stark drama, historic tales, and comedy (yes, early Bergman films, like *Smiles of a Summer Night*, were often funny). And, like Shakespeare, he tapped into a universal and timeless reservoir of deeply meaningful reflections on the experiences of life and death. Additionally, even more than Shakespeare, Bergman explored his own upbringing with a stern minister-father and a warm mother in richly autobiographical segments in many of his films, especially near the end.

Bergman may have been, as Woody Allen has argued, the greatest single filmmaker in the history of movies. I hope more of today's younger viewers of slam-bang cinema will one day develop the patience, values and concerns to discover this incredible artist, who has now faded, himself, to red.

ESSENTIAL INGMAR BERGMAN

Monika (1953)
Smiles of a Summer Night (1955)
The Seventh Seal (1957)
Wild Strawberries (1957)
The Virgin Spring (1960)
Persona (1966)
Shame (1968)
Cries and Whispers (1972)
Scenes from a Marriage (1973)
Face to Face (1976)
Autumn Sonata (1978)
Fanny and Alexander (1982)

STANLEY KRAMER

If you seek the liberal conscience of Hollywood in the 1940s, '50s and '60s, look no further than Stanley Kramer.

Kramer, who died Feb. 19, 2001, in Los Angeles at 87, consistently put his passionate beliefs on the screen, as a producer and director of more than a dozen memorable films, in a 36-film career, from 1941 to 1979.

Kramer's most consistent target was racism. He examined different aspects of prejudice in *Home of the Brave* in 1949, *The Defiant Ones* in 1958, and *Guess Who's Coming to Dinner* in 1967.

But the New Yorker also made viewers feel the waste of nuclear holocaust in *On the Beach* (1959). Kramer also put the spotlight on intellectual freedom with his screen adaptation of *Inherit the Wind* (1960) and brought Nazi villainy to justice in *Judgment at Nuremberg* (1961). And he tackled Hollywood's blacklist, albeit obliquely, in *High Noon* (1952), the classic Western parable about community responsibility.

For his first 19 films, Kramer worked exclusively as producer. But, like David O. Selznick, Kramer added his personal stamp as a producer. Then he started directing in 1955.

Since Hollywood stereotyped Kramer as a "message" filmmaker, he decided to go against the grain by making a comedy – the biggest comedy ever made. He hired every big-time comedian for the epic *It's a Mad, Mad, Mad, Mad World*.

Over his career, Kramer earned three best director nominations, and he was presented the coveted honorary Irving G. Thalberg Award in 1962 for lifetime achievement. His films earned 80 nominations and took home 16 Oscars.

Kramer's pictures weren't consistently brilliant, though they always seemed heartfelt. Because of his passion for topical subjects, depicted with the emotional fervor of their time, some films now seem dated. By today's standards, some content seems heavy-handed, for example in such films as *Guess Who's Coming to Dinner*. Still, any serious student of film would list *High Noon, The Caine Mutiny, The Defiant Ones, On the Beach, Inherit the Wind,* and *Judgment at Nuremberg* as key films. Kramer clearly used cinema to fight the good fight.

"A lot of young film guys say, 'I'm going to tell it like it is,'" Kramer told me as he was about to preview *The Runner Stumbles* in 1979. "Well, how is it? It's a very complex time. I don't mind if filmmakers speculate on the answers, but only if they ask the questions and satisfactorily speculate."

Karen Sharpe Kramer, the filmmaker's wife, told reporters when her husband died, "What epitomized Stanley Kramer … was that line from *Judgment at Nuremberg*: 'Let it be known this is what we stand for: truth, justice and the value of a single human being.'"

ESSENTIAL STANLEY KRAMER
The Defiant Ones (1958)
On the Beach (1959)
Inherit the Wind (1960)
Judgment at Nuremberg (1961)
It's a Mad, Mad, Mad, Mad World (1963)
Ship of Fools (1965)
Guess Who's Coming to Dinner (1967)
The Secret of Santa Vittoria (1969)

HENRY MANCINI

If Henry Mancini had composed only "Moon River," he would have been mourned around the world after his death on June 14, 1994, in Beverly Hills, Calif., at age 70.

"Moon River," one of the most beautiful songs ever written for the screen, has become a standard. Rooted in distinctly American folk melodies and myths, it's on a par with the best of Stephen Foster and Hoagy Carmichael.

Mancini said, "I hope I can paint pictures with my music." Working with lyricist Johnny Mercer, Mancini created his greatest images more than 30 years ago with "Moon River," composed for *Breakfast at Tiffany's*.

But the song was simply the most famous of a well-known repertoire, composed by a man who helped revolutionize the music of the movies. By incorporating elements from the jazz and Tin Pan Alley traditions, Mancini was among the first to offer Hollywood lighter alternatives to the lush, symphonic movie scores of Max Steiner, Erich Wolfgang Korngold, Bernard Herrmann and other studio composers.

Mancini, who died of complications of liver and pancreatic cancer, had been undergoing treatment for cancer for several months and had been hospitalized for blood clots. Still, he had continued work with lyricist Leslie Bricusse for a stage adaptation of *Victor/Victoria*. The two won an Oscar for their score of the 1982 film, which starred Julie Andrews and Robert Preston.

Victor/Victoria was part of an association between Mancini and director Blake Edwards that lasted for almost all of the composer's career. Mancini scored every Edwards film, including *The Great Race, The Days of Wine and Roses, 10, S.O.B.* and several *Pink Panther* comedies. His humorous, bouncy *Panther* theme has had additional life in a series of cartoons and even in ads for roof insulation.

"Blake and I have a great friendship," Mancini said in a 1984 interview. "We think the same way. And he doesn't stand over my shoulder while I work, like a lot of directors. He knows I won't abuse his trust."

The collaboration began on TV, with the landmark *Peter Gunn* detective series in the late 1950s. The show was set in a cool-jazz world of nightclubs and musicians, and featured a hard-driving, jazz-rock theme that remains a staple of both rock and marching bands.

Peter Gunn introduced jazz to TV, and the show was among the first to use newly composed music throughout. Previously, shows had used "canned" music from studio collections, except for main title themes. Mancini's 1958 album of *Peter Gunn* music became his first top-seller. The collaboration with Edwards continued with TV's *Mr. Lucky* in 1959 before the duo moved on to films. Scores for both shows featured what would become Mancini trademarks: clean, straightforward melody lines, frequently played on a piano and supported by a soft bed of French horns and strings, pushed along by steady, light-touch rhythms.

Interestingly, the piano player on a lot of the early Mancini jazz scores was John Williams, who would one day surpass even Mancini as a popular film composer. (And he paid tribute, in a way, with his Mancini-esque score for *Catch Me If You Can*.)

Jazz was Mancini's first calling card in Hollywood. A former pianist and arranger with the Glenn Miller – Tex Beneke orchestra, he was hired to arrange the music for the 1954 Jimmy Stewart film *The Glenn Miller Story*. This led to a similar assignment on *The Benny Goodman Story*.

Mancini's first film score was the moody jazz for Orson Welles' 1958 *Touch of Evil*. He then reunited with Blake Edwards, starting with a modest Bing Crosby film, *High Time*.

The second Mancini-Edwards movie effort, though, was a classic. *Breakfast at Tiffany's* remains one of the director's best films, and it gave birth to "Moon River." In 1961, the song and the score earned Mancini the first two of his four Oscars. (He also won for his song "Days of Wine and Roses" in 1963, and for the *Victor/Victoria* score in 1982.)

Breakfast at Tiffany's also was the first of several films in which Mancini music framed the magnificent face of Audrey Hepburn. He also scored two Stanley Donen films that featured Hepburn – *Two for the Road* and *Charade* – as well as the thriller *Wait Until Dark*.

Mancini studied flute and piano as a child in the steel town Aliquippa, PA. He began arranging music while still a teenager, and studied at the Juilliard School in New York City.

The style he eventually forged was his own: typically light and frothy, entertaining and relaxed, but still capable of stirring emotions. Like a midnight cruise on "Moon River."

ESSENTIAL HENRY MANCINI SCORES

Peter Gunn (TV)

Mr. Lucky (TV)

Touch of Evil (1958)

Breakfast at Tiffany's (1961)

Experiment in Terror (1962)

Hatari! (1962)

Days of Wine and Roses (1962)

Charade (1963)

The Pink Panther (and sequels)(1963-1993)

Two for the Road (1967)

Wait Until Dark (1967)

Victor/Victoria (1982)

ROD STEIGER

WHEN ACTORS TOLD ROD STEIGER, "I DON'T KNOW IF I SHOULD DO THIS ROLE. IT MIGHT be bad for my image," the intense actor would reply, "That's tough that you only have one image. My heart bleeds for you!"

Steiger, who has given filmgoers so many indelible images, died July 9, 2002, in a Los Angeles hospital, from pneumonia and kidney failure. He was 77. He'll be remembered for such diverse portrayals as Napoleon, Al Capone, Pope John XXIII, Mussolini and W.C. Fields. A powerhouse actor, he also played Julie Christie's cruel seducer in *Doctor Zhivago,* sang and danced as Jud in *Oklahoma!* and had his body covered in ink for *The Illustrated Man.*

Filmgoers first noticed Steiger in 1954's *On the Waterfront* as Charley "The Gent" Malloy, the brother of Marlon Brando's character. The two actors made movie history in the back seat of a cab when director Elia Kazan shot the famous "I coulda been a contender" scene.

Ten years later, Steiger created the role that he always said was closest to his heart: the Holocaust-scarred Harlem shopkeeper in Sidney Lumet's shattering *The Pawnbroker.* Steiger earned his second Oscar nomination for *The Pawnbroker* – and should have won. (Lee Marvin's victory over Steiger for *Cat Ballou* remains one of Oscar's most obvious miscarriages of justice.) Steiger finally took home the gold in 1967 as the redneck sheriff in the racially charged *In the Heat of the Night.*

Steiger was born in Westhampton, NY, on April 14, 1925, an only child whose parents divorced early on. After his mother remarried, young Rod moved with her to Newark, NJ. He left home at age 15, enlisted in the Navy the next year and served in the South Pacific in World War II. He returned from the war and used the G.I. Bill to study drama at the New School for Social Research, and was then accepted into the Actors Studio.

Steiger told me in 1999 that his career had been fueled by anger. "I had an incredible amount of rage," he admitted. "My family had disappointed me … I remember nights I had to go to bars and drag my drunken mother home, and the neighbors would laugh at us.

"I realized two years ago that I had spent my career trying to make sure the neighborhood never laughs at the name of Steiger again. Thank God I found a positive way to channel my rage."

ESSENTIAL ROD STEIGER

On the Waterfront (1954)
The Big Knife (1955)
Oklahoma! (1955)
The Harder They Fall (1956)
Al Capone (1959)
The Pawnbroker (1964)
Doctor Zhivago (1956)
In the Heat of the Night (1967)
The Illustrated Man (1969)
W.C. Fields and Me (1976)
The Chosen (1981)

MARCELLO MASTROIANNI

WHEN I ENVISION MARCELLO MASTROIANNI, I SEE HIM YOUNG AND EAGER, SITTING AT the head of a bed. Rubbing his hands gleefully and pounding his feet, he is thoroughly unnerved as Sophia Loren playfully strips for his pleasure. Here was the so-called Romeo, turned from wolf to puppy.

The moment is from *Yesterday, Today and Tomorrow* (1964), the greatest of 14 film collaborations between Mastroianni and Loren. It's typical of the humorous way Mastroianni often tweaked the myth of the Latin lover.

Mastroianni died Dec. 19, 1996, at his Paris home after a bout with pancreatic cancer. According to Italian state television, actress Catherine Deneuve was at the bedside of the 72-year-old actor, along with their 24-year-old daughter, actress Chiara Mastroianni.

Through the 1960s and '70s, Mastroianni was the biggest male film star on the European continent, reigning until the rise of France's Gerard Depardieu in the late '70s. But in some 120 films over a 46-year-career, Mastroianni became much more than a handsome Italian leading man. Among his many accomplishments:

– He was the on-screen alter ego of legendary director Federico Fellini, as important to the director's career as John Wayne was to John Ford's. The pairing began with *La Dolce Vita* (1960) and *8½* (1963), and continued in *City of Women* (1980), *Ginger and Fred* (1986), and *Intervista* (1987).

The connection between star and filmmaker was most obvious in *8½*, in which Mastroianni played a Felliniesque director in a dream memoir, and again in *City of Women*, in which he was Fellini's stand-in for a cinematic debate on women's rights.

– He was half of a romantic screen partnership that could be labeled the European equivalent of Tracy and Hepburn. His partner was Sophia Loren. Their films included *Yesterday, Today and Tomorrow*; *Marriage – Italian Style*; *Sunflower*; and *A Special Day*. They made a perfect match – two screen personalities that could be strong yet vulnerable, completely believable, funny and utterly passionate.

– Amassed over nearly a half-century, Mastroianni's filmography reads like a history of modern Italian film, with movies by Vittorio De Sica, Fellini, Luchino Visconti, Michael Antonioni, Pier Paolo Pasolini, Lina Wertmuller, Ettore Scola and Giuseppe Tornatore, among others.

– Though he worked less often outside his native Italy, his international successes included *Dark Eyes* by Nikita Mikhalkov, *Used People* by Beeban Kidron, and films by Robert Altman, Ida Lupino, Gene Saks, Jules Dassin and others.

– He collected three Academy Award nominations, for *Divorce Italian Style* in 1962, *A Special Day* in 1977, and *Dark Eyes* in 1987.

Mastroianni was born on Sept. 28, 1923, in Fontana Liri, Italy, and, like his frequent co-star Sophia Loren, into poverty. During World War II, he worked briefly as a draftsman, and was captured by Germans and sent to a labor camp. He escaped and spent the rest of the war hiding in a Venice attic.

After the war, Mastroianni went to Rome and spent evenings working with a group of university players. He joined Luchino Visconti's stage stock company and began appearing in films. Soon, his handsome looks and acting ability led to bigger and better things; he finally became an international star thanks to the success of Visconti's *White Nights,* Fellini's *La Dolce Vita,* and Pietro Germi's *Divorce Italian Style.*

Though his good looks led him to be labeled the Italian Clark Gable, Mastroianni rejected such comparisons. "If anything, I'm the anti-Gable," he once told an interviewer. He said Gable and Gary Cooper and the like "played strong, clean men, full of virtue and honesty. They were decisive and solid. But today, we don't know where we're going. In my roles, I reveal that I am simply human. In this sense, I play myself."

That's probably why he wasn't afraid to further tweak his Romeo image in one of his last performances, in Robert Altman's 1994 film *Ready to Wear.* The only magical moment in that lackluster movie was a sequence in which Loren and Mastroianni are reunited to recreate her striptease from *Yesterday, Today and Tomorrow.*

But now, many years have passed. Mastroianni's character is eager as the still-beautiful Loren begins to disrobe.

But, before she finishes undressing, he falls asleep.

ESSENTIAL MARCELLO MASTROIANNI

Big Deal on Madonna Street (1958)
La Dolce Vita (1960)
La Notte (1961)
Divorce Italian Style (1961)
8½ (1963)
Yesterday, Today and Tomorrow (1963)
Marriage Italian Style (1964)
Casanova 70 (1965)
Sunflower (1970)
A Special Day (1977)
City of Women (1980)
Henry IV (1984)
Ginger and Fred (1986)
Everybody's Fine (1990)
Ready to Wear (Prêt-à-Porter) (1994)

FRANK SINATRA

THE ULTIMATE SALOON SINGER TOUCHED US ALL WITH HIS HONESTY AND STYLE.

Nobody has ever sung the great American standards as well as Frank Sinatra, who died on May 14, 1998, at 82. Sinatra's way with "I've Got You Under My Skin" or "The Lady Is a Tramp" or "One for My Baby" is why we remember him so fondly. Nothing else matters.

Yes, he was a pugnacious, sometimes infuriating man, as likely to punch out somebody who bumped him in a bar as he was to buy a round for the house. And yes, he had a few shady friends.

As a movie actor, he was inconsistent. He could rise to the moment with an Oscar-winning turn in *From Here to Eternity* and impress critics as a drug addict in *The Man with the Golden Arm.* But he also phoned in duds like *Robin and the Seven Hoods,* which was little more than an excuse to party with his raucous Rat Pack.

Sinatra didn't even have the greatest voice among his peers. Mel Torme's is smoother, Tony Bennett's stronger and more enduring. But with Sinatra, it was never purely a question of pipes. He had a genius for how to use his voice, a rare talent for breath control, and an incomparable ability to understand and deliver a lyric.

"When he sings 'lovely,' he makes it sound lo-ovely, as in 'weather-wise it's such a lo-ovely day' (in 'Come Fly With Me')," lyricist Sammy Cahn once observed. "Likewise, when he sings 'lonely' (in 'Only the Lonely'), he makes it into such a lonely word."

This made Sinatra one of the great romantics of the 20th century. It's no accident that so many of his songs were about love or love lost.

When you heard Sinatra sing, on record or in concert, he seemed to be singing directly to you – whether he was knocking you flat with the brashness of "I Get a Kick Out of You" or moving you with the intimacy of "I'll Never Smile Again."

Sinatra's attitude offstage was all ring-a-ding-ding confidence, from the cock of his fedora to the snap of his fingers. But as a singer, ah, that's where his vulnerability and heart showed through. Maybe that's why so many of his songs survive as anthems, whether they're about romance ("All the Way"), geography ("New York, New York"), social conscience ("The House I Live In"), his philosophy of life ("My Way") or growing old ("It Was a Very Good Year").

The first big influence on Sinatra's style was Bing Crosby, whose influence is most obvious in Sinatra's smoother, early ballad performances, when he was billed as "The Voice." But the Sinatra style was truly forged after early stints with the orchestras of Harry James and Tommy Dorsey.

Sinatra studied Dorsey and the other musicians, and adapted their breathing techniques to vocals. He also developed a lifelong affinity for jazz and a rhythmic clock – a sense of swing – that remained unerring throughout his career.

Sinatra was not a jazz singer. He remained loyal to the original melodies and seldom improvised or sang scat. His knowledge of jazz, though, gave him a freedom to put a personal stamp on a song's rhythm and to emphasize key words in a lyric with the precision of a jazz drummer hitting a rim shot.

Generally, Sinatra stayed the course of the great American standard, singing the classic Tin Pan Alley songs well into the rock era. He won the gamble, remaining as popular in the 1980s and '90s as ever. Nearly 300 Sinatra albums have been available on CD. The 1996 movie *Swingers* was about today's cult of twenty-something Sinatra fans.

Ultimately, Frank Sinatra's greatness as a singer can be summed up in a single word: honesty. You believe everything he sings. And though his voice did not age gracefully as he tried to extend his career into his late 70s, his credibility as a singer never wavered. The emotional textures in his voice grew richer as his technical prowess diminished.

That's why I could still be moved on April 20, 1993, when I last saw Sinatra in concert.

Sure, there was much about that at Rochester's Community War Memorial which was depressing. Instead of the swagger, there was a bit of a stagger; the voice missed a few notes and failed to sustain even more. And even though he'd sung most of the songs for 30 years or more, he had to read the lyrics off TelePrompTers.

But, after the pianist played the bluesy opening notes of "One for My Baby," all was forgiven. Sinatra once again became the lonely man in a corner bar in Anywhere, U.S.A., mourning his loss over a glass of bourbon.

It is the greatest of saloon songs, being sung by the greatest saloon singer America had ever produced, and it replays in my mind as I write this: "We're drinking, my friend, to the end of a brief episode. Make it one for my baby, and one more for the road."

Movies:

Anchors Aweigh (1945)

On the Town (1949)

From Here to Eternity (1953)

Guys and Dolls (1955)

High Society (1956)

Pal Joey (1957)

Ocean's Eleven (2001)

The Manchurian Candidate (1962)

Come Blow Your Horn (1963)

Von Ryan's Express (1965)

The Detective (1968)

Albums:

"Swing Easy" (1954)

"In the Wee Small Hours" (1955)

"Songs for Swingin' Lovers" (1956)

"A Swingin' Affair" (1957)

"Only the Lonely" (1958)

"September of My Years" (1965)

"Sinatra at the Sands" (1966)

"Francis Albert Sinatra & Antonio Carlos Jobim" (1967)

WHY MOVIES MATTER

THE ARTS FORM THE TEXTURE OF OUR LIVES. THEY'RE THE WAY HUMANKIND PLAYS.

The arts are also the way we learn about life, the way we explore the human condition – each other and ourselves. The more understanding we bring to the arts, the more we will learn and enjoy.

The movies have been around for just a little more than a hundred years – and what have we done with that medium? What sorts of movies are people making and are we seeing?

If the movies are going to move forward as an art form in this digital age, if they're going to offer the same sort of information and inspiration that we find in literature or other art forms, filmmakers must consistently seek a higher vision.

We, as film watchers, need to demonstrate a greater understanding of how movies work, and be more demanding about what we expect from a motion picture.

That's why I believe the chief function of a critic is to increase the viewer's awareness and enjoyment of the arts. And the most important art form of the modern era is the motion picture – if only because we have such access to it, thanks to multiplex theaters, DVDs, pay-per-view, and cable television.

When I was young, I lived in a town with three movie theaters – and each of those theaters, of course, had only one screen. When I was 6, we got a television, but it only had three channels. Still, I grew to love movies, despite (or maybe because of) my limited opportunities to watch them.

If I wanted to see *Casablanca*, I had to hope that some revival house or college would screen it, or that it might surface on late-night television's Million Dollar Movie. And if I wanted to see a film by Ingmar Bergman or Akira Kurosawa, forget about it, unless I lived in New York or was blessed with a museum as rare and special as Rochester's Eastman House.

Today, I can see *Casablanca*, or a Bergman or Kurosawa film, by pulling it off the shelf and putting it in my DVD player. Or by streaming it online on my computer or iPad. The point is, we live at a great time to explore the world of motion pictures, to seek out good and entertaining films of all types.

Animation, for example, has made major inroads over the last two decades, first, with a revival of Disney's classic-styled animation (with *Beauty and the Beast, The Little Mermaid,* and *The Lion King),* and then with digital cartooning, with the very dependable Pixar leading the way (with the *Toy Story* films, *Wall-E, Finding Nemo,* and *Monsters, Inc.*). Like the best of the Disney features, most Pixar films find the balance between stories and graphics that enthrall youngsters and captivate adults at the same time.

Films in 3-D have also had a revival, with far more success than the original eruption in the 1950s. Granted, the impetus seems to be the opportunity to add a few dollars to the admission cost. Still, 3-D is occasionally used brilliantly to enhance stories, most notably in James Cameron's *Avatar* and in Martin Scorsese's wonderful *Hugo.*

No matter the technology, motion pictures are a wonderful way to experience various ways of life, to understand important issues, to get to know unusual people, to consider controversial issues – or just to have a lot of fun.

But it hasn't all been fun. Thanks to movies, I've stood alongside an angry Malcolm X and felt his rage about racial injustice; I've been a bystander to battles everywhere from Gallipoli to Gettysburg, from Montezuma to My Lai. Through the movies, I've witnessed lynching and murder, torture and rape, tyranny and holocaust.

Thank heavens, it's part of the magic of the movies that even when I have horrible, negative experiences, the lights eventually come up; I emerge safe and sound from the theater and go back to my comfortable middle-class life. I get the lessons without having to pay the price – except, of course, the fee to get into the movie or to rent the DVD.

Marshall McLuhan has said the literate person of the future will be visually literate – he or she will have an understanding and appreciation of the visual medium, of movies. McLuhan knew we needed a new visual awareness, in the way we make movies and in the way we view movies.

My function as a critic has been to help filmgoers enrich their lives by increasing their understanding of movies, and their appreciation for quality films. My hope is that I've been part of the process that has helped viewers better understand what they're watching.

Criticism of the arts also contributes to an overall sense of standards or aesthetics in a community. There may be no accounting for taste, but there is always a need to establish a challenging atmosphere for those who create films, music, books, artwork and plays. Everyone is a critic – or should be. Everyone should think about what he or she sees or hears or reads. I was simply blessed to be able to express my opinions far beyond the office water-cooler or the club luncheon.

What is a critic – in general, mainstream media?

1. A reporter first and foremost, responsible for the journalistic standard, the famous who, what, why, when, where and how of the beat.

2. A historian – providing historic perspective and pertinent background to increase

understanding and appreciation for the roots of a work, or an awareness of the inaccuracy of the work. Critics must do their homework.

3. A consumer advocate – keeping in mind the high cost of attending cultural events and entertainment or buying or renting DVDs or pay-per-views for the general public.

4. An advocate for the arts in general (though certainly not a booster of any specific institution or business). In other words, a film critic, for example, should like films, generally. I realize that sounds silly, but I've encountered a few instances over the years where I suspected that wasn't the case.

5. A critic – a person who expresses opinions about the quality of a work, and supports those opinions with examples and reasons.

A critic should approach a work with an open mind, with curiosity, and with optimism. We all have human prejudices about the things we like and dislike. We can't eliminate them, but we must be aware of them, and of how they may be influencing our attitudes.

A critic asks – and tries to answer – two basic questions about a work:

1. What is the artist trying to do?

2. How well is the artist succeeding or failing?

Films have different goals: to be a mindless roller coaster ride, to be an intellectually challenging puzzle, to be a moral statement. This goal must be determined, and acted upon, by the critic. If it is only a roller coaster ride, does it offer thrills and spills we haven't seen before?

These are the specifics I have tried to analyze over the years:

1. An originality of ideas. Is the basic concept or idea of the film fresh?

2. An originality of form, in aspects like script structure, visual texture, pacing, and editing.

3. An originality of technique – keeping in mind that the only good technique is the technique most filmgoers won't notice, including camera styles and angles, lighting, set design, special effects, and sound.

4. Honesty, passion, and engagement demonstrated by the actors.

But the most important element of a good movie is this: A film must have life – it should seem organic and alive, and remain alive in conversation and in your mind after you leave the theater or turn off the DVD. A creative work must move you. It must stir emotions of love or hate or fear or joy or sadness or fulfillment. A good film demands a reaction.

The great French director (and critic) Francois Truffaut wrote in his book, *The Films in My Life*: "I demand that a film express either the joy of making cinema or the agony of making cinema. I am not at all interested in anything in between. I am not interested in all those films that do not pulse."

ALL-TIME OSCAR WINNERS

During the run-up to a recent Academy Awards show, I put together a hypothetical list of my "All-Time" Oscars, an amalgam of my favorite performances and films over the decades to create one greatest-hits award collection. It was a fun exercise, and should serve, at least, to be a good argument starter.

The concept was to look at all the winners over the years in each of the major categories, and then select what I think are the greatest of them. In a few instances, I am championing performances that were unjustly ignored, and weren't even nominated.

JACK GARNER'S ALL-TIME ACADEMY AWARDS

Best Actor

Humphrey Bogart, *Casablanca* (1942)

Marlon Brando, *On the Waterfront* (1954)

Robert De Niro, *Raging Bull* (1980)

Peter O'Toole, *Lawrence of Arabia* (1962)

Daniel Day-Lewis, *Lincoln* (2012)

> My winner: Marlon Brando

Best Actress

Bette Davis, *All About Eve* (1950)

Faye Dunaway, *Chinatown* (1974)

Katharine Hepburn, *The Lion in Winter* (1968)

Marilyn Monroe, *Some Like it Hot* (wasn't nominated) (1959)

Meryl Streep, *Sophie's Choice* (1982)

> My winner: Meryl Streep

Best Supporting Actor

Ralph Fiennes, *Schindler's List* (1993)

Orson Welles, *The Third Man* (wasn't nominated) (1949)

Jack Palance, *Shane* (1953)

Claude Rains, *Casablanca* (1942)

Jackie Gleason, *The Hustler* (1961)

   My winner: Orson Welles

Best Supporting Actress

Linda Hunt, *The Year of Living Dangerously* (1982)

Peggy Ashcroft, *A Passage to India* (1984)

Hattie McDaniel, *Gone with the Wind* (1939)

Lillian Gish, *The Night of the Hunter* (wasn't nominated) (1955)

Angela Lansbury, *The Manchurian Candidate* (1962)

   My winner: Linda Hunt

Best Director

David Lean, *Lawrence of Arabia* (1962)

Alfred Hitchcock, *Rear Window* (1954)

Orson Welles, *Citizen Kane* (1941)

Francis Ford Coppola, *The Godfather* (1972)

Elia Kazan, *On the Waterfront* (1954)

   My winner: David Lean

Best Picture

Amarcord (1973)

Casablanca (1942)

Citizen Kane (1940)

Cries and Whispers (1972)

The Godfather (1972)

The Godfather, Part II (1974)

Lawrence of Arabia (1962)

On the Waterfront (1954)

Rear Window (1954)

The Searchers (1956)

   My winner: *Citizen Kane* & *Casablanca* (a tie!)

TWO HUNDRED ESSENTIAL FILMS

What films do I consider essential – at least to my life? Here's a list of 200, which I hope might give you some ideas when you're looking for something worthwhile to watch. I'll start with my favorite 10 films.

MY ALL-TIME TOP 10:

Citizen Kane (Orson Welles 1941). I don't care if they demoted *Kane* to the No. 2 spot behind *Vertigo* in the most recent *Sight & Sound* poll; this is still the all-time best in my book. The film incorporates every bit of technology of circa 1940 with a stunning multi-layered, flashback-upon-flashback script, astonishing breakthrough cinematography by Gregg Toland, and amazing performances and dialogue. It continues to take my breath away.

Casablanca (Michael Curtiz 1942). The most romantic film ever made, a stunning saga of lost love, found love, and human sacrifice, with some of the most memorable dialogue ever on the screen. Yes, we *will* always have Paris.

On the Waterfront (Elia Kazan 1954). A powerful landmark film, noteworthy for its relationship to the Red-baiting of that era, and much more so for Marlon Brando's astonishing performance, the greatest and most influential in the history of motion pictures.

Lawrence of Arabia (David Lean 1962). This is the thinking person's epic, with grand vistas and grand ideas, and a knockout performance by the young Peter O'Toole that stands as the greatest performance not to win an Oscar. (He competed against Gregory Peck's iconic Atticus Finch from *To Kill a Mockingbird.*)

Godfather I & II (Francis Ford Coppola 1972 1974). I consider this one great epic, a story of both family and Family, and a portrait of the corruption of power.

The Miracle of Morgan's Creek (Preston Sturges 1944). The funniest movie of my experience, a masterpiece from the always-underrated genius of film comedy.

Cries and Whispers (Ingmar Bergman 1972). A stark, emotionally draining portrait of Swedish sisters of the 19th century, gathered at the bedside of a dying sibling. Bergman has never been more eloquent or more painful.

Amarcord (Federico Fellini 1973). A warm-hearted memoir of the boyhood imagination of Fellini; touching and funny and poetic.

The Searchers (John Ford 1956). This film has grown in its stature in my eyes, most recently surpassing *High Noon* and *Shane* as my nominee for greatest Western. John Wayne is fabulous as a man in search of his kidnapped niece, either to kill her or save her. (Here Wayne eloquently defeats all those who belittle his abilities as an actor.)

Rear Window (Alfred Hitchcock 1954). The greatest film from the master of suspense. He examines the issue of voyeurism by exposing all of us as voyeurs. And he employs the most amazing set ever created on a soundstage, as well as memorable performances by James Stewart, Grace Kelly, and Thelma Ritter.

Silent Classics: (13)
Birth of a Nation (1915) and *Broken Blossoms* (1919) (D. W. Griffith)
The Gold Rush (1925) and *City Lights* (1931) (Charlie Chaplin)
The General (1926) and assorted shorts (Buster Keaton)
Safety Last (Harold Lloyd 1923)
Napoleon (Abel Gance 1927)
Sunrise (F. W. Murnau 1927)
Seventh Heaven (Frank Borzage 1927)
Pandora's Box (1929) and *Diary of a Lost Girl* (1927) (Louise Brooks in
G.W. Pabst's film)
Battleship Potemkin (Sergei Eisenstein 1925)
The Passion of Joan of Arc (Carl Theodor Dreyer 1928)

The Sound Era: (122)
King Kong (Ernest B. Schoedsack, Merian C. Cooper 1935)
Queen Christina (Rouben Mamoulian 1935)
Ninotchka (Ernst Lubitsch 1939)
Gone With the Wind and *The Wizard of Oz* (Victor Fleming both 1939)
The Bank Dick, with W. C. Fields (Edward F. Cline 1940)
Duck Soup, with the Marx Brothers (Leo McCarey 1933)
Double Indemnity (1944), *Sunset Boulevard* (1950), and *Some Like It Hot* (1959)
(Billy Wilder)
The Lady Eve (1941) and *Sullivan's Travels* (1941) (Preston Sturges)
It Happened One Night (1935), *Mr. Smith Goes to Washington* (1939),
and *It's a Wonderful Life* (1946) (Frank Capra)
The Adventures of Robin Hood (1938), *The Sea Hawk* (1940),
and *Yankee Doodle Dandy* (1942) (Michael Curtiz)

The Public Enemy (1931) and *The Ox-Bow Incident* (1943) (William A. Wellman)
Stagecoach (1939), *The Grapes of Wrath* (1940), *My Darling Clementine* (1946), and *She Wore a Yellow Ribbon* (1949) (John Ford)
The Maltese Falcon (1941), *The Treasure of the Sierra Madre* (1948), *The African Queen* (1951), and *The Man Who Would Be King* (1975) (John Huston)
White Heat (Raoul Walsh 1949)
His Girl Friday (1940) and *Red River* (1948) (Howard Hawks)
High Noon (1952) and *A Man for All Seasons* (1966) (Fred Zinneman)
The Best Years of Our Lives (1946), *The Big Country* (1958) and *Ben-Hur* (1959) (William Wyler)
The Third Man (Carol Reed 1949)
Great Expectations (1946), *Hobson's Choice* (1954), *The Bridge on the River Kwai* (1957), and *Doctor Zhivago* (1965) (David Lean)
The 39 Steps (1935), *Vertigo* (1958), *North by Northwest* (1959), *Notorious* (1946), and *Psycho* (1960) (Alfred Hitchcock)
Swing Time (1936), *Shane* (1953), and *Giant* (1954) (George Stevens)
Singin' in the Rain (Gene Kelly/Stanley Donen 1952)
The Hustler (Robert Rossen 1961)
A Streetcar Named Desire (1951) and *On the Waterfront* (1954) (Elia Kazan)
To Kill a Mockingbird (Robert Mulligan 1962)
West Side Story (Robert Wise and Jerome Robbins 1961)
The Manchurian Candidate (John Frankenheimer 1962)
Paths of Glory (1957), *Dr. Strangelove* (1964), and *2001 – A Space Odyssey* (1968) (Stanley Kubrick)
My Fair Lady (George Cukor 1964)
Anatomy of a Murder (Otto Preminger 1959)
Last Tango in Paris (Bernardo Bertolucci 1972)
In the Heat of the Night (Norman Jewison 1967)
Bonnie and Clyde (Arthur Penn 1967)
The Conversation (1974) and *Apocalypse Now Redux* (1979) (Francis Ford Coppola)
The French Connection (William Friedkin 1971)
Taxi Driver (1976), *Raging Bull* (1980), *GoodFellas* (1990), and *Hugo* (2011) (Martin Scorsese)
Jaws (1975), *Close Encounters of the Third Kind* (1977), *E.T. the Extra-Terrestrial* (1982), *Raiders of the Lost Ark* (1981), *Schindler's List* (1993), *Saving Private Ryan* (1998), and *Lincoln* (2012) (Steven Spielberg)
Bananas (1971), *Annie Hall* (1977), *Radio Days* (1987), and *Midnight in Paris* (2011) (Woody Allen)
The Pawnbroker (1964), *Dog Day Afternoon* (1975), and *The Verdict* (1982) (Sidney Lumet)
Eight Men Out (John Sayles 1988)

American Graffiti (George Lucas 1973)

Edward Scissorhands (Tim Burton 1990)

Treasure Island (Disney 1950)

Unforgiven (1992) and *Mystic River* (2003) (Clint Eastwood)

A River Runs Through It (Robert Redford (1992)

Picnic at Hanging Rock (1975), *The Year of Living Dangerously* (1982), and *The Truman Show* (1998) (Peter Weir)

Do the Right Thing (1989) and *Malcolm X* (1992) (Spike Lee)

Alien (1979) and *Blade Runner* (1982) (Ridley Scott)

L.A. Confidential (Curtis Hanson 1997)

Planes, Trains & Automobiles (John Hughes 1987)

L.A. Story (Mick Jackson 1991)

Pulp Fiction (Quentin Tarantino 1994)

A Beautiful Mind (Ron Howard 2001)

Brokeback Mountain (Ang Lee 2005)

Fargo (Coen brothers 1996)

A Hard Day's Night (Richard Lester 1964)

The Wild Bunch (Sam Peckinpah 1969)

The Night of the Hunter (Charles Laughton 1955)

The Graduate (Mike Nichols 1967)

Chinatown (Roman Polanski 1974)

Platoon (Oliver Stone 1986)

The Right Stuff (Philip Kaufman 1983)

Young Frankenstein (Mel Brooks 1974)

My Favorite Year (Richard Benjamin 1982)

The Chant of Jimmy Blacksmith (Fred Schepisi 1978)

From Russia With Love (Terence Young 1963)

Chariots of Fire (Hugh Hudson 1981)

Hoosiers (David Anspaugh 1986)

All the President's Men (Alan J. Pakula 1976)

The Silence of the Lambs (Jonathan Demme 1991)

The Hurt Locker (Kathryn Bigelow 2008)

Capote (Bennett Miller 2005)

Animation: (10)

Snow White and the Seven Dwarfs (1937), *Pinocchio* (1940), *Peter Pan* (1953), *Beauty and the Beast* (1991), *The Lion King* (1994) (Disney)

Toy Story 3 (2010) and *WALL-E* (2008) (Pixar)

The Illusionist (2010) (Sylvain Chomet)

The Fantastic Mr. Fox (2009) (Wes Anderson and Noah Baumbach)

The Old Man and the Sea (1999) (Aleksandr Petrov)

Foreign Language Gems: (36)

Nights of Cabiria (1957), *La Dolce Vida* (1960), and *8½* (1963) (Federico Fellini)

The Virgin Spring (1960), *The Seventh Seal* (1957), *Wild Strawberries* (1957),
and *Fanny and Alexander* (1982) (Ingmar Bergman)

Two Women (1960), *Yesterday, Today and Tomorrow (1963)*, and *Marriage Italian Style*,
(1964) all with Sophia Loren, and *The Bicycle Thieves* (1948) (Vittorio De Sica)

The Apu Trilogy – Pather Panchali (1955), *Aparajito* (1956), *The World of Apu* (1959)
(Satyajit Ray)

1900 (Bernardo Bertolucci, 1976)

Throne of Blood (1957), *Seven Samurai* (1954), and *Ran* (1985) (Akira Kurosawa)

Jules and Jim (Francois Truffaut 1962)

The Marriage of Maria Braun (Rainer Werner Fassbinder 1979)

Farewell My Concubine (Chen Kaige 1993)

Ju Dou (1990), *Raise the Red Lantern* (1991), and *Hero* (2002) (Zhang Yimou)

In the Mood for Love (Wong Kar-Wai 2000)

Babette's Feast (Gabriel Axel 1987)

Amélie (Jean-Pierre Jeunet 2001)

Jean de Florette and *Manon of the Spring* (Claude Berri, both 1986)

Fitzcarraldo (Werner Herzog 1982)

The Rules of the Game (1939) and *Grand Illusion* (1937) (Jean Renoir)

Seven Beauties (Lina Wertmüller 1975)

The Wages of Fear (Henri-Georges Clouzot 1953)

Volver (2006) and *Women on the Verge of a Nervous Breakdown* (1988)
(Pedro Almodóvar)

Documentaries: (9)

Woodstock (Michael Wadleigh 1970)

Gimme Shelter (Albert and David Maysles 1970)

Burden of Dreams (about *Fitzcarraldo*) (Les Blank 1982)

Hearts of Darkness (about *Apocalypse Now*) (Fax Bahr and George Hickenlooper 1991)

Brother's Keeper (Joe Berlinger and Bruce Sinofsky 1992)

A Brief History of Time (Errol Morris 1991)

The Battle of San Pietro (John Huston 1945)

Roger & Me (Michael Moore 1989)

4 Little Girls (Spike Lee 1997)

Favorite Actors and Directors

Actors: Marlon Brando, Humphrey Bogart, Meryl Streep, Sophia Loren,
Jack Nicholson, Robert DeNiro, Al Pacino, Morgan Freeman, Philip Seymour
Hoffman, Barbara Stanwyck, Henry Fonda, Michael Caine, Johnny Depp,
James Earl Jones, Michael Gambon, Toshiro Mifune, Liv Ullmann,

Marcello Mastroianni, Alec Guinness, Helen Mirren, Don Cheadle, David Straithairn, George Clooney, Daniel Day-Lewis, Richard Farnsworth, Groucho Marx, Woody Allen, Robert Forster.

Directors: Martin Scorsese, Billy Wilder, Preston Sturges, Federico Fellini, Ingmar Bergman, Akira Kurosawa, Elia Kazan, Clint Eastwood, Alfred Hitchcock, Spike Lee, Dave Lean, Woody Allen, Peter Weir, Francois Truffaut.

ACKNOWLEDGMENTS

It's important to acknowledge the support of people who helped me put together this book – and to that end, I thank Molly Cort, my editor at Rochester Institute of Technology. I'm a veteran writer, but a novice book author, and she's been a great help, guiding me through what it takes to get a book on a shelf. I thank my friend (and fellow RIT Press author) Scott Pitoniak for his advice and for his preface to my book. I'm grateful to Karen Magnuson, Editor and VP/News at the Rochester *Democrat & Chronicle,* for not hesitating for a minute in offering me the rights to reproduce my many features and interviews from my longtime home-base newspaper, and to the George Eastman House and the *Democrat & Chronicle* for access to photographs used in this book.

Since this is a survey of a life's work, I also wish to express gratitude to people who've been a big help over a career that's spanned more than 40 years, starting with teachers, especially Bill Byham at South Williamsport Area High School and the late Dr. Russell Jandoli at St. Bonaventure University. I've been given great guidance over the decades by a wide range of editors, especially the unrelated John Dougherty and Dick Dougherty, Tom Flynn, Jim Memmott, J. Ford Huffman, Sharon Hoffmann, Mary Holleran, and Cathy Roberts, and by the staff at the George Eastman House, who've been an essential part of my ongoing film education.

I especially want to thank my family, starting with my mother, who opened my eyes and ears to so much in the arts, from *On the Waterfront* to Duke Ellington, and my father, with whom I spent many a memorable night in the '50s, watching *Gunsmoke* and *Cheyenne,* when Westerns ruled TV, and my late brother, who introduced me to Ramsey Lewis and Dave Brubeck, and who snuck me into *And God Created Woman.*

My three children – Matt, Erica and Mary – deserve thanks for putting up with a father who spent many days away from home, watching movies in Manhattan or at film festivals, and for being attentive (and apparently appreciative) when I tried to expose them to great films and great music. They also served as great guideposts when I reviewed films aimed at children.

But mostly, I thank Bonnie, an incredibly supportive wife and fellow lover of the arts. She's always been my primary editor, giving me expert advice after careful readings of my work. And she's always been a welcome person by my side when I watch movies, for she often sees more and different things than I do.

I remember once when we were watching Clint Eastwood and Meryl Streep dancing romantically in the kitchen in *The Bridges of Madison County*, she leaned toward me to whisper in my ear. I figured, given the romance of the scene, it would be a sweet nothin'. But no: She said, "See the clock on top of the refrigerator? It hasn't moved since the scene started."

INDEX

COLOPHON

Composed in
Minion Pro, designed by Robert Slimbach
Univers, designed by Adrian Frutiger

Printed and bound by
Complemar Partners
Rochester, NY

Text and cover design by Lisa Mauro